Interactive Marketing

Routledge Interpretive Marketing Research

EDITED BY STEPHEN BROWN AND BARBARA B. STERN, *University of Ulster, Northern Ireland and Rutgers, the State University of New Jersey, USA*

Recent years have witnessed an 'interpretative turn' in marketing and consumer research. Methodologists from the humanities are taking their place alongside those drawn from the traditional social sciences.

Qualitative and literary modes of marketing discourse are growing in popularity. Art and aesthetics are increasingly firing the marketing imagination.

This series brings together the most innovative work in the burgeoning interpretative marketing research tradition. It ranges across the methodological spectrum from grounded theory to personal introspection, covers all aspects of the postmodern marketing 'mix', from advertising to product development, and embraces marketing's principal sub-disciplines.

Also available in Routledge Interpretive Marketing Research series:

Representing Consumers: Voices, views and visions
Edited by Barbara B. Stern

Romancing the Market
Edited by Stephen Brown, Anne Marie Doherty and Bill Clarke

Consumer Value: A framework for analysis and research
Edited by Morris B. Holbrook

Marketing and Feminism: Current issues and research
Edited by Miriam Catterall, Pauline Maclaran and Lorna Stevens

Interactive Marketing

Revolution or Rhetoric?

Chris Miles

Routledge
Taylor & Francis Group
New York London

First published 2010
by Routledge
270 Madison Avenue, New York, NY 10016

Simultaneously published in the UK
by Routledge
2 Park Square, Milton Park, Abingdon, Oxon OX14 4RN

Routledge is an imprint of the Taylor & Francis Group, an informa business

Typeset in Sabon by IBT Global.
Printed and bound in the United States of America on acid-free paper by IBT Global.

Library of Congress Cataloging in Publication Data

Miles, Christopher, 1967-
   Interactive marketing : revolution or rhetoric? / by Christopher Miles.
      p. cm. — (Routledge interpretive marketing research ; 12)
   Includes bibliographical references and index.
   1. Interactive marketing.   I. Title.
   HF5415.1264.M55 2010
   658.8'7 — dc22
   2009045446

ISBN10: 0-415-80171-0 (hbk)
ISBN10: 0-203-85207-9 (ebk)

ISBN13: 978-0-415-80171-3 (hbk)
ISBN13: 978-0-203-85207-1 (ebk)

For Şebnem

Contents

Figures

Introduction

THE TRIUMPH OF TALK

For all the dynamic visual and graphical power of modern communication media it is ironic that what the Internet is really about is *talk*. The chat room, the wiki, the forum, the blog, the comments on the blog, the adjudications of the blog on aggregator sites like Digg, the customer review site, and the social networking site: Everyone has something to say and everyone else has a comment on it.

This was not meant to be the way the world wide web evolved—the early days of Internet development looked forward to a future that was almost entirely visual in nature. We would have no need of something as mundane as 'chatting'—we would be using virtual reality interfaces to surf currents of pure information. William Gibson's (1984) *Neuromancer* provided the influential metaphors for this approach to the web, envisioning the knowledge worker as a "console jockey" interacting with data through virtual movement, a silent pilot rushing through monumental blocks of corporate data, deploying mute, pre-prepared modules of code that would grab just the right bytes before you turned a 180 and exited the area as fast as your hooped-up Ono-Sendai deck could take you. Yet the reality of the web in these early years of the new millennium is so utterly more quotidian—although in many ways far more surprising.

Talk rules the Internet. Even predominantly visual sites, such as YouTube, generate the buzz that they do because of their commenting system (both textual and visual) and it is telling that one of the latest and most heralded enhancements to YouTube is the ability to display textual annotations within a video stream—a postmodern simulacrum of medieval marginalia. Indeed, to most users now, the Internet appears founded upon the spirit of dynamic interchange of information and the tropes of chat room, forum and wiki that have come to be so characteristic of its discourse are strongly connected to ideologies of active, forthright communicators who expect to be active, forthright customers. In parallel, it would seem that commercial organizations, and the myriad forms of communication agencies that represent them, have had to realize that active listening to their customers (and other traditionally disenfranchised stakeholders) and the fostering of a continually evolving, interactive communication relationship with them is an absolute necessity in the contemporary webbed world. Whether it is through the tools and concepts of relationship marketing, customer communities, viral/connected/buzz marketing, corporate blogging, online advertising, marketing public relations or the whole panoply of Web 2.0 strategies[1], contemporary marketing has evinced an increasing and concerted espousal of the need to reach out to the customer and interact with them.

But what, really, does interactivity mean for modern marketing? How different are the communicative tropes of the Internet from those of traditional mass media? Is interactivity in marketing an identifiable feature of current practice or might it be only an illusion, a conceptual blind designed to further entrench existing methodologies and approaches? What exactly are companies doing when they say that they are listening to customers? What does dialog mean for the marketing practitioner? And who benefits from a belief that it is the customer who controls the dialog now?

This study examines these and other issues of interactivity in contemporary marketing. It looks at the ways in which both practitioners and academics have constructed a discourse of interactivity which revolves around rhetorics of customer involvement, community-created content and dialog-creation. I will argue that the use of such rhetorics is a function of specific language games within the field of marketing and has only a tangential connection with the way that interactivity is implemented in common industry practice. Furthermore, the study demonstrates the way in which the creation of this discourse of interactivity significantly impedes the evolution of interactive modalities that might provide richer and more effective ways of engaging with contemporary media, customers, and communities. At the core of the work is a radical new model of marketing centered upon an understanding of interactivity as an exploration of constructed understandings of value between stakeholders in a marketing system. This model, grounded in radical constructivist approaches to media and social systems and radical approaches to the rhetoric of invitation, is used to both critique the presentation and implementation of interactive, feedback-driven systems in contemporary marketing and provide an insight into how interactivity can more powerfully and consistently be applied to core marketing communication problem areas in networked and traditional media systems. Also foundational to my approach in this work is the belief that marketing *is* communication. I align myself with Ballantyne and Varey (2006) who see marketing as "grounded in interaction" (ibid., p. 228) and, consequently, my understanding of marketing is built upon an exploration of communicative interaction. For me, therefore, discussions of interactivity in marketing communication become discussions of fundamental issues in marketing theory and practice. The reasoning that informs this position will, I hope, become clearer as the study progresses although at this stage I would warn the reader that what looks like an obscuring of the difference between the terms 'marketing' and 'marketing communication' is, indeed, deliberate.

METHODOLOGY AND STRUCTURE

The methodological approach of the study is an unusual synthesis of rhetorical analysis and constructivist model-building. The first part of the book looks at the presentation and use of interactivity in the discourse of marketing. It examines the rhetorical strategies informing marketing's recent sanctification of interactivity and investigates the use of interactivity as a marketing concept (with all the attendant ambiguity such a phrase confers) and as a metaphor in public discourse about the relationship between mass media and mass audiences. As such it is an example of what is becoming referred to as "interpretive marketing research", in that it seeks to use techniques drawn from rhetoric, literary theory, and postmodern philosophy in order to interpret aspects of the discourse of marketing. However, in a significant departure from the existing interpretive range of references, the study grounds its core theoretical approach in the disciplines of radical constructivism, general systems theory, and cybernetics, particularly the recently emerged brand of discourse-focused cybernetics of observing systems that is termed second-order cybernetics. The study's methodological synthesis allows me to both analyze the discourse of current understandings of interactivity and to use the process of the creation and negotiation of discourse as the foundation for a new, evolutionary model of interactivity in marketing communication. I then use this model in turn to analyze the principle technologies and formats in networked marketing communication (web analytics, data mining, blogging, viral strategies, and online community creation) and suggest areas in which their application might be steered away from old assumptions of control and command and toward more truly interactive and revolutionary marketing practices.

My opening chapter begins by investigating the rhetoric and basic assumptions informing marketing's approach to communication. I use a number of exemplar texts from mainstream and marginal marketing discourses to delineate the powerful pull of the paradigm of control in their understanding of communication. This paradigm is seen to manifest itself in the wholesale adoption into marketing discourse of the Claude Shannon (1948) model of Sender–Message–Receiver and its accompanying implementation of the negative feedback loop. The connection between this model and early cybernetics provides a rich, though highly limiting, rhetoric of control metaphors and terminologies that have come to dominate not only mainstream marketing but also those self-identified revolutionary approaches that seek to overthrow the monological, linear management assumptions of that mainstream. The first chapter of the study, then, outlines what interactivity means within the 'traditional', cybernetic understanding of communication and how this is reflected in the use of language, metaphors, and discourse strategies associated with mainstream marketing communication and the 'alternatives' that seek to expand upon it or overturn it. In Chapter 2, I begin to focus my investigation upon the way in which the idea of interactivity has in recent years come to be presented as the key to a number of new or revitalized marketing theories. I examine the way in which these theories and the discourses that they generate portray constructions of empowered customers who need to be engaged in conversation or dialog. What conversation means in these discourses, and how it is entwined with the legacy of cybernetic control that continues to haunt all areas of marketing, are the questions that form the agenda for this chapter. I use rhetorical analysis to uncover the ideological forces and discourse streams that inform the refocusing of marketing communication toward the creation of apparent dialogs between the prospect/customer and representatives of the producer. In doing so, I seek to demonstrate that the discourse of interactivity employed by both marketing practitioners and academics is dominated by metaphors of dialog but underlying assumptions of control.

Chapter 3 serves as a form of 'prelude' to the final chapter of the study in which I present a new model of marketing interactivity based upon a recursive, invitational understanding of communication. In this chapter I discuss the connections between a radical constructivist approach to interactivity, an understanding of the generative nature of discourse that is foundational to the practice of rhetorical analysis as practiced in this study, and possibilities for an entirely new way of looking at marketing. I begin by contrasting the social constructionist approach to the analysis of marketing taken by Chris Hackley (2001) with the slightly different opportunities offered by a radical constructivist stance. Building particularly upon the work of Ernst von Glasersfeld, I look at the way in which our understandings of interactivity, and hence marketing, can be greatly enriched by examining them starting from the constructivist conjecture that the act of observation is, implicitly and necessarily, an act of creation. Step by step I build an initial constructivist model of marketing as a process of interaction (rather than exchange) in which stakeholders in a system explore and attempt to co-ordinate their constructions of value as they relate to their constructions of self and others in the system. This initial model serves as a preliminary framework for the introduction of recursive and invitational elements that are introduced in the final chapter. It also brings an added, constructivist dimension to the close readings that are the backbone of the next three chapters. Chapter 4 considers two areas of discourse that engage with marketing interactivity from what are superficially quite different perspectives; popular, 'practitioner'-focused marketing books that promote the use of blogging and social networking as keys to business success and texts originating in the technical discourse that shadows the use of data mining in the service of Relationship Marketing and Customer Relationship Management. High-profile books aimed at the general, non-academic business and marketing audience like Paul Gillin's (2007) *The New Influencers: A Marketer's Guide to the New Social Media* and David Meerman Scott's (2007) *The New Rules of Marketing & PR*, while often ignored by scholarly marketing research, are highly significant in the construction of the mainstream discourse around the subject. The understanding of interactivity evidenced in such texts reflects, and is reflected in, the academic and practitioner rhetoric around the issue and thus constitutes a fascinating setting for the exploration of tensions between different constructions of marketing reality. One of those tensions is that between the language of measurement and the language of dialog. As I will show, while measurement and control are intimately bound to each other in marketing discourses they simultaneously provide a source of discomfort and paradox in discussions of customer empowerment, conversational marketing, and service orientation. The last 10 years have seen significant advances in the way in which the Internet is used as a marketing tool. Technologies and algorithms from the field of computational linguistics and machine learning have found their way into the day-to-day networked marketing practices of text mining, search engine optimization, and social network analysis. Such mathematical techniques are designed to extract meaningful marketing information from the vast amount of text that is produced on the web in the form of customer interactions, blogs, community forums, wiki postings, public email exchanges, etc. Automated discourse analysis has become the driving force behind the fostering of ever more prolix expressions of opinion by prospects and customers—the more people talk, the more their words can be processed and mined for marketing significance. I take a close look at the way in which such technologies foster the production of discourse through the appearance of encouraging interactivity and boundless expression of personal opinion, while engaged in a far more control-orientated program of information analysis. In doing so, I consider the nature of the relationship between the traditional voices of marketing communication (agencies, marcom consultancies, and 'celebrity' practitioners) and the new (often occulted) voices of the scientists working at the forefront of marketing-orientated data mining. The enthusiastic adoption of a wide variety of data mining techniques in support of Customer Relationship Management strategies has, in particular, forced the tensions between rhetorics of dialog and control into increasingly stark relief. In addition to analyzing the discourse of marketers who use data mining in their construction of marketing realities, however, I look at the rhetoric of interactivity and control employed by those seeking to teach the programming of data mining applications for marketing, investigating how far the rhetorical tensions between control and dialog extend into the discourses of those in non-marketing fields who are nevertheless in crucial positions of support (in the sense of facilitating marketing use of customer data). I close the chapter with a look at how these rhetorical tensions spiraling around marketing's construction of interactivity are also to be found in the day-to-day discourse of the blogosphere itself.

Chapter 5 deals with the creation, monitoring, and management of customer communities in modern online marketing and brand management.

This practice appears to represent the perfect example of the synthesis between the latest trends in networking and software technologies and the power of marketing public relations techniques. However, the paradox of the marketing use of customer communities has been that such groupings are at their most vibrant and dynamic when clearly not controlled by one particular brand (therefore not regarded as public relations conduits for them). Consequently, the challenge of managing both the flow of information and the formation of opinion in customer communities is one riddled with paradox—how to control without appearing to control? This situation has led many marketing communication practitioners to adopt communication theories based upon the metaphor of the virus or "meme". These "connected marketing" paradigms appear to offer scientific models for the manipulation of information selection and retention across communities and yet there is a great reluctance in the marketing discourse to engage with the research (and controversy) that has been accruing around the 'thought as virus' trope outside of marketing over the past 30 years. The way in which the virus metaphor is implemented as a persuasive rhetorical strategy connected to the perceived threat of an interactive audience is examined through a consideration of key texts from the viral marketing discourse including case studies from the academic literature. Moving on from the way in which the viral trope constructs a particular idea of community, the chapter finishes with a discussion of the idea of community-created content and its peculiar manifestation in the recent work of the business strategy scholar C. K. Prahalad. Prahalad's championing of the co-creation of unique value is rooted in a comparatively radical interpretation of the role of interactivity between stakeholders in the contemporary business environment. The uneasy place which the idea of community has within this interpretation highlights the individualism that is central to Prahalad's rhetoric and allows me to discuss some of the polarization that exists within the many marketing and business theoreticians who celebrate the arrival of the era of co-production.

Prahalad's notion of the co-creation of unique value can be seen to connect into the foundational premises of the Service-Dominant Logic presented by Vargo and Lusch (2004) which, in turn, has served as a theoretical buttress for larger Relationship Marketing discourses. Chapter 6 consists of rhetorical analyses of the original paper by Vargo and Lusch that introduced the S-D orientation as well as key texts in the Relationship Marketing (RM) cannon by Evert Gummesson (2008) and Peppers and Rogers (1999). My argument in this penultimate chapter is that RM, and the S-D Logic that now accompanies it, can be observed to contain a deeply ironic turning away from communication and interactivity, a turning away that I metaphorically link with the behavior observed in those labeled with autism spectrum disorders. For discourses so ostensibly concerned with the construction and maintenance of relationships, RM and S-D Logics engage with issues of communication in general, and interactivity and dialog in particular, through elision and strategies of avoidance, often being reduced to the repetition of small rhetorical cells which serve to suggest an understanding that is never actually explicated.

The final chapter of the study presents the second stage of the model of marketing interactivity initiated in Chapter 3. Building upon the insights of the rhetorical analyses in the previous chapters, the model attempts to address many of the inconsistencies, tensions, and elisions around marketing's relationship with the issue of interactivity. Starting from the radical constructivist perspective outlined in Chapter 3, I go on to integrate into the model three elements that compliment and enrich that perspective; the radical "invitational rhetoric" suggested by Foss and Griffin (1995), Heinz von Foerster's (1981) notion of the "eigenform" which he created in order to discuss the apparent stability we afford our constructions of self and others, and Klaus Krippendorff's (1994/2009) recursive framework for communication. The resulting matrix of conjectures and re-definitions represents my own understanding of how a marketing based upon interactions might be constructed. As a 'model' it is intended to provide both a tool to reframe the existing discourses of interactivity within marketing as well as the beginnings of a suggested road-map for the discovery of future marketings focused around rhetorics of invitation and exploration of dynamic constructions of value.

INTERACTIVITY: CONTROL OR NEGOTIATION?

The main themes of the book are the tensions between control and interactivity, the ways in which these tensions are manifested in the discourse of contemporary marketing communication, and the part that a radical constructivist perspective can play in helping theoreticians and practitioners reconsider the assumptions that lead to these tensions. The principle objectives of the study therefore are, firstly, an examination of the place that interactivity has in marketing communication, secondly, a rhetorical analysis of the way in which marketing discourse reflects its assumptions of control, message management, and measurement in the language it uses to talk about its dialogical engagement with consumers and other stakeholders, thirdly, the presentation of a flexible, dynamic theory of marketing communication based upon an understanding of interactivity as part of a system of negotiated co-ordination of constructions of value rather than control and, lastly, a demonstration of the viability of a constructivist approach to the field of marketing theory.

This is the first book-length study of interactivity in marketing. While there have been many practitioner-focused books on approaches to advertising and PR which *imply* a focus on interactivity (such as advertising strategies for the Internet, permission marketing, customer community building, etc.) there have been no extended scholarly investigations of what interactivity actually means and how it is understood within these approaches. *Interactive Marketing: Revolution or Rhetoric?* thus provides a vital antidote to the rather woolly and unconsidered theoretical underpinnings of these contemporary, practitioner-focused manifestos. Part of the study investigates a powerful technological discourse that informs the day-to-day practice of networked marketing but which is rarely, if ever, addressed in academic or practitioner publications: the leveraging of machine learning algorithms and data mining techniques into systems of control and persuasion. Furthermore, my use of the radical constructivist paradigm represents a unique theoretical perspective in marketing communications research. The book's model of interactive marketing therefore offers a fresh and constructive alternative to extant conceptions of both networked and traditional commercial persuasion, foregrounding a dynamic of negotiation rather than control. It's implementation offers to build bridges between marketing theory scholarship and the innovative work being done in the areas of the sociology of communication, second-order cybernetics and the application of constructivism to the social sciences.

1 The Rhetoric of Interactivity

One way to get a sense of the real dynamics that characterize communication on the Internet is to spend a little time listening in on it. Listening in on Internet 'chatter' is something that this book will have a lot to say about but for now let me just quickly sketch a scenario for you. Ben Hedrington has created a Google App Engine project called 'spy' (available at spy.appspot.com) which allows a user to input a search term, say 'Nike', and then watch as the engine scrapes every use of that term, pretty much real time, from a number of the most popular social networking sites around the world. So, the results are a continuously streaming set of reports from users of Twitter, FriendFeed, and anyone who produces or comments on content with an RSS feed (which would include virtually all blogs on the net) who happens to be talking about Nike while you are sitting there at your computer. The talk that you can see is, naturally, international. Some of it clearly emanates from one aspect or another of Nike's corporate communication effort and some it is produced by retail outlets with RSS feeds from their websites but much of it represents informal chat between friends, colleagues, and acquaintances. Listening in on these short snippets of Nike-focused chat, one hears people complaining about their Nike + equipment not working properly, others stating how much they use the same equipment and how it has kept them running through the winter, while others remind each other of the Nike sponsored run in their area on the weekend, some compare other products to Nike's while others use Nike as a metaphor for a variety of characteristics. Hedrington's 'spy' application gives us an instant window onto the current state of Nike's brand identity and value—it can show us how, right now, a brand fits into the normal social life and rhetorical framework of people who live a significant portion of their life online. It would appear to be an excellent way to monitor and gauge the 'buzz' around a product, brand, or idea. Imagine that you were a marketing consultant working for Nike—surely such an application would provide you with a perfect way of constructing instantaneous communication audits for your client and then measuring the effectiveness of any marcom efforts you implement? You are literally eavesdropping on your stakeholders . . .

Hedrington's 'spy' is a good example of one of the ways in which the technological underpinnings of the Internet (in this case, RSS feeds and APIs for web sites like Twitter) are being used to gather the substance of "informal" conversations around the globe and present them for considered consumption by whoever is interested. This process is known as data or text mining and it is a vital part of the way in which organizations are trying to leverage the astounding urge to communicate that consumers display on the Internet. And the name that Hedrington has chosen for his application is demonstrative of the attitude toward the building of communication relationships with consumers that such processes are built upon. 'Spy', and all such data mining applications, can provide realtime feedback on the results of marketing communication but it is not the feedback of conversation or dialog. Rather, data mining is typified by a stance of 'listening in', of trying to 'overhear' what is being said about you (as brand). In learning what others might be saying about you behind your back (or when they think you are not listening) you may be able to use this information to alter your message or your presentation when you do address them face-to-face. Could we call this process interactive, though? Or, perhaps we might ask, who might call this process interactive and why?

In this opening chapter, I will be examining exactly how the terms "interactivity", "conversation", and "dialog" have been constructed and used within the academic and practical environments of marketing communication. In order to approach these issues effectively, though, we must first examine the way in which the concept of communication itself has been 'positioned' within the discipline of marketing. The way that marketing thinks of "interactivity" and uses the metaphors of conversation and dialog are inextricably linked to the understanding held by the founding and mainstream voices of marketing theory of what it means to communicate and how communication is carried out.

MARKETING AND COMMUNICATION

Marketing is highly uncomfortable with the idea of communication. In an academic environment, of course, this is easy to see. Marketing communication departments (including those specializing in public relations or advertising) are rarely situated within communication faculties. They are far more likely to be connected to business administration, MBA, or management programs. Occasionally, marcoms units might be found twinned with journalism departments, although such a relationship usually remains uncomfortable for both parties. Departments devoted to 'media studies' or communication theory will almost never include substantial components on marketing communication in their programs and the leading academic journals within the field of communication display little interest in covering the marketing communications territory. Furthermore, within marketing programs, marketing *communication* issues are often downplayed or marginalized to a few, often elective, courses.

Marketing academics are uncomfortable with the communication field, communication academics are uncomfortable with the marketing field, and *everyone* is uncomfortable with the marketing communication academics.

THE TRADITIONAL MODEL

Some of the reasons for this uneasy situation can be apprehended through an examination of one of marketing's most canonical texts, Philip Kotler's *Marketing Management*. First published in 1967 and now in its 12th edition (co-written with Kevin Lane Keller), Kotler's tome is the standard by which all other undergraduate and MBA marketing textbooks are judged. Marketing communication issues are afforded their own section (one of eight), under the rubric *Communicating Value*, comprising three chapters wherein the authors endeavor to introduce, contextualize, and strategize all of the elements of the Integrated Marketing Communication mix. As a natural overture to this enterprise, Kotler and Keller overview the concept of communication from a marketing perspective—in their rather instrumentalist terms, "how communications work and what marketing communications can do for a company" (Kotler & Keller, 2006, p. 536). The first thing that even a cursory engagement with the text makes clear is that there is no attempt made to define what communication might be outside of the marketing environment. The authors squarely treat communication as a component of marketing rather than choosing to situate marketing communication as a part of a larger field of communication. Instantly, therefore, marketing communication is isolated. It is purposefully cut off from the issues, theories, and discourses current in both the academic realm of communication studies and the more practitioner-focused areas of journalism and media production. Instead, Kotler and Keller construct a definition of marketing communication which is breathtaking in its presumption and (as I will show) so completely characteristic of the Kotlerite mainstream discourse of control:

> In a sense, marketing communications represent the "voice" of the brand and are a means by which it can establish a dialogue and build relationships with consumers. (ibid., p. 536)

Considered closely, the implications of this position are that communication within a marketing environment is something done *by* marketing *to* consumers; there is one "voice" and it is the voice of the brand and it is *used* to "establish" a dialog. Clearly, then, there can be no dialog that is not instigated by the brand and concomitantly there can be no relationship that is not initiated by the brand. The assumption here is that the consumer is passive, solely reacting to the initiative of the marketer. Perhaps it might be argued that one small sentence should not be held as representative of an entire authorial position. Yet, the assumptions that inform Kotler and Keller's definition of marketing communication are made even more manifest in their ensuing discussion of the two communication models they advance as the providers of "the fundamental elements of effective communications" (ibid., p. 539). The macromodel presented by the authors is an expanded version of the classic Sender–Message–Receiver model advanced by Claude Shannon (1948; see Figure 1.1) and then re-presented with an introduction by Warren Weaver in the 1949 study, *The Mathematical Theory of Communication*.

This model, variously referred to as the transmission model, the SMR model, or the injection or hypodermic model, although highly influential upon the communication theory of the 60s and early 70s now suffers from widespread dissatisfaction and mistrust in mainstream communication and media studies fields. In marketing, however, the opposite is the case and Shannon and Weaver's model has been adopted and maintained as the dominant communication paradigm, although those marketing academics and practitioners who have actually worked their way through the reasoning of the original mathematical treatise could probably be counted on the fingers of one hand. As an illustration of the distinct dichotomy between the two fields on this matter, an examination of *McQuail's Mass Communication Theory*, an undergraduate textbook written by Denis McQuail, first published in 1983 and now in its fourth edition, sees the SMR model presented as a historical artifact of a "largely unchallenged North American

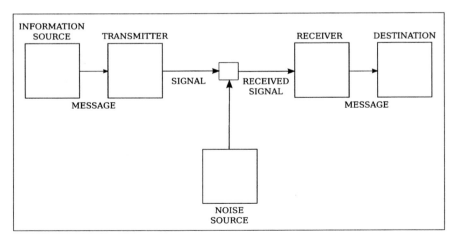

Figure 1.1   Claude Shannon's "Schematic diagram of a general communication system". (Source: Shannon, C. E., 'A Mathematical Theory of Communication', *The Bell System Technical Journal*, Vol. 27, July, 1948, p. 380, Figure 1. Copyright © 1948 Bell Labs. Reprinted with permission of John Wiley & Sons, Inc.)

hegemony over both the social sciences and the mass media" (McQuail, 2000, p. 46) that saw the mathematically-based transmission model of communication as able to "answer questions about the influence of mass media and about their effectiveness in persuasion and attitude change" (ibid., p. 47). McQuail quotes E. M. Rogers's judgment that the SMR model led the study of communication into an "intellectual cul-de-sac" that concentrated almost exclusively on mass communication *effects* while noting that "traces of functional thinking and of the linear causal model are ubiquitous" (ibid.) in communication research to this day. The tremendous power of the SMR, functionalist approach is readily acknowledged by McQuail and the other mainstream communication academics whose work his textbook is designed to summarize. As such, Kotler's presentation of the SMR model *topographically* appears to be identical to that found in current overviews of communication studies, in that it is the model that appears always at the start of a presentation on the theory of communication. Yet, what for most contemporary communication scholars is something to be historically contextualized and deconstructed, the starting point of the story, as it were, is for Kotler the fountainhead, the source. So, for example, McQuail continues his study by noting that the "rejection by researchers of this notion of powerful direct effect is almost as old as the idea itself" (p. 48) and goes on to outline the way in which the obvious failings of the model have even been used to help excuse its adoption by a western "liberal-pluralist society" which needs to downplay the possibilities of "subversion by a few powerful or wealthy manipulators" (ibid.). Alternative models and paradigms, based upon critical work produced by the Frankfurt School, are then presented and this leads onto a broad discussion of ideologies informing the communications field. Readers are specifically told that "they are not obliged to make a choice between" (ibid., p. 52) the dominant and alternative paradigms; McQuail suggests instead that these discourses of ideology and paradigm are involved in a continuing, polyphonic dialog. In Kotler's presentation there is no room for such considerations: A declarative reliance on the existential copula, coupled with that old advertising saw, repeated injunctions, means that alternatives cannot be countenanced:

> The model emphasizes the key factors in effective communication. Senders must know what audiences they want to reach and what responses they want to get. They must encode their messages so that the target audience can decode them. They must transmit the message through media that reach the target audience and develop feedback channels to monitor the responses. The more the sender's field of experience overlaps with that of the receiver, the more effective the message is likely to be. (ibid., p. 539)

The contrast between the two approaches is clear: Communication studies is wrestling with its instrumentalist, functionalist legacy while mainstream marketing continues to hold the transmission paradigm as central to its core theory.

An understanding of communication which unproblematically conceives of a unified 'sender' and a unified 'target audience', deliberate (and sanctioned) 'encoding' and 'decoding' and speaks of 'monitoring responses' is an understanding of communication founded upon a deep allegiance to a control systems paradigm. Kotler, after all, sees marketing as a *management* process and it should come as no surprise that he would view communication as a management process as well. Kotlerian marketing 'senders' seek to control the message and therefore the 'receivers' through a careful, informed management of message creation, presentation, and consumption. The more carefully the communication is managed then the more successful it will be: success, of course, being the achievement of specific marketing goals. Consequently, communication takes its place alongside the marketing channel, the product-line and logistics as simply another element that needs to be minutely controlled in the service of the organization.

Researchers from a communications studies background might feel themselves entitled, then, to look upon marketing communications as a field permanently stuck in embarrassing adolescence, fixated upon a model of communication that everyone else has grown out of. Indeed, there are even marginal voices within marketing academia that have been presenting alternative ways of approaching the communication process for almost 20 years. Communication theorists and marginal marketing mavens have taken the lessons of predominantly literary-based theories such as reader response, poststructuralism, deconstruction, and new historicism and applied them toward a rebalancing of marketing and marketing communication in favor of multivalent interpretations, active audiences, and a general problematizing of many of the management assumptions at the heart of mainstream marketing. Many of these (comparatively) radical voices point to the apparently more enlightened, grown-up discourses that constitute the communication and media studies disciplines as models of where marketing theory and research should be heading (Shankar, 1999; Robson & Rowe, 1997).

Yet, this wondrously evolved elder spirit of communication studies is itself very much a rhetorical construction, a strategic fiction designed to inculcate embarrassment in the country bumpkins of mainstream marketing communication. Pick up any issue of the *Journal of Communication, Human Communication Research,* or *Communication Theory* (to flagrantly single out the august organs of my own professional organization, the International Communication Association) and one will be greeted with predominantly instrumentalist research papers that assume discernible effects and are predicated upon essentially transmission models of communication. There are definite streams of postmodern critical voices in these journals but so there have been in quite traditional marketing and advertising publications for a considerable time. Perhaps more importantly, much of the postmodern thought in evidence in both communication and marketing theory remains tied to (often more subtly expressed) paradigms of transmission and control.

The influence of Claude Shannon's paper "A Mathematical Theory of Communication" in 1948 and Warren Weaver's subsequent introductory framing of it a year later in the book-length expansion have had a foundational effect upon both mainstream and marginal communication studies and marketing communication approaches to the idea of what communication actually is. Indeed, as Gary Radford (2005) has pointed out in his study *On the Philosophy of Communication*, the transmission model has come to dominate amateur as well as professional considerations of communication. Seconding Barnett Pearce's contention that "if you were to ask the first ten people on the street to define 'communication', all ten would likely give some version of what we call the transmission theory" (quoted in Radford, 2005, p. 1), Radford notes that "most people have a firm and quite unproblematic notion of communication" (p. 1) that is based around the quite "obvious" truth that communication is "a process of transmission" (p. 2). Shannon's work was born from and meant to be applicable to solving mathematical problems in the engineering of communications technology; he was certainly not advancing a 'theory of general communication' in the sense of a model that could be used to explain interpersonal discourse and the vagaries of semantic interpretation. However, because Shannon's work is grounded in the technology of communication it appeared to present a seductive (because scientifically rigorous) way of approaching the creation of a theory that could explain human communication across technologies of mass media. For a populace more and more used to thinking of communication as a function of technology, a technological model of communication appears quite natural. Electronic engineering terminology has become a part of our day-to-day lexicon: *broadcast, signal, distortion, reception, tether, coverage,* etc. The words have come to define our understanding of communication (both face-to-face and technologically-mediated) and they are infused with the assumptions of source, noise, receiver, and the process of transmission.

Intimately allied to the transmission model is the assumption of control that informs it. The most referenced author in Shannon's original paper is Norbert Wiener, the founder of cybernetics. Wiener's famous definition of cybernetics was that it was the "science of communication and control" and unlike Shannon he was far more happy to expand his work's applicability across disciplinary boundaries, investigating the fundamental role of control in human communication and social systems. The link between Shannon and Wiener, and between the transmission communication model and cybernetics, was strengthened by two important elements: Warren Weaver's "Introductory Note" to Shannon's 1949 book and Shannon's participation in the annual Macy Conferences held between 1943 and 1954. Weaver's commentary on Shannon's research boldly claimed that it provided a model of communication that was universal, applicable to "not only written and oral speech, but also music, the pictorial arts, the theatre, the ballet, and in fact all human behaviour" (p. 3, quoted in Radford, 2005, p. 76). Weaver then goes on to invoke Wiener's research as evidence that Shannon's model can be extended to the problem of communication effectiveness, reasoning that as Shannon himself has clearly been greatly influenced by the work of Wiener then it is only logical to carry (back) over his work into the arena of biological applications studied by Wiener. Effectively, Weaver conflates the two men's theories and thus merges the transmission model with the cybernetic paradigm of control. Wiener himself would take a similar approach to integrating Shannon's work into his own thinking and it was therefore only natural that the two would form the backbone to the Macy Conferences on Cybernetics that did so much to consolidate the assumptions of control across cutting edge work in biology, computation, robotics, and the social sciences in the 1950s. The conferences brought together a disparate group of anthropologists, philosophers, mathematicians, scientists, and engineers in an attempt to synthesize "the central concepts that, in their high expectations, would coalesce into a theory of communication and control applying equally to animals, humans and machines" (Hayles, 1999, p. 7). The early use of Shannon's information science approach to modeling communication in the building of an understanding of how control works across biological, social, and mechanical systems meant that when theoreticians of other fledgling disciplines such as management science and marketing had use for an accessible, cross-disciplinary way to discuss the process of communication they easily imbibed the paradigm of transmission and control that sits at the heart of what has become known as the first-order cybernetics of the Macy Conferences.

A further essential element in the wholesale adoption of the transmission and control model of communication in modern marketing, and the element that partly explains the way in which the discipline has so strongly resisted the reflexive questioning of this model when compared to the other social sciences, is the almost total dominance of the *management* paradigm since the publication of pioneering texts by Wroe Alderson, Gene McCarthy, and Philip Kotler in the late 50s and 60s. Indeed, Kotler's subtitle to his original 1967 *Marketing Management* text was *Analysis, Planning, and Control*—and this emphasis has been kept all the way through the 70s and 80s until the 10th, millennium, edition. *Control* was and is a central assumption of the management school of marketing, betraying its origins in the Operations Research application of cybernetics and informatics and the Ford Foundation-sponsored reframing of business education toward a tightly quantitative instantiation of the scientific paradigm. While Kotler's emphasis has appeared to change in later editions and texts, particularly in his adoption of the rhetoric of a 'holistic' approach, the goal of control remains the most essential component of the marketing management program. Communication, consequently, becomes a matter of control and the

Shannon/Weaver/Wiener transmission model is a perfect representation of the control perspective of the flow of information.

It is important to mention at this point the part played by the work of Paul Lazarsfeld in the elaboration and diffusion of the basic cybernetic model of communication as control. Lazarsfeld's research work at Columbia University produced the well-known "two-step flow of communication" theory which he co-authored with Elihu Katz in 1955. Katz and Lazarsfeld's (1955) theory has been seen as supporting the idea that the mass media has a much smaller direct effect on public opinion than it is often accused of having, although others (including C. Wright Mills [1959] who worked on some of the original field research for the book) have seen the theory as dangerously misguided and open to manipulation by the networks of power that control those media. The two-step flow theory alleges that the messages transmitted by mass media to the populace are heavily mediated by the social groups that individual citizens are members of. So, a newspaper article, radio broadcast, etc., is discussed at work, or on the train journey home, or at the dinner table with other people—its message is never simply injected into the minds of the audience but is always contextualized and interpreted by the opinion and commentary provided by those influential figures in an individual's social life. Now, I will examine the implications of the two-step flow of communication in greater depth in Chapter 5, when I come to discuss issues of interactivity and community in reference to viral, or connected, marketing. At this early stage, however, I would like to address the way in which the two-step flow mirrors the cybernetic approach to communication. Lazarsfeld, crucially, was a founding member of the Macy Conferences, attending the first six of the meetings (Heims, 1991). That the matrix of ideas contributing to the cybernetic approach had some form of attraction for Lazarsfeld seems obvious. Although he was not present for Claude Shannon's various presentations of communication theory (Shannon started appearing as a guest only after Lazarsfeld had stopped attending), the way that Shannon's approach suffused Wiener's own work meant that the milieu that surrounded Lazarsfeld was firmly rooted in assumptions of control. It is difficult not to see the influence of these assumptions in the focus on political and market opinion manipulation that typified his work at Columbia. The two-step flow of communication, while seemingly breaking the inevitability of the direct transmission of opinion between media and consumer, still presupposes the fundamental connection between communication and control. Influencers, those members in each small social grouping who are looked to (or who can effectively get their opinions heard) by those other members around them, become the substitute media; they interrupt the flow of the news or the advertising messages in order to transmit their own messages to those around them. The format of sender and receiver is still present, it is just that the media's message has now been intercepted by a local broadcaster (the influencer) who transmits her own take on it to her loyal neighborhood followers. The upshot, of course, was that the sponsors of Katz and Lazarsfeld's research (marketers), and those with a need to more effectively control public opinion, held the two-step flow of communication up as a model for the use of grassroots, community message transmission (Bennett & Manheim, 2006), while at the same time using the research to initiate the design of more effective means of transmitting messages directly to the consumer without them being distracted by the 'noise' of local opinion. Furthermore, the two-step flow of communication formed a central component in the communications science that provided the "historical roots of the marketing communication approach" (Hackley, 2001, p. 110). Lazarsfeld's perspective was always a heavily empirical one, using statistical modeling in pursuit of more effective understandings of the mechanism of opinion formation in mass audiences. The two-step flow of communication contains the same assumptions of feedback-driven control that Shannon and Wiener's work displays, and, although Lazarsfeld was also personally responsible for the transplantation of the Frankfurt School of critical communication studies to the U.S., it is the communication as control paradigm that went on to inform the understanding of the dominant mainstream of communication and marketing.

FEEDBACK AND THE TRADITIONAL MODEL

In the decades since Shannon's model was adopted by the discipline of communication studies, there have been a number of attempts to 'improve' it, particularly in response to concerns that it makes the receiver too passive. Ironically, the addition to the model that has been most successful in appearing to take into account the active nature of an audience (and thus is used to counter uneasiness with the simplistic injection nature of the straight SMR diagram) is the tagging of a feedback loop from the receiver back to the sender. This was first instituted by Melvin DeFleur in his 1966 study *Theories of Mass Communication* but has now become part of the standard presentation of the Shannon model. This is ironic, of course, because the feedback loop is the one mechanism that typifies the classic first-order cybernetic approach. DeFleur's addition simply makes explicit the strong historical and conceptual relationship between informatics and cybernetics, communication theory and control theory. As such we are able to see the feedback loop for what it really represents rather than what it has come to be used to signify.

When Kotler, in his presentation of the "macromodel of the communication process" (see Figure 1.2), delineates the flow of "response" back from the "receiver" as it turns into a "feedback" input into the "sender" what he is describing is an element of a control flow. There is one channel present and its purpose is to convey the response back to the receiver to the message from the sender. When this "response" gets transmuted into "feedback" the model is explicitly referencing the cybernetic use of the term to indicate

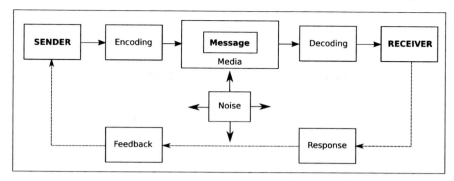

Figure 1.2   Philip Kotler and Kevin Keller's "Elements in the communication process". (Source: Philip Kotler and Kevin Lane Keller, *Marketing Management: Analysis, Planning, Implementation and Control*, 12th edition, ©2006, Electronically reproduced by permission of Pearson Education Inc., Upper Saddle River, New Jersey.)

the observation of a signal from the environment that enables the adjustment of an output in order to bring a process closer to a desired goal state. The response from the receiver, in other words, is useful only in so far as it enables the sender to adjust the message until the desired goal of communication has been reached.

Feedback ensures effective control. Kotler's discussion of the key elements of the model is clearly predicated upon this basis. He writes that the sender "must know what audiences they want to reach and what responses they want to get" and that they must then "develop feedback channels" in order to "monitor" those responses (Kotler & Keller, 2006, p. 539). In this scheme, the receiver is given a voice, is listened to, but is not allowed agency. Noticeably, the feedback channels are developed by the sender. There is no possibility that the receivers themselves might initiate such channels or indeed might actually wish to communicate with the sender outside of the context of the sender's own message. The receivers only exist when the senders send them messages and they can only possibly communicate when they are being targeted by the sender. Furthermore, any communication, or feedback, that the receivers do partake in is entirely framed within the terms of the goals of the sender, the responses that they know they want to get. When the receivers talk their words are being judged according to predetermined criteria—does what they say match what the sender wants to hear? If not, then the message must be adjusted or the channels must be recalibrated. It is also important to note that the use of the Shannon model means that communication is concerned with information and therefore it is in no way necessary for the feedback from the receiver to take the form of conscious or direct communication. The receiver's buying behavior, for example, would constitute a communication response. In Kotler's terms, the receiver is 'monitored' for output signals that can constitute feedback.

PROBLEMS WITH THE TRADITIONAL MODEL

The consequences of mainstream marketing management's adoption of the Shannon/Wiener model of communication as control are significant and multitudinous. Firstly, it neatly positions communication as simply another tool of the larger management control system thus strengthening the legitimacy of the marketing as management paradigm. Secondly, it provides the impression that a message selected by the marketing agent can be successfully delivered in a considered manner to a pre-selected audience. Thirdly, it understands communication as something that produces effects—effects that can be monitored as part of a control system and therefore corrected if not consistent with management goals. Fourthly, it thinks of the receiver as lacking agency. Fifthly, it frames all communication under its remit as subservient to the formulated marketing goals. Clearly, some of these points arise from a motivation to persuade the target audience of marketing management textbooks that the information contained in such books is directly transferable and applicable to 'real life', quotidian management scenarios. The presentation of the logical empiricist, mathematico-cybernetic marketing communication model thus serves to instill confidence and certainty in the reader; marketing is a calm, considered, scientific system of control. All this would be highly attractive to anyone wishing to see the world of business, enterprise, and organization as *manageable*. Marketing management and its view of communication stands as a beacon of sanity to anyone who is worried about the unpredictability and unknowability of humanity; follow the right steps and your message *will* get through and it *will* have the effects you want.

The problem occurs when this approach to communication becomes manifestly unworkable. Despite the many voices in the liberal arts and softer social sciences from the 1960s onwards, the communication as control model has remained basically unassailable in marketing theory and practice (Buttle, 1995). As Mark Tadajewski (2006) has shown, marketing academics in the U.S. (and hence the most powerful voices in the field globally) have experienced since the late 1950s a strong process of reinforcement (through tenure criteria, journal inclusion, conference selection, and grant allocation) toward a quantitative, objective "scientific" paradigm and away from qualitative, subjective, "liberal" modes of investigation and expression. So, those voices of discontent with the transmission model of communication, although strong in other fields and even influential in communication studies, had little effect in marketing because there was little sense that their discontent emanated from anything other than an ill-advised liberal dissatisfaction with the whole scientific paradigm. Marketing knew where it was going and it knew who its friends were. In all fairness, the liberal arts and social sciences that began to slowly take up more reflexive positions toward such issues had never experienced the sort of public tongue-lashing that business schools in the U.S. had received in the Ford and Carnegie reports on business education. It is no wonder that ever since, marketing has consistently nailed its colors to the quantitative, empiricist mast even while its sister disciplines in the social sciences and humanities were questioning and examining the claims of objectivity and normativeness. And it is no wonder that alternative voices within marketing theory have, until very recently, found it so difficult to be heard.

ALTERNATIVES

Ironically, while marketing has stuck to a mid-20th century understanding of control and communication, the disciplines that gave birth to such a perspective have themselves evolved almost beyond recognition. Cybernetics, systems dynamics, and general systems theory (GST) have become areas of research that are infused with the knowledge that the process of observation is a creative act, and consequently any model, any description, any data set is, before anything, a construction of the researcher. These disciplines have been able to evolve highly sophisticated approaches to the integration of theories of control with ideas of communication based upon perception as construction. Recently, Chris Hackley has put forward a reading of marketing theory's history that uses a "social constructionist ontology" (Hackley, 2001, p. 46) that bears many similarities to current GST and second-order cybernetic thinking. As Hackley notes, social constructionist theories are far more the province of modern sociology departments rather than business, marketing or (indeed) humanities departments. Interestingly, this is also the case with cybernetics and systems—the evolution of which has tended to take place, in Europe, within sociology departments that are interdisciplinary schools with a strong sociological component. Given what I have written above regarding the strong historic tendency within marketing academia to favor quantitative, empirical arguments it is perhaps more realistic to expect the marketing management mainstream to be influenced in its understanding of communication and control by paradigms originating in 'harder' social sciences (with experimental traditions) such as sociology and psychology rather than the softer, militantly qualitative disciplines of rhetoric, literature, and critical theory. In this regard, I will argue that constructionist/constructivist approaches, like those advanced by Hackley and by modern systems/cybernetics schools, have a real chance of supplanting the traditional Shannon/Wiener communication and control model at the heart of marketing. A full exposition of the constructivist approach to communication will be provided in Chapter 3; for now I will discuss the degree to which rhetorical and 'postmodern' analyses of marketing communication have attempted to challenge the hegemony of the Shannon/Wiener model.

THE RHETORICAL MODELS

The meaning of the term 'rhetoric' has evolved significantly since its coining in Athens in the fifth century BCE. Originally referring specifically to "the civic art of public speaking as it developed in deliberative assemblies" (Kennedy, 1994, p. 3) it soon came to denote the persuasive use of language in any context and more recently has taken on a wider definition as the art and discipline "that facilitates our understanding of the nature and function of symbols in our lives" (Foss, Foss, & Trapp, 2002, p. 1) therefore moving outside the realm of the word and including images, rituals, music, etc., and also more explicitly encompassing the study of how the choices of such symbols reflect the larger worldviews of those who use them. This evolution of meaning, and the fact that earlier understandings of the term continue to co-exist with these more expanded ones, has meant that for some contemporary researchers there is little difference between the words *communication* and *rhetoric* while for others the difference is clear and necessary. This variance is mirrored in the history of rhetorical approaches to marketing communication over the last few decades, which would include such core examples as Barbara Stern's (1988, 1990) articles on the use of allegory and metaphor in advertising messages, Linda Scott's (1994) foundational analysis of the "visual rhetoric" of advertising, Stephen Brown's (1999) notorious (to some), hilarious (to others) comparison of the rhetorical tropes of Morris Holbrook and Theodore Levitt, not to mention significant papers by Barbara J. Phillips and Edward McQuarrie (2002, 2004), McQuarrie and David Mick (1992, 1996, 1999) and Mark Toncar and James Munch (2001). The use of rhetoric as a means of discussing, analyzing, and framing marketing communication artifacts, practices, and theories takes a number of different forms as evidenced in the work of these authors. Phillips, McQuarrie, Mick, Toncar, and the early work of Barbara Stern can be said to exemplify a more traditionalist stream which applies classical rhetorical typologies of the figures of speech to discussions of advertising texts in order to illustrate the way in which commercial copy from the 20th century often follows classical models of persuasive technique. This research emphasis has a number of consequences. Firstly, it 'legitimizes' advertising texts as a form of discourse that can be discussed using the same terminology and considerations as one might use to examine the language of Shakespeare, Joyce, Cicero, or Lincoln. Secondly, it offers a powerful vocational reason for the teaching of rhetoric in communication faculties, advertising and, even, marketing departments. Thirdly, it presents an understanding of direct effects which harmonizes very nicely with the Shannon/Wiener communication model. Fourthly, it serves to historically contextualize the advertising enterprise within a long and complex tradition of attention to persuasive effect (significantly deepening advertising's historical legacy beyond the ideas of maker's mark and craftsman's signpost).

The problem with this classical approach, as suggested in the third point above, is its intimate connection to the 'classical' communication model. Although Shannon, Weaver, and Wiener can be said to have perfected and 'empiricized' the model of communication and control, the idea of direct communication effects inculcated in a target audience through the deliberate strategies of a sender belongs to Arsitotelian formulations of rhetoric. As Benoit and Smythe put it in their landmark article in *Communication Studies*, "traditional rhetorical theory adopts the standpoint of rhetors instead of auditors, or privileges invention and message production over message reception and interpretation" (Benoit & Smythe, 2003, p. 96). Seen from this point of view, analysis of advertising or PR copy using classical rhetorical approaches, although seeming to hale from a humanities-inspired appreciation of texts, in fact compounds the assumptions of communication and control that mainstream marketing management theory is built upon. As the discipline of rhetoric has developed over the 20th century, scholars have sought to widen it scope and examine many of its classical assumptions. However, there remains across much of the theoretical work a central focus on the rhetor rather than the auditor, so whether a scholar is examining a discourse for its ideological assumptions, gender assumptions, or assumptions of metaphor, the emphasis is still upon the creator of the message, the text, and how whatever rhetoric he or she might be said to be using is going to have an effect upon the audience. Only very recently, with the importation of reception theory (see next), has rhetoric begun to really, systematically question this focus.

Another, more recent, use of the term rhetoric has origins outside of the specific discipline (as it is understood particularly in the U.S.), being more connected with the work of Michel Foucault and his theory of discourses of power. For example, in Routledge's *Interpretive Marketing Research* series, both this book and Chris Hackley's use the word "rhetoric" (or "rhetorics") in their subtitles to reference this contemporary academic understanding of the word to mean the investigation of how "everyday linguistic usage has a history and reflects relations of power and authority which we unwittingly reproduce through the rhetoric we choose" (Hackley, 2001, p. 11). So, I might speak of the 'rhetoric of mainstream marketing management' by which I would mean the way in which discourses engaged in by marketing management scholars will (re)produce, through their choice of terminology, their favoring of certain approaches, terms, methodologies, perspectives, ways of saying and ways of speaking, particular systems of knowledge, power, and authority. Implicit within this stance is the idea that there is no actual, correct truth outside of a particular discourse— knowledge is not absolute but rather generated from eternally reproducing, revising, recombining discourse streams and is therefore completely contingent. This use of the word 'rhetoric' is clearly linked, then, to a form of constructionist paradigm but there is a danger here too that the communication that underlies such a radical conception is still fundamentally one that privileges the rhetor over the auditor. In uncovering the systems of power, authority and knowledge reproduced within the discourses of such groupings as doctors, lawyers, politicians, and marketing academics once again we have the portrayal of the receiver as powerless, lacking agency, controlled by the language of the sender. The transmission model of communication runs deep within Foucault's own discourse and even though some of his acts of investigation and analysis serve as examples of a receiver actively interpreting and exposing the reproduction of power systems that have been transmitted to him, the assumption is that such a transmission is made and most of the time succeeds. Kotler's macromodel is thus, ironically, just as Foucauldian as Hackley's social construction stance.

Rhetoric is something to be careful with, then, particularly in an examination of the 'rhetoric' of interactive marketing. So, while I will be making use of the term in the sense outlined above, because it implies a constructionist paradigm I will be treating sympathetically and because it usefully signals this text as a member of a larger, academically 'hip' discourse ('hipness' being a metric of power within certain contexts), I will also be trying to subvert the transmission nature of its communication assumptions ('subvert' being another one of those words that attempt to flag membership of a particular discourse stream).

THE POSTMODERN MODELS

The term 'postmodern' in relationship to research methodologies or critical approaches is used to refer to a number of (sometimes easily allied, sometimes not) discourses and authors. Notoriously difficult to define, Jonathan Potter's attempt to sum up the difference between a modernist and postmodernist approach via personification perhaps remains the most immediately effective. Imagining the pair as if they were two of his friends, Potter describes the modernist as "well meaning and hard working, but she has not got much of a sense of humour: she is constantly struggling to get to the best understanding of what is going on in any situation" (Potter, 2005, p. 88). The postmodernist, on the other hand, "talks more about work than actually doing it; she is witty and ironic—you never know whether she is making fun of you or sending herself up", adding that "she is many things at once, and none of them seems more true than any other" (ibid.). Fundamental concerns of postmodernist writers and artists have been the link between language and perception, the use of 'metanarratives' to legitimate social and cultural paradigms, the trope of self-reference or reflexivity (often connected with an ironic attitude toward infinite loops as metaphors), the need to investigate and challenge the process of representation wherever it might be found (though perhaps not in the postmodernists' own backyard), and the consequent collapsing of such constructed binary oppositions as fact and fiction, good and evil, past and present. The works of Derrida, Lyotard, Foucault, Bakhtin, Lacan, Deleuze, Guattari, and Baudrillard are the most canonical and provide continual touchstones in the teaching and dissemination of this complex polyphony of critical ideologies.

The influence of postmodernist discourse upon the humanities has been considerable. A graduate student in Western literatures, histories, or philosophies is generally expected to have mastered the discourses of 20th century postmodernism and would be expected to be able to reproduce the rhetorics of deconstruction, hyperreality, and schizoanalysis in conference presentations, article submissions, and theses. In the social sciences the hegemony of such discourses has been more subtle, although in both sociology and anthropology the strong lineage of influential scholars who have arrived at similar positions to those of postmodern researchers in the humanities means that there has evolved a mutually-supporting cross-pollination between the fields that can sometimes give the impression of a remarkably pervasive monoculture (to use a rhetorically loaded term redolent of a dangerous poverty of variety). Marketing's response to these discourses has been notably cool. With a few telling exceptions, mainstream marketing management has refused to adopt the rhetoric of postmodernism. Understandably, perhaps, for a discipline that is almost paranoid in its attempts to maintain the appearance of generating an approved scientific discourse, any connection with an ideology that so consistently points out the constructed, arbitrary, power-serving nature of the empirical scientific paradigm is going to raise severe discomfort. The mainstream journals in marketing and advertising have acted to keep a thick boundary between their statistics-driven, quantitative concerns and the rising tide of subjectivist, reflexive voices to be heard in other disciplines. There have appeared, however, a small number of publications, such as the *European Journal of Marketing* and *Marketing Theory* which pursue a pluralistic editorial agenda and are happy to provide a space for research applying postmodern or critical perspectives. Allied to the inclusive spirit displayed by these titles is the alternative nature of much work conducted under the rubric of consumer research. Since 1974, the *Journal of Consumer Research* has specifically stood as a "medium for interdisciplinary exchange" and has carried a significant amount of 'postmodern' writing on consumer attitudes and behavior. Unfortunately, its coverage has become so broad that it has effectively encouraged the establishment of consumer research as a separate discipline outside of marketing with the consequence that the alternative, qualitative voices it publishes have become easier to ignore within the marketing management mainstream because they no longer represent a relevant internal disciplinary force. Furthermore, as Wilkie and Moore (2003, quoted in Shaw & Jones, 2005) discovered, the influx of non-marketing academics into the realm of consumer research has meant that the emphasis on marketing per se has severely diminished.

At the beginning of the 21st century, then, postmodernism has a place in marketing management discourse but that place is a neatly fenced ghetto. A growing ghetto, to be sure, but still not a neighborhood that the conservatively-attired mainstream academic would like to be seen walking around by her colleagues. The presence of the ghetto means that marketing can at least appear to be engaging in this increasingly popular discourse and so, when needed, can point to the work of, say, Stephen Brown (1993, 1995, 1998a, 1998b), Stephanie O'Donohoe (1997, 2001), Linda Scott (1992, 1993, 1994), Chris Hackley (1999, 2001), Barbara Stern (1994, 1996, 1998) and A. Fuat Firat (1993; with Venkatesh, 1993, 1995; with Dholakia & Venkatesh, 1995; with Dholakia, 2006) to prove its currency. As Brownlie and Hewer (2007) have pointed out, this type of critical marketing research has a strong part to play in making mainstream marketing competitive in a higher education world dominated by Research Assessment Exercises (the UK league-table system designed to evaluate scholarship levels of university departments) and their equivalents. The integration of alternative voices into the mainstream is slow, however. Additionally, for the purposes of this study, what is important is how far postmodern and alternative discourses themselves advance models of communication that depart from the Shannon/Wiener paradigm of control. The most obvious area in which this can be examined is the work done in advertising research to implement the insights of reader-response theory into the mainstream communication model.

READER-RESPONSE THEORY

It is telling that the one alternative voice that Kotler allows into his presentation of the transmission macromodel of communication (though only to the extent of a brief endnote at the end of a *very* long chapter) is Barbara Stern's Revised Communication Model of Advertising, which Kotler references as "an alternate" model "developed specifically for advertising communications" (Kotler & Keller, 2006, p. 564) but, crucially, does not explain. In characterizing Stern's model as "specifically developed" for advertising, of course, Kotler dismisses its relevance to the larger area of marketing communication in general, although its principle features are entirely transferable across the gamut of communication systems employable in marketing. The reference to Stern's article is a piece of rhetorical strategy, then. Kotler is seen to allow an alternative voice into his discourse but strips it of all power by at the same time noting that it is only applicable to a small, specific area of marketing communication—the Shannon/Wiener macromodel thus remains unassailable because there is no alternative general model of marketing communication. The alternative voice is both invoked and banished at the same time.

Since the publication of Stern's Revised Model in 1994 there have been almost no published attempts to re-examine it, build upon it or offer further alternatives to it, which is not to say that it has in any way supplanted the dominance of the transmission model in marketing, marketing communication, or advertising discourse. Rather, this comparative silence demonstrates the hegemony of the Shannon/Wiener model across mainstream *and* alternative discourses in marketing. A careful examination of the way in which Stern uses an approach influenced by reader-response theory to modify certain aspects of the transmission model will enable us to highlight the elements of that model which appear to be untouchable and unquestioned.

Stern opens the paper by pointing out the ways in which the traditional model of communication "fails to capture the interactivity of communicative discourse between advertisers and consumers":

> it presumes that the source and the recipient are singular constructs; it does not account for message content that can be activated in a variety of forms; and it assumes a passive message recipient as the object of information transmitted by the source. (Stern, 1994, p. 5)

Stern describes how her revision "expands the traditional triad" (ibid., p. 8) of "who—tells what—to whom" in three ways (see Figure 1.3). Firstly, she makes the "source" multidimensional, so that instead of being represented as a single, homogeneous element, the sender is fragmented into three principle voices: the sponsor (who pays for the ad, dictates what it should say, and approves its final form), the author (who is paid for the ad and is responsible at a microlevel for the creation of the message), and

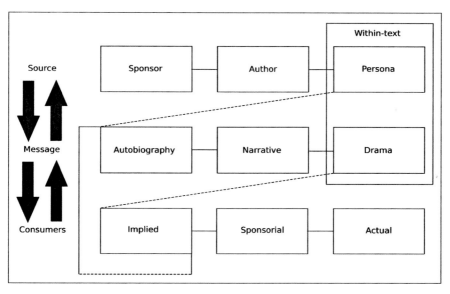

Figure 1.3 Barbara Stern's "Revised Communication Model for Advertising". (Source: *Journal of Advertising*, Vol. 23, No. 2 (June 1994): Figure 2. Copyright © 1994 by American Academy of Advertising. Reprinted with permission of M. E. Sharpe, Inc. All rights reserved. Not for reproduction.)

the persona (the representation of the advertiser within the message itself, whether that be an anonymous voice-over, a spokesperson, or perhaps an animated product). Secondly, the simplistic conception of the "message" is developed into a triadic matrix of choices between the framing devices of autobiography, story, or drama. These three different forms of discourse effect the type of persona embedded within them and also frame the receivers in the sense of placing them in particular roles characteristic of drama, third-person, or first-person narrative (audience as "empathetic, vicarious participants", "students in need of data", and "eavesdroppers sharing private personal experiences", respectively). Thirdly, then, Stern expands the traditional model's element of "receiver" into a further triumvirate: the "implied consumer" (the construct of the consumer implicit within the message), the "sponsorial consumer" (the initial audience for all advertising message being the advertiser themselves who need to grant approval before the message can be presented further), and finally the "actual consumer" ("individuals in the real world who comprise the target audience at which advertising aims"). Stern's conception of the implied consumer is directly influenced by the work of the reader-response theorist Wolfgang Iser (1990, 1991). The text's author fictionalizes an 'ideal' reader to whom the text is optimally directed and who would represent the perfect interpreter. The implied reader therefore exists within the text as a construct of the author but at the same time, precisely because of its privileged position within the text, stands to dominate the interpretative presence of the actual reader. Stern quotes Susan Sulieman's explication of this subtle play for control: "only by agreeing to play the role of this created audience for the duration of his/her reading can an actual reader correctly understand and fully appreciate the work" (Stern, 1994, p. 11). Similarly, the "sponsorial consumer" is depicted by Stern as a controlling force over the "actual consumer's" reception and interpretation of the discourse. Both in their role as a message source and a message consumer, sponsors are "market representatives who collectively shape the cultural tradition of advertising by determining what enters it and what is excluded". The sponsors' control is thus over the message received by the "actual consumer" but also over the attempts at message production made by the "author" (the multi-agent agency). Stern's revised model of advertising communication, particularly in its engagement with Iser's reader-response theory, appears to offer a perspective where the "actual consumer" engages in the active construction of meaning by "cooperating with the communicator". This cooperation, however, takes the form of an agreement to adopt the perspectives of the communicators, to mimic the ideal interpretation of the "implied consumer". So, it is "active" in the sense of agreeing to conform. Control, then, remains at the heart of Stern's communication model. The "sponsor" controls the "author" and both control the "actual consumer" who is expected to cooperate in the correct interpretation of the message. Stern's consideration of an interactive component within this model is a very cursory implementation of what is effectively the traditional marketing communication feedback loop whereby the "actual consumer" is able to "respond to the message in real-time by means of seeking information or making a purchase" (ibid., p. 13). In other words, the consumer is producing a real-time response that can be fed back to the sponsorial source and author and used to measure the effectiveness of the transmission and interpretation (i.e., how closely the actual consumer is mimicking the implied consumer). Stern's model is therefore an expansion of the control flow delineated in Kotler's macro-model, an unfolding of some of its elements, rather than a radical alternative to its control-centered assumptions.

In her examination of future research directions that may emanate from her revised model, Stern does problematize the assumption of consumer cooperation by noting that some researchers have discussed the idea that consumers "may behave in an uncooperative way, invoking a special and cynical code for interpreting advertising" (ibid., p. 13). This facet of consumer interpretation is of vital importance to an effective, realistic modeling of market communication and has been taken up in the work of a number of scholars, most enthusiastically by Stephanie O'Donohoe (1994, 1997, 1998, 2001) who has contributed much insightful theorizing and field research to the examination of the way in which (particularly young) audiences make use of advertising messages in manners at distinct variance with the authorized "implied consumer" profile. O'Donohoe's findings provide much food for thought when examining the rhetoric of interactivity and I will return to her work later in this study.

Stern's revised model of advertising communication significantly expands the traditional Shannon/Wiener paradigm of communication and control but does little to overturn its basic assumptions. Despite its use of tropes from Wolfgang Iser's theory of reader-response (generally included within the corpus of postmodern literary schools) it only implements very particular aspects of his work and in quite limited ways, leaving the ramifications of the reader's cooperative creation of meaning for future researchers to investigate. The limited scope afforded the explication of the revised model is perhaps a result of the publication that it appears in, the *Journal of Advertising* being the most conservative (and the most powerful) academic organ devoted to that area of marketing communication. It would be unlikely that highly radical revisions of the communication model central to the academic study of advertising would be presented within its pages. The dyadic relationship between communication and control that the Shannon/Wiener model embodies remains mostly uncontested in Stern's paper, although in its radical fragmentation of the principal components it brings a multidimensionality to the model that had been lacking for almost 50 years.

Kotler's assertion that Stern's paper is only applicable to the arena of advertising is disingenuous. The fragmentation of the traditional components of sender, message, and receiver has obvious analogues in each of the marketing communication elements. It is the lesson of reader-response theory, for example, that there is an implied reader (or viewer or auditor) in *every* text, whether it be a novel, a print ad, a press release, a company statement, or an op-ed piece written by a consultant. Similarly, Stern's placing of the sponsor as both a 'sender' and 'receiver' component holds for PR practice, sponsorships, the presentation of sales promotions, and even the face-to-face realm of sales representatives (if one considers the heavy control of message format and content that constitutes the training of most sales forces). Unfortunately, Stern's article positions itself in a way that allows Kotler to marginalize it. In that the piece is published in the *Journal of Advertising* it must clearly demonstrate its relevance to advertising in particular as opposed to marketing communication in general. In order to fulfill the requirements of the journal, Stern sets up a binary opposition between oral communication and advertising communication by asserting that the traditional, linear tripartite communication model (which she interestingly locates in the "information processing theory" of Laswell and the linguistics of Jakobson) does not account for the "interactive network of advertisers, promotional text, and consumers as co-creators of communication" (Stern, 1994, p. 5). There is no hint that the traditional model is in any way deficient in describing any other form of communication other than advertising. Yet, the theoretical work that Stern uses in the principle arguments of the paper, work by literary theorists such as Iser and Prince, is based on the contention that all texts, all discourses (and therefore all communication) contain implied readers and implied authorial personas and that their meaning is the result of a cooperative interaction. But such universal implications are quite openly excluded from the presentation of the revised communication model. Now, as a reader familiar with the way in which academic peer review and journal publication processes work, I would venture the interpretation that this clear positioning of the article as relevant exclusively to advertising communication is a result of an expressed (or perceived) direction from the sponsor (the editorial voices at the journal) to the actual author (Barbara Stern) to keep the focus of the article tightly relevant to the journal's scope, and therefore not to muddy the waters and talk about the way in which this revised model for advertising communication is not in fact just for advertising communication but actually for all forms of mediated communication. In this way, the journal limits the scope of the article which in turn allows mainstream arbiters such as Philip Kotler to highlight the marginal nature of the work and thus strip it of the power to effect the broader macromodel he is presenting as the explanation for how marketing communication in general functions.

Marketing management's emphasis on practical instruction rather than theoretical speculation might make it hesitant in dealing with expanded (and potentially far more complex) versions of the traditional communication model. How might an advertising manager *make use* of the difference between "implied consumer" and "actual consumer" and what does it really matter if we say that there is a "typological trichotomy" of forms of advertising message? How might 'knowing' these things change the way that advertising is 'done'? If the answer is not clear and immediate, then the tendency is always going to be to return to the traditional understanding of the traditional model.

The problem comes when that traditional understanding no longer seems to work.

2 The Interactivity Crisis and Marketing Discourse

Nostalgia for simpler, more profitable days appears to be a constant feature of popular books on marketing communication. These are the types of books written by successful professionals in the marcoms business (or occasionally by successful academics who also have consultancy positions) and which purport to instruct readers in the latest, sure-fire techniques for closing that sale, reaching that prospect, persuading that switcher, or using the web to monetize their customer database. It is a tradition that the opening chapters of such texts must include a (sometimes bordering on the hysterical) lament for the fact that the marketing business isn't what it used to be, that the reliable tools of old are no longer up to the job of communicating effectively with new types of audiences exhibiting new types of behaviors and attitudes. One of the most common sources of disruption identified by these books is what has come to be called "clutter"—the sheer, vast tidal wave of media messages that we are subjected to from when we open our eyes in the morning to when we close them to sleep at night. So, Al Ries and Jack Trout, in their influential book, *Positioning: The Battle for Your Mind*, after providing the reader with a flood of figures regarding the information overload that besets us all in the "overcommunicated society", note that:

> The average mind is already a dripping sponge that can only soak up more information at the expense of what's already there. Yet we continue to pour more information into that supersaturated sponge and are disappointed when our messages fail to get through. (Ries & Trout, 2001, p. 7)

Ries and Trout offer their theory of positioning as the way to cut through this clutter and reach the mind of the prospect. And they have been doing so since 1972. Seth Godin plays the same cards in the opening of his *Permission Marketing*:

> This is a book about the attention crisis in America and how marketers can survive and thrive in this harsh new environment. Smart marketers

have discovered that the old way of advertising and selling products isn't working as well as it used to and they're searching aggressively for a new, enterprising way to increase market share and profits. (Godin, 2002, p. 23)

The problem is the same, then, but the solution is different—instead of positioning, Godin is offering permission marketing. And this pattern continues across the years and at different resolution levels. David Ogilvy comments in his *Confessions of an Advertising Man* that the "sad truth is that despite the sophisticated apparatus of the modern agency, advertising isn't getting the results it used to get in the crude days of Lasker and Hopkins" (Ogilvy, 2004, p. 47). It seems that wherever and whenever you look, marketing communication professionals are complaining that marketing communication doesn't work in the way it used to. The trope is echoed in the work of academic researchers. So, Sut Jhally, quoting a J. Walter Thomson report from 1984, writes that "commercial viewing levels are decreasing" (Jhally, 1990, p. 89) and notes that consequently "advertisers are starting to voice their discontent at having to pay for viewers who may not be watching their advertisements at all". Similarly, the academic/practitioner team of Wright-Isak, Faber, and Horner writing in the late-90s speak of advertising agencies being "on the defensive" and having to "scramble to produce facts that indicate a positive evaluation of the advertising contribution" due to the "recurring recession" and "environment of advancing globalization" (Wright-Isak, Faber, & Horner, 1997, p. 3). Paul Marsden of the London School of Economics, writing in 2006, devotes the introductory chapter of *Connected Marketing* to delineating the "state of turmoil" in the marketing industry by citing a barrage of dire U.S. figures that illustrate amongst other things, that the "failure rate for new product introductions" is 95%, that the "proportion of B2B marketing campaigns resulting in falling sales" is 84%, and that the "proportion of TV advertising campaigns generating positive ROI" is 18% (Marsden, 2006a, p. xix). There is, without a shadow of a doubt, a significant rhetorical element in this constant depiction of crisis. Every voice here is trying to persuade the reader that they have the solution or the answer or, at least, the most effective analysis of the condition, and talking up "the crisis in marketing" (as Marsden refers to it) is a way to try to increase the audience's perception of the need for a new approach. We can see Kotler taking advantage of the same rhetoric in *Marketing Management* when he writes in the opening paragraph of the marcom section:

But communications gets harder and harder as more and more companies clamor to grab the consumer's increasingly divided attention. To reach target markets and to build brand equity, holistic marketers are creatively employing multiple forms of communications. (Kotler & Keller, 2006, p. 535)

In other words, holistic marketing joins positioning, permission marketing, marketing public relations, viral marketing, or connection marketing as the answer to the (seemingly ongoing) marcoms crisis.

Perhaps the most consistent theme across all such discourse is that the customer is not as easily reached, or persuaded, as they once were. Customers have become empowered (ibid., p. 14), we are told. Indeed, the choice of this word is telling: When A empowers B, they give power to them, they allow them to have it. It is not as if B decided to get more power and went out and empowered themselves. No, once again, the customer is portrayed as a passive receiver. Even in their moment of seeming dominance, the rhetoric of marketing management robs consumers of agency and independence. When Kotler and Keller provide a list of "new consumer capabilities" they compound this portrayal of the passive prospect by referring to the way in which "the digital revolution has placed a whole new set of capabilities in the hands of consumers and businesses" (ibid., p. 11), the idea that they might have grabbed these for themselves being utterly alien to the control assumptions fundamental to marketing management. This perspective is even repeated in postmodern-inspired academic overviews such as Firat and Dholakia's recent article for *Marketing Theory,* in which the authors declare that marketing is no longer a "somewhat occult art" focused on satisfying consumer needs, but rather:

> a process available to consumers in order to *empower* and *enable* them to construct the realities they intend to experience through the construction of communities. (Firat & Dholakia, 2006, p. 136)

The ambiguity in the initial phrasing leads one to ask 'Made available by whom?' The sense seems to be that marketers now have to empower consumers to create communities. Certainly, through the use of "empower" and "enable", consumer agency is being subtly undermined. As I will show in later chapters, there is a very real sense in which traditional conceptions of marketing control are indeed feeding into 'postmodern' implementations of consumer communities. For now, however, what I wish to highlight is the rhetoric used by practitioners and academics alike in discussing the strategy to be adopted when faced with consumers who can talk quickly and freely to each other. And that rhetoric can be seen to contain a deeply patrician attempt to portray the consumer as somehow *allowed* the means to communicate, *enabled* to form communities by the brands and media conglomerates. Perhaps what we have here is an attempt by the traditional creators of both academic and practitioner marketing discourse to put up a rhetorical front of control when that control is being potentially threatened; by talking *as if* the consumer still has no real agency they attempt to allay fears that the consumer really does have agency.

The marketing trend that has most consistently exemplified the paradox of consumer agency is "relationship marketing". First proposed by L. L.

Berry (1983) in a volume devoted to new approaches to service marketing, the idea of relationship marketing (RM) has come to occupy a central place in the academic response to perceived changes in consumer attitudes and media use at the end of the 20th century. As John Egan notes, "during this period RM was probably the major trend in marketing and certainly the major (and arguably the most controversial) talking point in business management" (Egan, 2003, p. 145). In that a relationship marketing approach seeks to build and maintain strong relationships with the stakeholders of a company in order to become and remain competitive, communication is necessarily fundamental to its paradigm. Relationships, surely, are built upon communication? Yet explicit engagement with issues of communication appears only tangentially within the body of RM research. Words such as "interaction" and "dialog" are liberally strewn across RM discourse but rarely held up for examination or amplification. Instead, conceptual discussion amongst RM researchers has tended to focus around issues of which stakeholder relationships are essential for long-term competitiveness, how fundamental is the supplier-customer dyad or how the different relationships within the "relationship portfolio" (Gummesson, 1999, quoted in Hunt, 2002, p. 283) support each other. In this sense, the most significant piece of *communications* research relating to RM theory is Stern's 1994 article discussed previously, because the revised model's fragmentation of sender and receiver provides a view of the communication relationship between a number of stakeholders in the client–agency–audience system. Even though the growth of RM has meant that a lot of academic and practitioner attention has been focused on the adoption of new communication technologies and resources in pursuit of enhancing the effectiveness of the relationship networks of companies, the assumption of control remains central to the communication model implicit within this work. However, RM and the Customer Relationship Management (CRM) perspective that has grown out of it are primarily responsible for the rhetoric of communicative interactivity that has pervaded all levels of marketing management for the last decade. It is the RM paradigm that speaks through the countless paeans to the customer voice in contemporary industry journalism, doorstopper textbooks and airport bookstore, help-yourself, marketing-miracle, eureka-texts. Yet, as Stephen Brown has so directly put it, RM is "little more than a rehash of the original marketing concept" (Brown, 1998b, p. 273). It is a rehash because, behind the rhetoric of interactivity there is no revolution in communication model to back it up. And without a substantially different approach to communication, marketing is doomed to repeat the same patterns of control that it so vociferously contends it wishes to avoid. As we have already seen in both Kotler and Firat and Dholakia, the language of empowerment and enablement suffuses discussion of the modern consumer's participation in community-formation and information-sharing. That such disparate authors use the same, patrician rhetoric is a consequence, I would argue, of the way in which the discourse of RM has convinced stakeholders in marketing that the Internet and mobile communications technologies are tools to be used to *control* the management of customer relationships. In other words, it is an implicit assumption within industry paradigms that the consumer has been *allowed access* to the technologies so that they can be *empowered* to construct communities and so *enabled* to render up the data that feeds relationships to companies. One need only regard the phrase "customer relationship management" to take Brown's point: To momentarily adopt the marriage metaphor that is popular amongst RMers, if a husband was to express the desire to *manage* his relationship with his wife, most balanced people would tend to think that his words expressed a woefully controlling and fundamentally flawed attitude to the partnership of marriage.

RELATIONSHIP MARKETING AND INTERACTIVITY

In order to more deeply explore some of the rhetorical connections between the theory of RM and its use of the concept of interaction, I will examine a number of representative texts from the corpus in this study. While I have devoted the whole of Chapter 6 to an in-depth examination of the way in which RM, and the Service-Dominant Logic that supports it, sets up rhetorical elisions and maskings in order to avoid engaging significantly with issues of communication and interactivity, in the current chapter, as an initial exploration of the dominant rhetoric that manifests itself in RM discourse, I will be focusing on Susan Baker's book, *New Consumer Marketing: Managing a Living Demand System.* Baker's (2003) text is a good example of the current stage of evolution in academic thought on RM. The author begins with a rhetorical trope we have already become quite familiar with, the declaration of imminent marketing crisis: "a new marketplace is emerging and bringing with it a host of challenges never before encountered". This new marketplace represents a "root-and-branch upheaval" that, in a highly dramatic use of association, Baker further describes as a "paradigm shift" occurring at "the start of the third millennium" (ibid., p. 9). If this isn't apocalyptic enough, Baker rams it home with the following startling sentence:

> Marketing, especially consumer marketing, faces a daunting prospect: quickly undergo profound change or prepare for certain death. (ibid., p. 10)

At the heart of this life-threatening paradigm shift is, what Baker calls the "New Consumer". Fueled by the effects of globalization and the Internet,

> Instead of being the focus of persuasion to buy what producers wished to produce, consumers became the focus of production itself; they could influence to a great extent the nature of products. (ibid., p. 11)

The move away from production-focused toward consumption-foc economies is the "seismic shift" that Baker asserts has led to the need radical change in the marketing paradigm. Interestingly, Baker sees RM and CRM as natural, but fundamentally flawed, marketing responses to the "fact that the certainties of the production-driven economy have been replaced with the uncertainties of the consumption-led economy" (ibid., p. 21). RM and CRM ostensibly place the customer at the center of the marketing system, with the realization that "the customer has an intrinsic and dynamic value to the supplying organization and vice versa" and that "commercial transactions are not isolated events but that they take place within a live and continuous context of engagement" (ibid., p. 14), which takes the form of a relationship that needs to be nurtured by the company. For Baker, though, both RM and the more technologically-driven CRM, have proved to be disappointments. RM, while promoting a more "holistic" approach than traditional transactional marketing was difficult to actually implement within companies and although CRM, with its heavy use of database technologies, offered to solve the issue of exactly what tools should be used to manage the customer relationship, Baker supplies a depressing list of statistics to show that the large amount of money companies have spent on retooling for a CRM focus has apparently been for nothing. The principle problem with CRM has been, according to Baker, the fact that there are too many diffuse understandings of what the approach actually means and that fundamentally, "most CRM systems are not conceived with the active, demanding, IT-literate consumer in mind" (ibid., p. 17). Although the implementation of CRM has been highly problematic, however, it has "established the business case for adopting the customer's perspective and involving the customer in the formulation of product and service strategies".

Baker's narrative of the evolution of customer-focused marketing approaches is a tale of misunderstanding and lack of perception. Marketing management has recently begun to define itself as a discipline that has always been customer-focused. Indeed, as Kotler tells it these days, the marketing concept, emerging in the 1950s, was a shift away from a "product-centered, 'make-and-sell', philosophy" toward a "customer-centered, 'sense-and-respond' philosophy" (Kotler & Keller, 2006, p. 16). Logically, then, for the past 50 years, marketers *should have been* responding to the customer and placing them at the center of their processes. If this position is to be taken seriously, then the development of RM and CRM can be interpreted as indicators of the failure of marketing to effectively stay 'on message'; if marketing was always about making the customer the center then it has always been about relationship management. Unfortunately, Kotler's current version of marketing history is at variance with much of that history written by other pens in earlier years. Indeed, in reading through Shelby Hunt's overview of the birth and development of the marketing paradigm in *Foundations of Marketing Theory*, there is no mention of customer-focus or customer-centeredness. Through an examination of the work of Leavitt, Levy, Lazer, Luck, Ferber, Lavidge, Zaltmann, the AMA, and (even) the pre-1990s Kotler himself, Hunt never once notes the issue of customer-focus as central to any of these scholars' understanding of marketing. A similar observation can be made of Shaw and Jones's recent overview of schools of marketing thought (Shaw & Jones, 2005). Kotler's (re)construction of marketing history (and let us remember that it is no more or less a construction than Hunt's, Baker's or anyone else's) is designed to position marketing management as a cohesive discipline with a stable and consistent sense of core values and concerns—the projection of a definition that neatly reflects contemporary business concerns. In the same way, the regular redefinitions of the American Marketing Association and the UK's Chartered Institute of Marketing come to reflect contemporary trends and concerns whilst inevitably giving the impression that things have always been like that; the current CIM definition, for example, faithfully mirroring Kotler's own current approach (marketing is "the management process responsible for identifying, anticipating and satisfying customer requirements profitably", quoted in Jefkins, 2000, p. 4). Baker's version of marketing history serves her own argumentative concerns: A "growing realization that a manufacturer is not so much a product company as a service company with a product offering" is combined with the growth of the consumer rights movement to produce a "confluence" which serves to question "the way in which consumption is managed" (Baker, 2003, p. 27). The consequences of the failure of RM and CRM to adequately engage with the New Consumer is, as we have seen, framed by Baker in catastrophic, apocalyptic imagery; this rhetoric compliments her assertion that her work offers a new, vital approach that can save marketing from the accusations of irrelevancy and failure that she relays in her introduction. Kotler, on the other hand, seeks to project a sense of ordered, logical evolution culminating in the refinement of the "holistic marketing" orientation, which provides a "more complete, cohesive" (Kotler & Keller, 2006, p. 16) approach to the modern (never postmodern) market place.

Baker writes of RM as an orientation which has failed, while Kotler unquestioningly integrates it into his "holistic" conception. But in the end, both end up saying basically the same thing; modern marketing should be "an interactive dialogue between the company and its customers" where companies "must ask not only 'How can we reach our customers?' but also 'How can our customers reach us?'" (Kotler & Keller, 2006, p. 603) and the goal of marketing today "is to ensure that consumers have a perfect experience across whatever media they use to interact with the organization" so that "relationships are developed through the empowered engagement of both participants in a two-way interaction process" (Baker, 2003, p. 136).

Dialog with empowered consumers (and other stakeholders) has become almost a mantra to contemporary marketing. Time and time again, marketers and scholars point to the interactive technology of the Internet and make the connection between highly networked consumers and the need for a new communication paradigm. Relationship Marketing and Customer Relationship Management represent the practical outcome of making those connections. Yet, as Hackley, Baker, and Kotler all demonstrate in their different ways, these have not proved to be the panaceas everyone has wished for. For Hackley, this is because there is no real difference between RM and any previous instantiation of the marketing management impulse. For Baker, too, RM and CRM have not demonstrated a sufficiently revolutionary approach to dealing with changes in the marketing environment. Kotler, politically unable to admit the failure of RM, (and therefore the crisis in marketing management) instead subsumes it into the grab-bag of 'holistic marketing' (where there is strength in numbers). It appears that the interactive nature of the Internet remains at the heart of the modern marketing malaise. Everyone knows that it is vital to engage with it, or to solve it, yet, this interactivity has proven to be an elusive goal.

I will return to a deeper analysis of Relationship Marketing's construction of interactivity in Chapter 6, where I will also discuss broader issues of communication arising from the service-dominant re-orientation in marketing theory.

My argument in this book is that the reason that marketing responses to interactivity have been so markedly unsatisfactory is that they are all based upon the traditional control paradigm of the Shannon/Wiener communication model. An examination of the few scholarly attempts to provide a theoretical underpinning to interactive marketing communication is therefore called for.

MODELS OF INTERACTIVITY

In addition to Stern's work already outlined, there have been two further significant attempts to provide models of interactive marketing communication. Hoffman and Novak's "Marketing in Hypermedia Computer-Mediated Environments: Conceptual Foundations" appeared in the *Journal of Marketing* in 1996 while Rodgers and Thorson's "The Interactive Advertising Model: How Users Perceive and Process Online Ads" was published in the *Journal of Interactive Advertising* in 2000. As I have pointed out elsewhere (Miles, 2007), both of these articles advance a view of interactive marketing communication as inherently separate from all other forms of advertising. Stern's model, on the other hand, seeks to provide an inclusive, integrated view of the communication process that is applicable to all forms of advertising (and, as I have pointed out, is therefore also extensible to other forms of marketing communication).

Hoffman and Novak define a hypermedia computer-mediated environment (CME) as "a distributed computer network used to access and provide hypermedia content (i.e., multimedia content connected across the network with hypertext links)" (Hoffman & Novak, 1996, p. 50). As such, the World Wide Web on the Internet is the "first and current networked global implementation" (ibid.) of a hypermedia CME, and it is the marketing use of the Web that the authors are concerned with discussing and modeling. Hoffman and Novak see hypermedia CMEs as typologically separate from other advertising media due to a number of unique characteristics: machine-interactivity, telepresence, hypermedia, and network navigation. Fundamental to their conceptual approach is Csikszentmihalyi's (1977) idea of "flow" which they use to discuss the state of mind that a user enters when navigating the hypermedia CME network.

> When in the flow state, irrelevant thoughts and perceptions are screened out and the consumer's attention is focused entirely on the interaction. Flow thus involves a merging of actions and awareness, with concentration so intense there is little attention left over to consider anything else. (ibid., p. 58)

Indeed, the language used by Hoffman and Novak (following Csikszentmihalyi's lead) when they talk about the state of flow has decidedly mystical connotations: "self-consciousness disappears, the consumer's sense of time becomes distorted, and the resulting state of mind becomes most gratifying" (p. 58). Web site design from a marketing perspective thus becomes an attempt to keep the consumer "in the flow state" (p. 17) for as long as possible so that they are more likely to remember and learn the information they come across, more likely to perceive that they are in control of the communication (even though they might not be, see p. 27), more likely to further explore the structure of the site that provides a state of flow to them, and more likely to have a positive experience that will lead to them wanting to come back to the flow-enabling site. As Hoffman and Novak summarize, "we anticipate that the positive affect generated by flow will translate into longer duration time spent visiting a CME, and increased repeat visits" (p. 65) and consequently, because

> we believe that repeat purchasing behavior, that is, repeat visits to a hypermedia CME, will be increased if the environment facilitates the flow state, the marketing objective at trial will be to provide for these flow opportunities. (p. 66)

It is not far-fetched to describe this as a trance-based theory of marketing and it has much in common with some of the blithely optimistic discourse that surrounded virtual reality research in the 1990s, discourse which saw enhanced telepresence as a manageable, controllable alternative to the use of hallucinogens for entertainment and self-discovery. Naturally, if usage of certain well-designed websites can induce a state of consciousness that so neatly fits the goals of marketers then it is understandable why Hoffman and Novak maintain that the hypermedia CME of the Internet is to be differentiated from the traditional media channels. Csikszentmihalyi's work on "flow" originated in his research on its appearance in those pursuing creative activities (music, painting, even group brainstorming in business contexts) and other enterprises that are considered rewarding "in and of themselves" (Nakamura & Csikszentmihalyi, 2002, p. 89). Interestingly, in the outline of the criteria that appear to produce the "flow" state, we come across some highly telling use of language:

> Being "in flow" is the way that some interviewees described the subjective experience of engaging just-manageable challenges by tackling a series of goals, continuously processing feedback about progress, and adjusting action based on this feedback. (ibid., p. 90)

Nakamura and Csikszentmihalyi are using the language of classic cybernetics here, characterizing their human respondents with mechanical and computing metaphors (they 'process' feedback and then adjust their actions). The state of "flow" is also explained as "one of dynamic equilibrium", a construction with clear connections to Ross Ashby's cybernetic principle of "homeostasis" (Ashby, 1960), the way in which a system regulates itself toward stability. If "flow" is, in the end, a term to describe the perfect functioning in a human of a cybernetic control system, what does Hoffman and Novak's adoption of Csikszentmihalyi terminology say about their underlying communication paradigm? How deep does the cybernetic influence go?

The communication model informing Hoffman and Novak's flow-based approach to consumer navigation of hypermedia CMEs is characterized by its attempt to radically rewrite the SMR schema by holding that the "primary" communication relationship is not built between sender and receiver but rather between the "mediated environment" and the sender and receiver. Additionally, the roles of sender and receiver are interchangeable and duplex. Their model is based on work by Jonathan Steuer in the early 1990s which considered the communication implications of virtual reality and telepresence technologies and which defined interactivity as "the extent to which users can participate in modifying the form and content of a mediated environment in real time" (Steuer, quoted in Hoffman & Novak, 1996, p. 53).

Hoffman and Novak call their formulation a "many-to-many communication model for hypermedia CMEs" and there are significant differences between their model and that of Shannon/Wiener (see Figure 2.1). The principle distinction is that, for Hoffman and Novak, the 'target' of communication is not the receiver but rather the media. Multiple receivers and senders converge, as it were, upon the media channel. This is a radical change to the traditional model and potentially promises a revolutionary perspective on contemporary communication. However, as I have already begun to point out, the assumptions of traditional cybernetic control are buried deep within the theoretical frame that Hoffman and Novak bring to

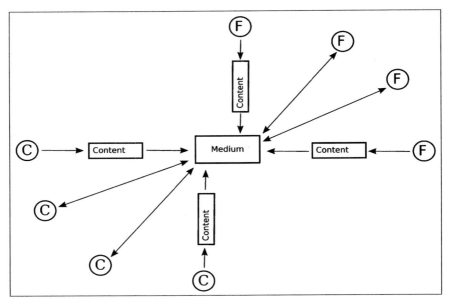

Figure 2.1   Hoffman and Novak's "New Model of Marketing Communications in a Hypermedia Computer-Mediated Environment." (Source: Reprinted with permission from the *Journal of Marketing*, published by the American Marketing Association, Hoffman, D. L., & Novak, T. P., 1996, Vol. 60 (July), pp. 50–68.)

bear upon the elaboration of their model. Before I address the full consequences of these assumptions of control, I would like to examine the many-to-many CME communication model for the very valuable reorientation that it offers marketing communication.

Steuer's theory is based around the idea of 'telepresence', defined as "the mediated perception of an environment" (ibid., p. 61). Clearly, in the area of virtual reality, telepresence is an important focus for research, relating to the feeling of 'really' being in a virtual environment. For Hoffman and Novak, telepresence is used to describe the immersion in the hypermedia environment of the Web, so that "the strength of the experience of telepresence is a function of the extent to which one feels present in the hypermedia CME, rather than in one's immediate physical environment" (ibid., p. 54). The higher the extent to which this mediated environment can be manipulated by the viewer, the higher the feeling of telepresence. This is the reason why Hoffman and Novak differentiate so strongly between their many-to-many communication model for hypermedia CMEs and the traditional communication model. For them, there is no way that traditional media can be manipulated by the 'receiver'. Hypermedia CMEs offer this possibility and therefore require a new communication model. Importantly, then, Hoffman and Novak see no particular problem with traditional models; they suffice to explain the communication that occurs in broadcast mass media and one-to-one situations. Hypermedia CMEs are unique in their integration of audio, video, text, and hypertext and therefore require a unique communication model that allows for senders and receivers to interact *with* the mediated environment as well as *through* it. Hoffman and Novak present their many-to-many model as the last in a series of three: First the traditional SMR, able to model broadcast and mass communication, then a one-to-one schema for modeling interpersonal and "computer-mediated" marketing communication which embodies a "feedback view of interactivity" (ibid., p. 52), and finally their model designed for the explication of marketing communication over hypermedia CMEs. Although never openly stated, there is an undeniable sense of evolution in this presentation: from print and broadcast, to computer-mediated (and word-of-mouth) and then finally to the hypermedia of the Web; the models follow a path of apparently increasing technological sophistication. Interactivity gradually becomes present in communication as increasing technology leads to a physical manifestation of the medium. For Hoffman and Novak, full interactivity is not typified by the classic cybernetic feedback loop which can exist between two communicators, each altering their output in accordance with the input they receive from the other. Instead, full interactivity occurs when the *medium* is alterable by both communicators. The apparent consequence of this is that there is no more 'targeting' of the customer by the 'firm'. Indeed, in a not-very-subtle use of visual rhetoric, Hoffman and Novak *reverse* the traditional placement of elements from the SMR, so that in their diagrammatic representation of the many-to-many model, the 'firm' is on the right hand side (the traditional location for the receiver or target) and the customers are on the left (traditionally occupied by the 'sender'). Inevitably, this serves to give the impression of reversal in essence and consequences (which is why it is a piece of visual rhetoric). The many-to-many model thus overturns the assumptions of previous models—is, literally, revolutionary. Hoffman and Novak make no reference to this change in placement—it is presented in the diagram for readers to notice or not. Additionally, the arrows that serve to indicate direction of communication (one assumes) appear to all converge upon the central element of the "medium". The visual effect is that of a wheel, with the "medium" at its hub, the spokes of communication flow radiating toward that hub and, at the rim, the customer and firm communicators. Closer inspection reveals that there is a differentiation between some of the communicators. For both the "firm" and "consumer" elements, there are some that display a one-way, two-step communication flow (from communicator to "content" to "medium") and others that demonstrate a synchronous single-step flow (to and from communicator and "medium"). Again, there is little gloss upon these distinctions by Hoffman and Novak, who other than simply explain that the figure "shows the range of communication relationships possible in a hypermedia CME", largely let the diagram speak for itself. The diagram appears to be saying, therefore, that some communicators will create "content" and, as a consequence, their communication will be one-way only, while others, who do not create content, will enjoy a two-way (synchronous) relationship with the "medium". The implication of this is that content creators are not receivers. If this is the case, though, how can a communicator who does not produce content be a transmitter? And look, I am using those words *transmitting* and *receiving*—words that Hoffman and Novak are careful to avoid as much as possible but words which seem to be implicit (or, perhaps, complicit) in their diagrammatic use of arrows. A bi-directional arrow symbolizes two-way communication flow and therefore we might use the phrase "interactive communication" to describe it, but a one-way arrow has no other reasonable interpretation in a communication context other than transmission or reception. Indeed, the visual instantiation of the concept of interactivity into a bi-directional arrow reveals the basic assumption that interactivity is the facility to both transmit and receive. So, what is the significance of the distinctions between communicator elements present in Hoffman and Novak's visual formulation of their model?

Content creation and hypertextual interaction are two separate things, two of the "communication relationships possible in hypermedia CMEs". Pointing and clicking as well as filling in search boxes and web forms are part of surfing the Web and represent a two-way interaction with the medium, whereas the creation of a website would constitute a one-way transmission to the medium. Hoffman and Novak are careful to distinguish between *providing content to the medium* and communicating to people through the medium, this latter being an instance of computer-mediated rather than many-to-many communication. So, consumers and firms can (within a marketing frame of reference) surf the web interactively, provide product-related content, engage in computer-mediated, one-to-one communication or attempt one-to-many broadcasts. As Hoffman and Novak point out, "the Web combines elements from a variety of traditional media, yet it is more than the sum of the parts" (ibid., p. 55). Both Web content creation and hypermedia interaction are described as being between a communicator and the medium, so that, for example, a Website creator provides the content to the Web rather than to other creators. This assertion obviously lies at the heart of the hypermedia CME but is a difficult one to fully understand. When I create a website I am creating it for the purpose of communicating to a number of sometimes known, sometimes unknown visitors—the content that I upload to the site can be video, audio, hypertext, or links to non-hypertext files (in PDF format, for example). Although I am using the Internet to construct and serve up to the public this collection of material I am still creating the content *for* visitors, not for the medium. Furthermore, when I serve up this content I might allow people to comment on it (although I do not have to) in which case they will be adding their own words (content) to my website and so (in a strict sense) altering the content of my site. In such a scenario (occurring on the Web everyday), my content creation is focused upon communicating with the visitors to my site. While technically I might have to concern myself with how I must "markup" my content in HTML code in order for it to appear and function on the web page in the way that I wish, surely these concerns are the same that a director might have in choosing camera angle and lighting setup or that a playwright might have in thinking of stage directions. They do not imply that I am principally providing content to the medium rather than communicating with an audience. Let us consider a letters page in a hypothetical photocopied fanzine of the mid 1980s devoted to punk music. A small group of friends united by a common appreciation for a particular type of music (as well as, inevitably, a number of other things), decide to try and put together a fanzine reaching out to the like-minded in their metropolitan area. They cut and paste typewritten stories, personal photographs, and commercial images into a set of masters that are then photocopied or offset and distributed to local record shops and venues. A contact P.O. Box address is supplied in the ranting editorial's first edition. Slowly, over the initial months of distribution, the readers' letters file grows and, amid much argument regarding publication policy between the friends, many of the pieces of readers' feedback are incorporated into later editions of the fanzine. The principle difference between this scenario and a modern web page is the speed at which content can be delivered and updated by the site/fanzine owners and the speed at which readers can comment on this. Additionally, the web page can contain audio and video material which fanzines, unless they were distributed on videocassette rather than paper, were unable to do. My point here is to establish that Hoffman and Novak produce no logical reason to construct a distinction between media that a communicator provides content *to* and media that communicators communicate *through*. Furthermore, the lack of clarity in the diagrammatic representation of the many-to-many model leads to the suggestion that content providers are in some sense transmitters and not receivers; clearly a position that doesn't make sense in a world of bloggers and commentators and probably a position that Hoffman and Novak did not mean to assert. Indeed, perhaps the presence of the one-way communication lines from content producers to medium is exactly that—a mistake, a telling slip of the pen (or mouse) that betrays the pervasive influence of the communication as control paradigm even in the most radical of thinkers. Yet, the visual rhetorical strategies of reversal and the conjuration of the ectoplasmic to/ through distinction make me, as a reader, wary of the larger construction that Hoffman and Novak build. Yes, the Web provides a unique integration of media and content types and this means that users can be content providers (as people could be in the early days of radio in the U.S., for example, and as the printing press has consistently allowed us to be) and yes, visitors to web pages can experience an active engagement with the structure of their journey through them. But the understanding of communication that underlies Hoffman and Novak's explication of the Web is still one where people do things to other people.

Network navigation is controlled. A site designer must, at a very deep level, make decisions regarding how a visitor is allowed through the network of pages, how they should be steered to different locations in order to receive (and give) different information. Hoffman and Novak's presentation of the marketing use of hypermedia CMEs is premised upon controlling how visitors are led through the network, how they are steered and challenged in order to experience maximum flow. Once in the state of flow, the visitor is primed for the marketing message—more likely to give it time, more likely to remember it, more likely to respond positively to it. The discourse's focus on the differentiation of 'providing to' the medium is a blind—distracting the reader from the heavily control-centered assumptions that infuse the discussion of marketing use. Hoffman and Novak's paper, while promising a revolutionary approach to *consumer-controlled* hypermedia, delivers instead a refined, flow-based approach to *consumer control*. Marketing communication, for them, is still based upon marketers trying to produce desired responses in targeted consumers through communicative control—the content-producing ability of the consumer is provided as a context in the mediated environment they discuss, but ends up having no actual influence on the marketing concerns and procedures they concentrate on.

Hoffman and Novak's paper has been highly influential in academic considerations of Internet marketing (Ozuem, 2004). Its use of "flow" to conceptualize the marketing consequences of site navigation continues to be elaborated upon by researchers (see, for example, Sicilia & Ruiz, 2007) and is often referenced outside the marketing literature as a source of corroboration for 'flow'-based approaches to issues of telepresence in hypermedia CMEs. It has been reprinted in the *Marketing Communication Classics* collection and is available for free online at the University of Vanderbilt's website as a working paper for their 'Project 2000: Research Program on Marketing in Computer-Mediated Environments'. In other words, the Hoffman and Novak model of marketing communication is "rapidly achieving the status of a true classic" (Fitzgerald & Arnott, eds., 2000) and is thus instrumental in setting the terms for academic discourse in this area. The visual and textual rhetoric that Hoffman and Novak employ in the service of their own model is both reproduced and amplified by later researchers. This is particularly interesting in the case of Wilson Ozuem's (2004) implementation of the many-to-many model, where Hoffman and Novak's rhetorical reversal of the sender ("firm") and receiver ("consumer") locations is compounded by the elimination of all but one of the "firm" elements.

Ozuem's diagrammatic representation of the Hoffman and Novak communication model (see Figure 2.2) surrounds the "medium" with seven "consumer" elements (in synchronous interaction with the "medium" or as transmitting-only content-providers to it) with the single "firm"

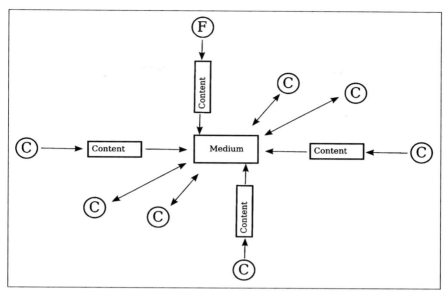

Figure 2.2 Ozuem's Rendering of Hoffman and Novak's "New Model of Marketing Communications in a Hypermedia Computer-Mediated Environment." (Source: Ozuem, Wilson F., 2004, *Conceptualising Marketing Communication in the New Marketing Paradigm: A Postmodern Perspective*, p. 217. © Ozuem 2004. Reproduced with the permission of the author.)

element present only as a content-provider, and thus not portrayed as an interacting element. Although Ozuem's figure is clearly captioned as "Hoffman and Novak (1996) New Model of Marketing Communication in Hypermedia Computer-Mediated Environment" (Ozuem, 2004, p. 217) it has significantly changed the representation of the many-to-many model found in the 1996 original. The result is a portrayal of the hypermedia environment in which the consumer is the *dominant* actor and voice. The "firm" is presented as a simple content-provider to the medium and in that sense disengaged from the exchange fundamental to the hypermedia CME. The firm is *disempowered* visually; indeed, it is almost entirely surrounded by consumers who have been granted far more access to content production and are able to engage in interactive relationships with the medium. A further detail of Ozuem's *tour-de-force* of rhetorical framing is the fact that he has placed the single "firm" element at a further distance away from the central "medium" than all the "consumer" elements: The firm has literally become the outsider in his schema, squeezed out to the margins to eke out a precarious existence in the content trade. This is made all the more remarkable when considered in conjunction with Ozuem's own diagrammatic representation, following a few pages after his rendering of Hoffman and Novak's model, of what he terms "Marketing Communication in Computer-Mediated Marketing Environments (CMMEs)" (see Figure 2.3).

Here, in what is presented as an evolution of the Hoffman and Novak framework, the proper ordering of the SMR model has returned ("Marketers" on the left, "Customers" on the right) along with an explicit rendering of the cybernetic feedback loop, although this loop is bi-directional and described as "Gestalt Feedback". Explaining the use of gestalt theory in this conception of feedback, Ozuem writes that "every activity in the gestation stage engenders gestalt feedback where communication becomes co-productive interaction (conjoint action)—meanings are not transferred but jointly produced in social interaction" (ibid., p. 219). The hypermedia CME interface thus is a medium for the co-production of meaning between users. As noted, Ozuem characterizes users as either "Marketers" or "Customers" and in his diagrammatic representation does not explicitly allow for customers to interact and create meaning with other customers. It is unclear if this is deliberate or not, but it surely represents, once again, the powerful rhetorical hold that the SMR has over discourse on communication models. It is almost as if Ozuem, having radicalized Hoffman and Novak's own model to the point of almost pushing the "firm" out of the 'picture' altogether, succumbs to the gravitational force of the SMR schema and produces, as the final flourish in his analysis, an image that returns us to the safe ground

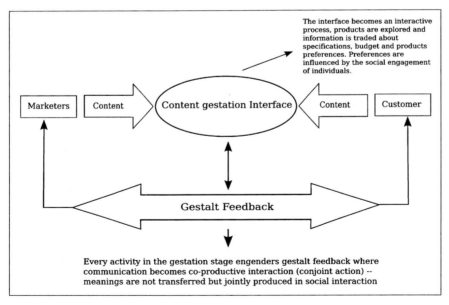

Figure 2.3   Ozuem's "Marketing Communication in Computer-Mediated Marketing Environments (CMMEs)". (Source: Ozuem, Wilson F., 2004, *Conceptualising Marketing Communication in the New Marketing Paradigm: A Postmodern Perspective*, p. 219. © Ozuem 2004. Reproduced with the permission of the author.)

(even if only superficially) of the Kotlerian macro model, with "Marketers" and "Customers" positioned opposite each other. What of control, though? Does Ozuem's gestalt feedback surrender the assumption of control implicit within the concept of feedback? Unfortunately, Ozuem does not elaborate beyond the already quoted explanation in his 2004 book, so next I will try and (re-)construct (and, inevitably, rhetorically frame) an understanding of control in Ozuem's implementation of gestalt feedback.

If meaning is the result of "conjoint action" between Marketer and Customer, then the status of the "content" that each of these two agents produce is necessarily that of "preliminary"-meaning, in the sense that the content is produced, say by the Marketer, with a particular meaning in mind, but that meaning only has reality for the Marketer, it can only become a *communicated* meaning once it has passed into the realm of the "content gestation interface" at which point it must inevitably *change*. The meaning that the Marketer communicates never reaches the Customer because it cannot survive the process of gestalt feedback without mutation. Interaction with the Customer, and with the customer's own meaning, produces a new, co-produced, meaning belonging to both agents. This, surely, is a reasonable interpretation of Ozuem's assertion that "meanings are not transferred but jointly produced in social interaction"; a new meaning emerges from the interaction of the constituent agents' meanings. This shared meaning is an "emergent property", in the language of General Systems Theory. As the cyclic nature of Ozuem's figure suggests, this meaning is not necessarily ever fixed, rather, it undergoes constant creation as the two agents continue in their relationship.

The previous description of a gestalt feedback-based model of interactive marketing communication is designed to extrapolate the consequences of Ozuem's sketch. From the control perspective of traditional marketing management, the model is a nightmare. The intended meaning of the Marketer, like the intended meaning of the Customer, becomes subordinated to the emergent meaning of the gestalt interaction. Thus, all attempts to control the reception of information and persuasive arguments become moot: because the very idea of "reception" is absent from the model. More confusingly (and perhaps frighteningly) even if one were to argue that attempts to control the reception of information and persuasive arguments could be somehow kept so structurally integrated as they pass into the interface zone that they might have the ability to effect the Customer's 'meaning', the same is true in the reverse direction! The Marketer, also, faces the inevitable prospect of the Customer's content changing her meaning. And if there is no end to this? If the process continues for the length of the communicative relationship, then the emergent meaning can never be said to be finished; there can be no point where the Marketer could say to the Client (Stern's insights in the polyphonic nature of the marcoms model are unfortunately missing from Ozuem's consideration, largely because he follows Hoffman and Novak's typology), "we've finished, the message has been received, we've got them thinking like we want them to". The marketing management paradigm is redundant for this model of marketing communication; similarly, the traditional marcom understandings of control, reception, effect, and persuasion are rendered meaningless.

Ozuem's 2004 sketch is a highly significant can-of-worms. Taken to its logical conclusion, the gestalt feedback model frames most marketing communication practice involving the Internet as woefully misguided and laughably ineffective. However, Ozuem does not build up the sketch in the way that I have done in the preceding paragraphs. He does not draw conclusions and refrains from examining any consequences. Indeed, as I have already shown, much of the visual rhetoric around the figure is strongly redolent of the most traditional renderings of the SMR. In addition, some of the rubric alongside Ozuem's gestalt feedback figure demonstrates a quite conservative approach to what the "content gestation interface" really means for marcoms practice. As an example of what he means by content co-creation, Ozuem explains that in the interface, "products are explored and information is traded about specifications, budget and product preferences" (ibid., p. 219). The presentation of *exploration* and *trading* as analogues of co-creation is rhetorically interesting. From a postmodern cultural anthropology perspective (not invoked by Ozuem), both processes can be seen as creative in the sense that an explorer inevitably changes the territory and peoples they explore (leaving traces and trails) whilst the act of trading creates change in the traders (in new balancings of power and knowledge). How appropriate is this understanding of creation in the context of Ozuem's focus on practical marketing communication issues? While the explorer might come back from her explorations a changed person and while the people she has encountered can be changed by their experience of the explorer, where exactly can we situate the emergent, co-created meaning that Ozuem speaks of? What is for sure is that the unglossed choice of these two words to exemplify the co-creation of the interactive process is problematic in its ambiguity. We can choose to interpret them in very simplistic, traditional marketing terms or we might choose to see them as referencing well-problematized issues within the discourses of cultural anthropology. Some help might be provided to us by a later, 2008, article of Ozuem's, co-authored with Kerry Howell and Geoff Lancaster, entitled "Communicating in the new interactive marketspace". This article returns to a number of themes present in the 2004 text but framed within a "constructivist ethnographic"/phenomenological investigation of how a group of respondents compared their experiences on the Web to their experiences of traditional mass media. In discussing respondent comments regarding interactivity on the Internet, Ozuem et al. describe the way in which users can "modify" content on the Web:

> Individuals in computer mediated marketing environments were able to access retrospective content and modify it. As noted by some respondents, users have twin accessibility traits: input and output. Consumers can interact with each other whilst simultaneously having direct

access to companies. Consumers participating in computer mediated marketing environments are adventurous in exploring product details. (Ozuem, Howell, & Lancaster, 2008, p. 1072)

This rather brief note is almost all that is left of Ozuem's 2004 conception of the co-creation of marketing meaning, joined only by the assertions toward the close of the article that "products and messages should be co-created in the consumption process" (Ozuem, Howell, & Lancaster, 2008, p. 1079) and that consumers are "creative and innovative partners in the creation of experiences in the consumption process" (ibid., p. 1080). 'Modifying' content, as discussed in the previous extract, is far less ambitious than the idea of "jointly produced" meaning. Indeed, meaning has altogether disappeared as an emergent property of the new interactive marketplace; "marketing practitioners" and customers are "partners" (a nice and acceptable business word) in the creation and modification of content experiences, products and messages. But not meaning.

Ozuem appears to be in a constant backing-off from the implications of his 2004 model. He backs off from them in the original text and continues to back off from them through a process of rhetorical re-direction and re-presentation in his later work. In the end, the co-creation of an emergent meaning is a deeply problematic concept; its ramifications, as I have outlined previously, call for a radically different marketing communications paradigm, one that surrenders the prospects of control, planned and measurable effect and strategy. In other words, a paradigm that is entirely non-management orientated. Such a form of marketing communication would be viewed with ridicule, impatience, frustration, dismissal, and anger by the current gatekeepers of the discipline and its practice. Additionally, one would have to ask how could the field of marketing communication function if it was to be split between a radical non-management approach to interactive media and a control-based management enterprise for traditional media?

Ozuem's 2004 outline raises many uncomfortable questions and many startling possibilities. The fact that they have been largely unvoiced (or camouflaged) by Ozuem himself is reminiscent of the way in which Barbara Stern's advertising communication model has remained largely undeveloped or simply conveniently reframed. On the other hand, the widespread influence of Hoffman and Novak's model of interactivity can be attributed to the comparatively conservative, control-orientated management paradigm that suffuses its every paragraph. The marketing management status quo is thus preserved even in the supposedly 'revolutionary' field of hypermedia CMEs.

INTERACTIVITY, CONTROL, AND THE WEB

The relationship between interactivity and control is at the heart of this study. So far, we have seen that marketing communication's attempts to engage with issues of interactivity have revolved around making statements

structing models that, in contrast with earlier conceptions, appear
ender some amount of control to the consumer. As I have shown,
however, there is a great deal of ambiguity in the terms of this surrender. It
is necessary at this point to consider in a little more depth the exact nature
of the relationship between interactivity and control. Certainly, the manner
of marketing's presentation of interactivity has framed it as a form of *liberation* for the consumer—they have been given power (empowered) and,
as such, released from a condition of powerlessness. Whether we should say
that the consumer has been liberated or whether instead we should describe
them as having seized the means of production, the consequence is that
interactive media (give? provide? I am trying to search for a word that does
not imply some form of patrician control) are controllable by consumers
(grammar to the rescue!). But is all this talk of liberation and empowerment
really warranted? Perhaps we are so used to (re-)spouting the platitudes of
the networked revolution that we forget to ask whether the Internet is really
all that special? Certainly, the social systems theory of Niklas Luhmann
has a quite different interpretation of the presence and significance of interactivity in the modern mass media.

Luhmann defines "interaction" as "episodes of societal process" (Luhmann,
1995, p. 406). One of its principle defining characteristics is its *temporality*
and this is what makes a conversation between two people in a supermarket,
or over a telephone, or a speaker addressing a public rally, different from a
television broadcast, a newspaper article, a homepage on a website or a blog.
Technological mass media communication is typified by the fact that "no
interaction can take place between sender and receivers" (Luhmann, 2000,
p. 2) because technology is 'interpositioned' between them. In a public rally,
communication occurs in a shared immediate space and time, and although
a rhetor can speak any member of the audience can try and shout her down.
The mass media, on the other hand, are instantiations of "copying technologies" and enable mass communication without any need for "spatial and temporal contact" (Moeller, 2006, p. 123) and therefore "episodes" of interaction
are alien to their nature. As Luhmann points out, what we are sometimes presented with as being 'interactive' experiences through mass media are in fact
carefully "staged" elements of tightly scripted programs where the interaction
is highly simulated. For Luhmann, the interactive aspects of the mass media
face of the Internet are as equally staged as a Jerry Springer live audience
extravaganza. Moeller notes the important distinction that:

> . . . not all communication performed with the help of computers is
> mass media communication: private email exchange in the intimacy
> system or the [economic] purchase of an airline ticket is not, whereas
> logging on to cnn.com or the Playboy Web site is. (ibid., p. 123)

The staging of pseudo-interactive episodes is, I would contend, the real subject of Hoffman and Novak's article. Their concern with the control of a navigator's sense of presence and flow as he or she journeys through the structure of a site is the concern of a labyrinth builder who takes care to think through how the questing guest will respond at each twist and turn, dead end and grotto, preparing unnerving surprises and enlightening tableau, making sure not to test the visitor's patience, taste, or credulity but giving them just the right amount of experience and information to keep them interested and motivated. But the builder is unable to communicate in the same temporal moment with the navigator—and so there cannot be, for Luhmann, an episode of interaction between the two. Luhmann's very stringent conception of interaction encourages us to interrogate some of the assumptions informing marketing communication's engagement with the so-called interactive technology of the Internet. Interestingly, unlike the vast majority of social theorists of media, Luhmann sees absolutely nothing suspicious, debilitating, or *wrong* with mass media—its lack of episodic interaction is not a fault, but rather simply a characteristic of the mass media system. As Moeller explains:

> Technology separates senders and receivers, but this is for Luhmann, unlike for Heidegger or Baudrillard, not reason enough to decry the inauthenticity of this type of communication. It is just a defining characteristic of a rather peculiar type of communication that only becomes possible with the existence of certain technologies . . . [. . .] . . . The separation of sender and receiver in space and time makes it impossible to centrally coordinate the transmission and the 'tuning in'—newspaper editors or movie producers have no direct control over their audience. (ibid., p. 123)

The Internet, in Luhmannian terms, is a compound mixture of systems: mass media, intimacy, economic, and so on. While Hoffman and Novak also describe the World Wide Web as a form of media that shares "characteristics with a wide variety of other media types" and can therefore be thought of as the most "typical" of all media (Hoffman & Novak, 1996, p. 12), their conclusion is that this mixture makes it the most interactive of media channels. For Luhmann there are only a very few specific aspects of the 'net (real-time chat, email) that can be said to not partake of the non-interactive technological mass media system. The division between web surfing and real-time chatting is analogous to the difference between watching a TV broadcast and talking with someone on the telephone. To adopt the posture that web navigation is an example of interactive communication is, in this context, nonsensical.

Luhmann's formulation of interaction points to an interesting precedent in the history of rhetoric which can demonstrate the intimate connection between the immediate temporal presence of sender and receiver and the processes of control and co-production of meaning in communication. *Kairos* (often translated as the sense of the "right time" or the "opportune moment") is an element of rhetorical practice that was essential to early Greek thought on the discipline and eventually evolved into the Roman idea of *decorum*. It has, over the centuries, become a rather submerged strain in the study of classical rhetoric, so much so that it usually warrants only a few incidental remarks in most contemporary studies. Isocrates and Gorgias afford *kairos* an important place in their systems of rhetoric and, indeed, Plato is credited with reserving for *kairos* the position of capstone of his rhetoric. James Kinneavy (1984) notes that even though pre-Aristotelian theoreticians like Plato considered *kairos* to be central to a conception of rhetoric, it:

> has never received the attention it deserves, possibly because it seems to be at variance with the general direction of Plato's thinking. Indeed even in antiquity, no one seems to have analyzed the notion of kairos very carefully, as Dionysius of Halicarnassus remarked. This is probably true, despite the fact that Gorgias built his entire system of thought from sense perception through ethics to aesthetics on kairos and despite the attention given the concept in medicine. (Kinneavy, 1984, p. 72)

Recently, however, the tide has been turning and more attention is being paid to this vital aspect of persuasion. This is possibly due to the influence that the practice of improvisation has had in the late 20th century, particularly its popularization in music, stand-up comedy, and 'flash' writing. Certainly, the ability to respond rhetorically to the pressures and opportunities of the moment has become something which the creative disciplines are tending to examine, codify, and teach more systematically. And this is, in the end, what *kairos* means, thinking on your feet in the most persuasive manner possible, responding to the emotional dynamic of the audience, what Craig Smith defines as the "adaptation to or taking advantage of an opportunity through fitting response and proper timing" (Smith, 2003, p. 68). In the highly structured and prescriptive model of rhetoric that Aristotle built (and which laid the foundation for so much of the later Western understanding of the field), the rhetor must take into account the nature of her audience in the preparation of the speech[1] but there is barely any engagement with the sense of moment once the rhetor is in front of the audience (though see Kinneavy & Eskin, 2000, for a recent rehabilitation of a *kairotic* Aristotle). It is rather understood that if everything has been planned correctly, then the rhetor will be successful accordingly. *Kairos*, on the other hand, is a sense of the rich, complex dynamic of situational context that exists between the speaker and the audience at the moment of the speech. Charles Bazerman has been responsible for elucidating a reading of *kairos* that links it convincingly with both a Luhmannian sense of interaction as social episode and the constructionist motif of discourse as the creation of social reality. Bazerman sees *kairos* as "a means of locating oneself in a world of evolving action with others, linked together by the fragile threads of symbols handed back and forth among us" (Bazerman, 1994, p. 189). Adapting Bazerman's development of the *kairos* concept and Luhmann's theory of episodes of interaction to the issue of interactive marketing communication is something that I will be doing in much greater depth in Chapters 3 and 7, at this stage, however, these concepts allow us to problematize many of the assumptions that inform existing approaches to interactivity in marketing space.

The tendency to speak of the World Wide Web as a coherent, homogeneous 'thing', even when codified in the techno-jargon of "Hypermedia CMEs", brings with it the practice of conferring across its breadth an equally homogeneous construction of interactivity. Yet, if we are to consider the immediate social moment of an IM chat between prospect and sales advisor as possessing the equivalent quality and typology of interaction as a questing consumer's navigation of a product's website (replete with Flash animations, web forms, embedded audio, etc.) then we are left with an understanding of 'interactivity' that is useless in its generality of reference. Real-time chat partakes of the *kairotic* moment of social creation; in their immediate interaction, **both parties** are engaged in the production and reproduction of social moments. Each party creates, through their experience of their interlocutor's discourse, a sense of who that person is and how they fit into their idea of larger social structures; in other words, such interactions help us to create in our minds a stable sense of who the other is[2]. We construct an idea of them. In 'interaction' with a website, however, there are a number of significant factors, determined by the technology, that distance the consumer from her interlocutor.

Firstly, the practice behind the construction of commercial websites means that it is almost completely certain that the person responsible for the design of the site is not the same person who is creating the marketing 'content'. Failure to heed the lessons of Barbara Stern's 1994 article means that the multiple dimensions of the message source in web marketing are completely overlooked by most researchers who act as if there is a single authorial voice that speaks through each site. Indeed, it is highly likely that, in the same way that an advertising agency's creative output represents the combination of a large number of voices (artists, copywriters, account planners, executive personnel, as well as the client themselves) so too the final presentation of a commercial website will be the result of the concerted expressions of graphic artists, web designers, copywriters, software developers, managerial personnel, and client representatives. Although it is quite possible for one person (given the required knowledge and skill sets) to create every aspect of a website, such situations are largely restricted to non-commercial concerns. Additionally, while it is possible for one person with little 'coding' and design know-how to take advantage of turnkey blogging solutions like WordPress[3], it must be recognized that the very turnkey nature of such packages means that the voices of the software developers (through the choices that they have already made regarding availabilities of structure, style, and presentation of content) are inevitably to be found within the resulting sites. All this means that a visitor to a website or a blog is not interacting with a single interlocutor. Rather, a complex of voices, at varying temporal and spatial distances from each other, broadcast out from the site's content (content, of course, referring to everything from text, audio, and images through to navigational structure, graphic design, typography, etc.).

Secondly, the voices emanating from the website are not addressing a particular visitor. In that sense, the voices are blind—they can speak but they have no idea of who they are speaking to. There is, it is true, a certain amount that can be gleaned from a visitor (through the *automatic* examination of the IP address, browser and cookies, all of which a user may either mask or delete) but this information is only going to be responded to in real-time by the software running the website and so therefore can only be subjected to a series of 'if, then, else' rules which at best serve up a series of scripted responses. The level of complexity that automated interactions (such as Amazon.com's contextual recommendation system) can achieve is impressive and will be examined in Chapter 4, but it is important to acknowledge at this stage that this is completely anchored in *machine learning*, and although humans write the programs that implement the algorithms that make the 'machines' learn, it is nevertheless central to the use case of such systems that they provide a degree of automation so that a human does not have to be present (or at least intellectually engaged) when a dataset is analyzed and a response is produced. Only through *later* analysis of reports (whether automatically generated logs or web forms voluntarily filled out by visitors) will a human be in a position to make judgments or comments about the 'input' from the visitor. Putting these issues of automation to one side for the moment, however, it is clear that even for the human voices aggregated on the website, there is little possibility of direct interaction with a visitor. The content is created, edited, approved, and presented in a manner almost identical to broadcast media. Yes, the characteristics of the technology allow for the flow of Internet content creation to be potentially handled much faster than on earlier broadcast technologies (though that in no way guarantees that it will be) and the synchronous nature of the channel allows for a much speedier gathering of input from the consumer. This, however, is just a feature of the different technological structure of the medium—it does not constitute a typological difference. In Luhmannian terms, the technology distances the visitor and the site creators too much for there to be episodes of interaction.

Finally, there is the issue of control. The *kairotic moment* of interaction can be thought of as an instance of communal creation, where social meaning is created in and between all the interacting parties (though importantly this does not necessarily mean that each party creates the same social meaning). In other words, interaction changes all participating actors.

However, common commercial and marketing uses of the webpage channel are not founded upon such an assumption. Instead, befitting the legacy of cybernetic communication and control, the design and operation of such websites is informed by the desire to direct, constrain, and sculpt the user's 'navigation'. From the very early days of the public Internet, metaphors of uninhibited travel have dominated descriptions of the user experience: 'navigation', 'surfing', riding the 'information superhighway'. The metaphor of surfing, in particular, has anchored itself in popular discourse on the Web experience and carries with it a complex of associations such as individualism, freedom, an exhilarating relationship with natural forces, and counter-culture motifs from American lifestyle mythologies. Surfboarding is a renowned demonstration of the individual's ability to control her passage through the dynamic, disengaged momentum of the sea. For all that surfing is about control, however, the limits of navigation are starkly drawn. One 'hitches' the wave, after all—the ability to 'ride' it implies the canny harnessing of an unstoppable natural energy, but one is always headed, throughout however many tacking vectors, toward the shore, the ultimate, unchanging destination of the wave. The freedom implied in the act of surfing is a tightly curtailed one: You can go anywhere you want, *as long as it's toward the shore.* The rhetoric of web surfing might alert us to some of the features of the communication relationship implicit within the contemporary implementation of hypermedia CMEs. Sites are built to be navigated in certain ways: Hyperlinks cannot generally be added into the structure of a web page by the visitor. A web designer, when commissioned to create a site for a client (whether it has a manifest marketing function or not), first builds an outline of the site's potential navigation architecture (this often takes the form of a 'wireframe'; for an example and explication, see Mayhew, 2005, pp. 343–345). The intention here is to work out in advance what visitors can access and from where, what they will be asked and how they will be asked it, what the visitor can leave behind and how they might be allowed to leave it behind. Essentially this is the design of the interaction between the user and the site. It is a plan in spirit very much like a playwright's directions in a script, although it takes advantage of the branching nature of the hypertext format in order to map out a number of possible pathways. To go back to the surfing metaphor, then, the visitor has a fair number of ways of navigating the site, but the site is always moving in one, inexorable direction, transporting the surfer along with it. The visitor might be encouraged to leave a message (as in the commenting system of a blog or some form of 'white wall' or guest book) but the framing of that message and the choice as to whether it is publicly viewable or moderated or not is entirely up to the site designer(s). Lest we forget that this level of control is not a natural, inherent feature of hypermedia CMEs, let us recall that the inventor of the hypertext concept, Ted Nelson, had (indeed, *still has*) a significantly more ambitious vision of the way in which navigators of a hypertext document would be intimately involved in altering that document's content and context. Nelson's *Xanadu* project is founded upon the idea of "open hypertext publishing", which "means both that your link can reach into the original document it points at and that FROM that original document you can find your link", effectively enabling anyone "to publish a footnote to any book" (Nelson, interviewed in Rucker, Sirius, & Mu, 1993, p. 148). This utterly egalitarian approach to the creation of a universal document sea would truly mean that a user might navigate anywhere they wish and link, for all to see, her own comments with any pre-existing document or set of comments and, most importantly, those links would be internal to the text. This, however, calls for an ethic of surrendering on behalf of *all* content producers. When Novak and Hoffman, Ozuem, et al., talk of the consumer as an empowered content creator and reify the interactive nature of the contemporary Web, we must realize how much the assumption of control is fundamental to commercial Web design as we know it. Bellman and Rossiter (2004) have shown that users' experience of web sites appears to be more satisfactory when their internal "schema" of how the web site is structured and navigated is closely aligned to the way that the designer has thought of the structure. If a website's navigational structure is clearly designed (and so easily learned) or conforms to schema that the visitor has already learned from other sites, then the user will experience less incongruity between her internal web navigation schema and the structure of the web site she is visiting; this, Bellman and Rossiter show, has a consequently positive effect on the visitor's attitude toward the brand that the site is promoting. The scenario that is painted here is a rather depressing, classical stimulus and response situation where users are initially trained in information retrieval by the first sites that they visit (or the favorite sites that they habituate) and then expect homogeneity in navigational structure from new sites that they are exposed to (and get irritated if they do not meet it). Control in this context becomes a carefully judged process of the creation and meeting of expectations in order to keep visitors as in the 'flow' as possible, steering them through familiarity and similarity. As Geissler's web designer respondents indicated,

> Controlling the navigation process helps expose customers to the entire Web site and may increase consumer involvement and comfort levels. The notion is that the more involved and comfortable consumers are with the Web site, the more likely they are to purchase online. (Geissler, 2001, p. 497)

The irony implicit in much web design rhetoric is that through control of the navigation, the designer may produce the feeling of involvement in the user, which is in turn then reframed as the user's ability to control the site. For example, Shih's (1998) explanation of how the consumer can be said to control the content of a web site that they visit demonstrates perfectly the rhetorical reframing of terms that transforms a scripted choice regarding the order to visit a series of linked pages into a shining beacon of user-created content:

> With the Internet, although users cannot modify the actual content of the Web pages, they have the ability to modify the order of the presentation by selecting the links they want to follow. This affords users the power to tailor certain aspects of the contents to their needs, making them the authors of the content because they alone determine the content they see. (Shih, 1998, p. 657)

Shih contrasts this utopic vision with the way in which a print magazine's "presentation is largely left to the discretion of its editors" so that the readers are left in the "passive position of message recipients, having little input into the makeup of the magazine and the order of the information delivery" (p. 657). This assertion blithely ignores the ways in which readers make any print publication their own, turning to their favorite columns first, skipping whole sections known to carry nothing other than adverts, using (heavens forbid) the contents page to locate articles they might wish to read first, and so on. The existence of such active readers is, naturally, inconvenient to those who wish to frame the Internet as something qualitatively different from all other media, and Shih's comment that choosing which hyperlink to follow makes a visitor an "author" of content is a good example of just how far scholars will go to construct a discourse of exceptional interactivity and content-creation for the Internet. Choosing between three pre-determined hyperlinks that will take you to three different pages is no more or less control than a reader of a book with a table of contents or an index has— in fact, the reader of the printed publication has a lot more freedom as to when and where to dip into the text and, furthermore, may rip out entire sections, mark them up and glue in whatever they please.

In Chapters 4 and 5 I will be examining in detail the contemporary marketing use of the Web and its relationship to issues of control, information, and interactivity. What I hope I have shown so far is that the design of commercial Web sites, so important for the idea of interactivity in hypermedia CMEs, is predicated upon the need for control: control of 'flow', control of navigation, control of experience. Web sites are highly designed collections of multimedia scripts—their commercial use is predicated upon their ability to lead visitors to particular presentations of product and brand information and to extract as much data from them as possible. Due to the very nature of the planning that must go into the construction of such sites, the *kairotic moment* of interaction is pushed far away from any interchanges that visitors might feel they are having with the hypermedia CME. The automation of such interchanges (in the form of web forms, hyperlinks, email buttons, animations, etc.) enables the site authors to maintain a distance of time and location from the experience of the visitor. The Human–Computer interaction that results is interaction by proxy. It is *not* the case that the human visitor is interacting with the computerised site (which seems to be the subtle inference of Hoffman and Novak's conception that in the many-to-many communication model, it is the medium that is being interacted with). The interactive ability of a computer-controlled site is entirely planned and scripted by the complex of authors I have already mentioned. And it is this planning and scripting that excludes the possibility of the *kairotic moment* being invoked in any form of web-hosted interaction. Such a state of affairs is tacitly recognized in the rhetorical deflection and reframing that occurs in the academic literature surrounding marketing's use of the Internet.

Before closing this chapter, there is an aspect of the rhetorical framing of interactive communication models which calls for some further consideration. I have already made reference to a number of interesting features demonstrated by the illustrative figures used by Kotler, Stern, and Ozuem in the explication of their different communication models. Now I would like to take a step back and ask a number of questions regarding the place of such figures in the discourse of marketing communication theory.

DIAGRAMMATIC REPRESENTATION AND VISUAL RHETORIC

All of the models that I have been discussing so far, irrespective of their theoretical orientations, have one thing in common: their dependency on the diagram. Diagrams are used to present the communication models advanced by the authors concerned and this is often at the expense of sustained textual explanation. Diagrams, like tables and all other figures or visual representations, have a rhetorical component. As Linda Scott puts it, in her seminal paper instituting a rhetorical approach to advertising images:

> The rhetorical intention behind a visual message would be communicated by the implicit selection of one view over another, a certain style of illustration versus another style, this layout but not that layout. (Scott, 1994, p. 253)

Additionally, the decision itself to instantiate the message in the form of a diagram rather than as text has a rhetorical weight. For reasons that I have discussed previously, there is a strong bias toward the scientific, empirical method that is prevalent throughout marketing theory. In order to be taken seriously in the mainstream academic and professional discourse of marketing, the patina of scientism needs to be confidently projected and nothing says 'science' better than numbers (hence the barrage of statistical analysis papers that greet the readers of the major marketing and advertising journals). But when numbers aren't appropriate, the table and the diagram serve as worthy replacements. The origins of communication modeling in the cybernetics and information theory of the 1940s and '50s means that control flow diagrams and telecommunication block diagrams act as touchstones of empirical authority, affording an instant connection with a scientific legacy that confers the values of rigor, certainty, and practicality. This is evident in the way that the diagram is used in communication and marketing theory as something that both speaks for itself and stands for a fact, a self-explanatory artifact of power—a talisman. Its presence serves to identify the text as part of scientific discourse. One of the long-standing assumptions of scientific discourse is that it has no rhetorical element. As James Anderson explains:

> The antirhetorical position—the claim that science writing has no rhetorical dimension—argues that there is no audience intended in this writing and, hence, no need for a rhetorical effort. Instead this writing is deliberately directed toward an archive of written discourse rather than a reader. Its entrance into that archive is determined by whether it meets the standard for veridical claim not its persuasability. (Anderson, 1996, p. 193)

Ironically, then, the use of the graphical trappings of scientific discourse in marketing communications writing can be said to be a rhetorical strategy attempting to persuade the reader of the non-rhetorical status of the text. Of course, as Anderson goes on to show (citing the recent work of a raft of rhetorical scholars), scientific discourse is highly rhetorical and science "scholars do not trust in only the truth value of their claims to carry the field and, in fact, embrace very mundane efforts to persuade" (ibid., p. 194). In marketing, the use of what Hackley calls "grandiose scientific rhetoric" (Hackley, 2001, p. 71) is part of the accepted language game that the academic and practitioner complex uses to construct a particular reality. Furthermore, George Lakoff and a string of co-authors have shown the fundamentally *metaphorical* nature of mathematical, psychological, and scientific discourse. In the case of mathematics, for example, Lakoff and Núñez (2000) have demonstrated how that discipline "turns out not to be a disembodied, literal, objective feature of the universe but rather an embodied, largely metaphorical, stable intellectual edifice constructed by human beings" (Lakoff & Johnson, 2003, p. 270). In Lakoff's terms, a communication model diagram would be an attempt to visually express "a set of ontological and structural metaphors" (ibid., p. 220). Remembering that metaphor is the source of a large number of rhetorical figures, it is worth examining what metaphors are present in these diagrams and just how they are visually expressed. I have shown, already, a number of peculiar rhetorical features of the diagrams that I have been considering, but I would now like to make some more general remarks about the common metaphorical system that these diagrams demonstrate.

ARROWS AND LOOPS

The element of interactivity that is present to varying degrees in the diagrammatic representations of the marketing communication models that I have examined previously is symbolized in two principle ways. Firstly, we have the two-way (bi-directional) *arrow* and secondly we have some form of the feedback *loop*. It is worth spending a little time considering the rhetorical implications of the use of these two symbols.

A one-way (uni-directional) arrow is generally understood to signify a number of possible things. In terms of direction (of a force, a body, an object) it is taken to be an analogue for "this way". Following on from this, in mathematics and logic it is also often used to stand for the idea of entailment, where one thing leads to (entails) another. In Shannon's original communication model diagram (refer back to Figure 1.1 in this study), the one-way arrow from "information source" to "transmitter" represents the direction of the "message" as it is passed from the one element to another. A bi-directional arrow, according to such conventions, represents the idea of a message flowing simultaneously in both directions. There is an obvious issue here regarding the choice of a single bi-directional line versus two uni-directional lines pointing in opposite directions; there must, surely be a difference in meaning? A single bi-directional line implies the lack of a distinction between the message streams that are being directed from one position to the other. In other words, there is something about the substance of the message stream that serves to make it indistinguishable whether it is traveling from A to B or from B to A. Whereas, if there are two uni-directional lines pointing in opposite directions, this tends to imply that the two message streams *have to be* differentiated, that there is something inherently distinct about the message traveling from A to B and that traveling from B to A.

A further point of interest is the semantic difference between a line that has opposing arrow heads at either end and a line that has converging arrow heads toward its center. In the case of the former, the pictorial logic would tend to suggest that the center point of the line is the source of the message (rather than element A or B); the arrows are, after all, radiating out from that center point. In the case of the latter, with the arrow heads traveling from opposite directions (emanating from A and B respectively) the center point of the line stands as the location for a future clash between the two arrow heads (standing for the messages).

Simple choices of arrow style and usage therefore contain rhetorical significance in the metaphorical presentation of interactivity in marketing communication diagrams. This is usually made all the more important because there is so little attempt to explain the conventions (the metaphors) used in these diagrams. Arrows, indeed, are almost *never* explained even in the most careful and reflexive of authors (Lakoff himself is a prime candidate, here; see, for example, his diagram of metaphorical entailment, Lakoff & Johnson, 2003, p. 94).

Diagrammatic representation of the feedback loop has a long and august history in the annals of engineering, biology, Operations Research, system dynamics, and so on. As the name implies, the feedback loop is a metaphor of circularity. As Ross Ashby put it, it is concerned with a "circularity of action" between "the parts of a dynamic system" (Ashby, 1957, p. 53). However, even though its essence might be circular there is not an overwhelming tradition of circular diagrammatic representation for feedback. For example, Ashby's graphic representation takes the form of two elements (A and B) each surrounded by a square (boxed in, as it were) with one unidirectional arrow traveling from A to B and then another uni-directional arrow traveling from B to A. This represents a "coupling" (ibid., p. 87) between the two elements such that "the two together form a system with feedback". Ludwig von Bertalanffy (considered by many to be the founder of General Systems Theory), in his diagrammatic representation of a "simple feedback scheme" (von Bertalanffy, 2001, p. 43) uses a gently curved uni-directional line originating from the "response" element and feeding back into the "stimulus" element. Kenneth Boulding, an economist central to the uptake of GST principles in certain areas of the political and social sciences, illustrated his normative feedback model of hierarchical organizational structures with a diagram where the undoubted circularity of what is being proposed is implemented in a linear, pyramidal form (reproduced in Hammond, 2003, p. 209). We see in Shannon's "schematic diagram of a correction system" (see Figure 2.4) again a similarly linear, though quadrilateral, representation of the feedback control cycle.

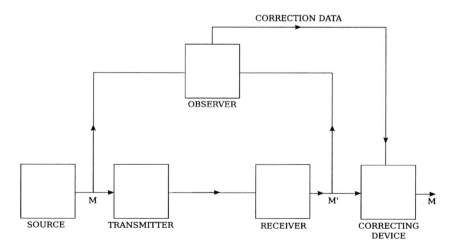

Figure 2.4   Claude Shannon's "Schematic diagram of a correction system." (Source: Shannon, C. E., ' A Mathematical Theory of Communication,' *The Bell System Technical Journal*, Vol. 27, July, 1948, p. 401, Figure 8. Copyright © 1948 Bell Labs. Reprinted with permission of John Wiley & Sons, Inc.)

To give yet another example, William T. Powers, the originator of Perceptual Control Theory, presents his "general form" of a "feedback control system" as a diagram utilizing straight and right-angled uni-directional lines that describe a square, even though he repeatedly uses the word "loop" to describe the nature of the system (Powers, 1989, p. 8). Powers has himself written a critique of Wiener's (1948) original feedback diagram from *Cybernetics* (which is, once more, a linear graphic of a circular process) arguing that the ambiguous way in which it was embedded in the text has led to a quarter century of misunderstanding (Powers, 1992, pp. 17–29). The point I am making here is that in this broad spectrum of diagrammatic representations of the feedback loop, all originating from either an engineering or a mathematical perspective, there is a common desire to visually present something clearly described as being circular or a loop as instead *linear* and *angular*; there is little attempt to instantiate the circularity in a graphic manner. This must be regarded as a rhetorical trope, in the sense that the vagaries of the printing process cannot be held responsible for the linear nature of the schematics (examination of the surrounding printed context for all of these instances reveals that arcs and circles are perfectly capable of being represented). As we have seen, this particular trope of visual rhetoric is reproduced in marketing communication scholarship—Kotler, Stern, and Ozuem all using straight lines to represent something usually referred to as a circular process. What is the rhetorical strategy that informs this visual squaring of the circle?

MECHANISM AND ORGANICISM

Rhetoric can be thought of as, in the words of Jonathan Potter, "a feature of the antagonistic relationship between versions: how a description counters an alternative description, and how it is organized, in turn, to resist being countered" (Potter, 2005, p. 108). In this respect, we might identify a curious antagonism within the legacy of description that surrounds the study of communication and control. Textual descriptions speak of loops and circularity (which are metaphors, of course) whereas the visual descriptions speak of lines and angles (again, metaphors). The two sets of metaphors, two versions of description, oppose each other within the same discourse stream, each vying for dominance. It is very tempting, perhaps, to interpret this antagonism as an extension of the struggle between mechanistic and biological paradigms, straight lines and right angles speaking of artificial control and circles and loops arguing for organic, developmental process. Certainly, such a division can be easily discerned in the intellectual history of control systems and their reception and interpretation; N. Katherine Hayles' (1999) study of the human body's place in cybernetics and informatics provides a highly nuanced exposition of this tradition. Projected into the realm of interactivity in marketing communication, such an antagonism between textual and visual rhetorics underlines the deep, troubled coupling that exists between paradigms of control and paradigms of communicative liberation that lie at the heart of marketing engagement with the issue of interactivity.

As I shall show in Chapters 4 and 5, marketing's response to the quandary of consumer-control (the ambiguity is intentional) in hypermedia CMEs has been a hysterical flip-flopping of hyper-mechanization and biological spasming. Indeed, the control paradigm in marketing has always been locked in a mutually-reinforcing, symbiotic coupling with the matrix of *humanness* and I will be contending that the spectacle of this coupling in contemporary interactive marketing is mirrored across the legacy of marketing history.

3 A Radical Constructivist's Marketing Construction

In Chapter 7, I will be presenting a communication model that shares many of the ramifications of Ozuem's 2004 gestalt feedback model, attempts to clearly problematize the management assumption of control, incorporates a number of Stern's innovations, and integrates the use of 'interactive' and traditional media. Based upon a radical constructivist reading of the marketing communication concept, this model attempts to follow the ramifications of emergent meanings as they would play out both in day-to-day practice and in a new marketing theory. In this interlude I would like to more clearly lay out the meaning of radical constructivism, argue for its applicability to the marketing paradigm, and demonstrate the particular perspective it brings to considerations of interactivity and persuasion.

"YOU'VE BEEN FRAMED!"

Chris Hackley's work (1999, 2001, 2002) has sought to integrate contemporary, postmodern approaches to marketing with an explicitly social constructionist perspective. Although much recent writing that ostensibly flies the postmodern flag shares a mildly constructionist turn, Hackley is alone in so openly aligning himself with a "social construction" stance. However, it is clear from Hackley's own clarifications of his position that he is not comfortable being interpreted definitively as a social constructionist, particularly in any sense that such a term might be used to refer to the body of theory that has developed around Berger and Luckmann's (1991) foundational *The Social Construction of Reality: A Treatise in the Sociology of Knowledge*. Hackley asserts that his social construction:

> . . . is more informed by post-structuralist and critical traditions than by the phenomenological social constructionism social researchers know from Bergman and Luckmann. (Hackley, 2001, p. 1)

It is to discourse analysis that Hackley looks for his social construction principles, particularly the work of Jonathan Potter, and it is certainly in discourse analysis that social construction has tended to neatly integrate with much postmodern critical theory. Furthermore, Hackley is keen to point out that he 'invokes' such apparent "unities" as 'marketing' and 'social construction' "merely in order to destabilise and then reconstruct them in the pursuit of my own literary marketing agenda" (ibid.). Hackley is not just being 'honest' here, boldly admitting his own agenda in disarming postmodern reflexivity (though, such a display has its own rhetorical purpose in arguing for the *ethos* of the author); rather, this framing of the phrase 'social construction' serves to forestall any criticism that might be made of Hackley's own construction of the "diverse archeology" (ibid., p. 56) of social construction (as if to say, don't expect too much from this, after all, I'm not really claiming to be a social constructionist). This is reinforced by the curious outburst on p. 64 in which he apologizes for the "cod philosophizing and bowdlerized social research" that have resulted from his "desperate attempt to be taken seriously". All of this means that Hackley doesn't have to get too bogged down in discussing differences between schools and interpretations and can instead move on quickly to doing what he really wants to do, which is demonstrate the constructed, contingent nature of marketing theory. The opening comments from *Marketing and Social Construction* quoted previously also serve to rhetorically construct a specific vision of the disciplinary landscape of social construction, where the Berger and Luckmann legacy is presented as in some way separate from the assumptions of discourse analysis and where other significant constructionist schools are occulted through Hackley's lack of reference or marginalization.

Constructivism raises difficult questions regarding the nature of the 'reality' we perceive as existing outside ourselves and that reality includes, naturally, other people and the act of communicating with these people. If knowledge is socially constructed, then how much of our personal knowledge of other people is constructed by our own language, our own thought? Such questions might appear to have no place in a marketing book and it is entirely understandable that for Hackley, whose principle target is marketing discourse, such apparently 'philosophical' issues would threaten to cloud the points he is trying to make regarding the 'real' hegemony of the marketing management paradigm. However, I contend that some constructivist approaches to dealing with these questions can provide us with very interesting, practical insights when dealing with marketing issues like communication and interactivity.

The understanding of constructivism that I will be creating here is one that is built upon a number of complementary streams of thought, including the work of Berger and Luckmann, the theories of discourse analysis, and Hackley's own formulations. However, my presentation of the paradigm is grounded also in the field known as *radical constructivism* which has been built up around the work of Ernst von Glasersfeld and which seeks "to model the generation of knowledge without reference to an ontic reality" (von Glasersfeld, 2005, p. 11).

"IS THERE ANYBODY OUT THERE?"

Watzlawick, Bavelas, and Jackson (1967) define an "interactional system" as "two or more communicants in the process of, or at the level of, defining the nature of their relationship" (ibid., p. 121). I would like to use this definition as a sort of beacon to travel toward in my exploration of a radical constructivist approach toward marketing communication because it seems to me that it both immediately invokes an idea of a mutual, continual process of definition (which potentially has much to say regarding the business of marketing communication) and at the same time seems to raise one of the biggest hurdles to any rigorously constructivist approach, namely, the apparent necessity in any definition of a communication process for "two or more communicants". Paul Watzlawick himself has written explicitly constructivist texts (Watzlawick, 1984) and his work with Bavelas and Jackson is a seminal application of constructivist philosophies of language to problems in human interaction and mental health, situations where most of the time there is a clear sense of there existing communicants (in the plural). How can a radical constructivist talk about *others*, however? If we are unable to make reference to "an ontic reality", how can we fruitfully talk about communication between individuals? Answering these questions will bring us closer to an understanding of interaction that has significant implications for marketing practice.

Radical constructivism holds that we construct our external reality. What we think of as the 'out there', real, concrete world can have no meaningful status separate from our own perception. Our senses provide us with data and it is the natural work of the mind to find connections in the arrangements of light and shade and color values (in the realm of visual data, for example), to try and fit the connections into 'recognizable' patterns. As von Glasersfeld explains:

> The drawing of connections in perception has the goal of yielding coherent patterns and, wherever possible, familiar ones. That is, patterns that prior experience has shown to be useful in the generation of meaningful action. One of the main tasks of perception is, after all, to put the perceiver into a position to decide which ways of acting seem viable. In short, perception serves to make predictions. (von Glasersfeld, 2008, p. 61)

The process of prediction is seen by constructivists to be central to the character of the human brain because it is intimately connected to the idea of 'viability', or usefulness; if we can, through the observation of patterns in our perceptual field, predict which of our actions may produce apparently useful consequences for us, then we may come to a way of being, of surviving, of developing. Recent constructivist work integrating research in the areas of cognitive psychology, neuroscience, computer modeling, and linguistics has led to the formation of the theory of the "anticipatory drive", a concept heavily developed in the work of Butz, Hoffman, and Hoffman (see Butz, 2008, for a literature review), and which they propose "concurrently biases and guides brain development, decision making, and control" (Butz, 2008, p. 1)[1]. So, according to von Glasersfeld, the knowledge that we construct about the 'external' world,

> . . . does not represent the world at all—it comprises action schemes, concepts, and thoughts, and it distinguishes the ones that are considered advantageous from those that are not. In other words, it pertains to the ways and the means the cognizing subject has conceptually evolved in order to fit into the world as he or she experiences it. (von Glasersfeld, 1996, p. 114)

It is, perhaps, important at this stage to recall von Glasersfeld's dictum that constructivism "has nothing to say about what may or may not *exist*" (ibid., p. 113, emphasis in original); it is an epistemology, not an ontology. The question of whether the external world exists or not is entirely outside its scope precisely because constructivism holds that our knowledge is not a representation of something outside and independent of us but rather a "re-presentation" (in von Glasersfeld's phrase) of something inside us. Much radical constructivist scholarship has concerned itself with arguing and demonstrating that what we traditionally conceive of as representations of the real world are in fact constructions that spring from "individual thinkers as an adaptation to their subjective experience" (von Glasersfeld, 2000, p. 4). In mistaking their knowledge as a 'true' representation, or in trying to move ever closer to achieving such 'true' representation, objectivists (or realists) completely ignore what radical constructivists hold is the actual source of knowledge: subjective experience. Now, the school of social construction, founded upon the work of Peter Berger and Thomas Luckmann, does not see individual, subjective experience as the source of knowledge, but instead "understands human reality as socially constructed reality" (Berger & Luckmann, 1991, p. 210). Their emphasis is therefore upon the way in which language, ritual, social structures, and institutions (and institutionalizations) serve to legitimize the 'realities' of social groups. Much of what Chris Hackley proceeds to do in his 2001 book on marketing and social construction can be unproblematically (despite his strategic protestations) viewed as originating from this theoretical perspective. The selection criteria and power-brokering of academic journals, the rituals of conferences, the language use of dominant marketing intellectuals, the canon-creating course reading lists—all of these elements (and more) of the society of marketing academics serve to construct a "notion of a unified and objective science of marketing" (Hackley, 2001, p. 65). Radical constructivism, however, while certainly agreeing with the broad assertions of social construction, identifies individual subjective experience as the root of 'reality' creation.

"YOU SAY CONSTRUCTIONISM, I SAY CONSTRUCTIVISM"

Hackley's own take on the difference between social construction and constructivism is interesting for the way in which he seeks to allegorize the fundamental dichotomy between the two approaches through his own caricature of the traditions of research in advertising and consumer behavior. Beginning by claiming that "constructivist theories of knowledge generation have been influential since Plato" (ibid., p. 59), Hackley then defines constructivism by referencing exactly two thinkers, Plato and Piaget (perhaps another instance of the will to alliteration demonstrated throughout his text). The Platonic "tradition" of "cognitive epistemology" is summarized with the following words:

> . . . we look out into an unknowable world armed only with our sense and our reason. What we learn about the world is in some sense imperfect, a poor reproduction of the real thing: a sort of mirror image, in fact. But humans are solitary thinkers who can attain insight through rationality. Knowledge is generated in a social vacuum. (ibid., p. 59)

Hackley then proceeds, with no explanation whatsoever, to link this "tradition" directly to Jean Piaget's "constructivist developmental epistemology", which is described as influencing "much social psychology of adult thinking" (ibid.). Now, let me leave aside for a moment the fact that this characterization is completely at odds with the basic premise of *radical* constructivism, and instead let me take a quick look at the rhetorical strategies implemented by Hackley in this construction of a "tradition". Firstly, constructivism is subtly presented as a hegemonic tradition through the bookending claims that constructivist theories have been "influential since Plato" and Piaget's constructivism is the source for "much" "social psychology of adult thinking". In portraying constructivism as highly influential, Hackley correspondingly frames social construction as a marginalized underdog, bereft of power and influence, the Rocky Balboa in this intellectual arena. Furthermore, by speaking as if with the voice of constructivism, Hackley is able to place quite damning words into its 'mouth'; so, the sentence "Knowledge is generated in a social vacuum" is presented to the reader as a tenet of constructivism, whereas it is instead a careful characterization designed to undermine it. The word "vacuum" carries connotations of emptiness (and at the same time reminding us of the principle that "nature abhors a vacuum"), while the phrase "social vacuum" implies that the "social", though existing somewhere else, has been expelled from this particular place. In other words, constructivism is presented as an unnatural attempt to expel social considerations from epistemology, an attempt, furthermore, that appears to stand for an influential, mainstream (and we have already been taught to deeply mistrust *this* word 60 pages into Hackley's argument) hegemony.

The crowning coup-de-grace of Hackley's positioning of social construction as the *un*constructivism occurs with his virtuoso rhetorical linking of constructivism with everything that is unholy in research on advertising, consumer behavior, and marketing communication in general. Clearly echoing his earlier formulation of constructivism, Hackley asserts that advertising research, while in many ways "less bound to economic models of consumer rationality" has generally "presumed that consumers consume advertising in a social vacuum" (ibid., p. 60)[2]. Additionally, "a constructivist view of knowledge" is deemed to be at the root of marketing communication's understanding of such "constructs" as consumer attitudes and satisfaction and this has led to the primacy of "a notion of socially solipsistic consumers, constructing their marketing experiences in the void of their own head" (ibid.). Against this finely constructed straw man, Hackley contrasts (in the upstanding tradition of binary opposition), a "social constructionist ontology" which enables us to see "that consumption is constructed in engagement with the social world" (ibid.).

For Hackley, then, social constructionism "is first and foremost an ontological position" (ibid., p. 61), whereas he describes constructivism (quite fairly) as an epistemology. I am not going to pretend to fully understand what is going on here—it seems to me as if Hackley is trying to say that ontological issues are traditionally not addressed in management and psychological research, whereas they should be because all forms of social research have an "implicit or explicit" ontological component. And that therefore, in claiming that social constructionism is an ontological position, he may assert that its application to marketing research will "turn attention to the deep assumptions about the social and psychological, and political order in marketing issues" which are usually "discursively silenced". The implication appears to be that such assumptions are issues of ontology, rather than, say, epistemology.

In the end, Hackley's construction of constructivism serves to rhetorically strengthen his claim that the *social* construction of reality premised by social constructionism offers a perspective that is substantially different to the assumptions informing research strains in marketing communication. Hackley's position is that social constructionism holds that "representations of 'facts' and 'knowledge', like any other descriptions, cannot be seen simply in terms of their correspondence to a version of reality, but must be seen as constitutive of it" (ibid., p. 65) and that, therefore, the discourses created by the social groupings that construct marketing and marketing theory need to be interrogated for their constitutive force. The application of social constructionism can connect marketing research back to the societies that construct it, and so offers to embed understandings of marketing within long-denied, or long-marginalized social contexts.

The construction of rigidly exclusive binary oppositions does nothing for the establishment of nuance, complexity, and depth in the alternative discourse of marketing theory. It is not the case that one either has to accept that knowledge is socially constructed or believe that it is the result of individually, subjective experience, and it is also not the case that the latter hypothesis should be equated with "private" and "mysterious" forces of social vacuity within the mind. What a sad sight it would make for the constructivists and constructionists to flay each other alive while the good burghers of the mainstream 'tut tut' and turn back to their veal. The navigation of an inclusionary course is both possible and desirable. So, how can we negotiate such a course and what might it mean for marketing?

"THE TWO FACES OF THE FEEDBACK LOOP"

There are two cybernetics. So far, I have been using the term in reference to the work on systems of self-regulation (whether mechanical, biological, or social) that is typified by the research of Norbert Wiener, Ross Ashby, and Stafford Beer. This highly functional school of thought has branched off into many different areas; robotics, computer science, artificial intelligence, Operations Research, and, as we have seen, important aspects of management and marketing 'science' (see Rudall, 2006 for a good overview of current applications of such research). Some of the central problems of this cybernetic heritage, particularly in relation to the modeling of communication, have been laid out in the first and second chapters of this work. However, one of the greatest ironies, for me, regarding the influence of cybernetics upon communication theory (and consequently marketing communication theory) of the late 20th century, is that there has existed for at least 40 years a *second* cybernetic tradition that has concerned itself with such issues as the observer's position as creator, reflexivity in self-organization, reality construction, communication as creative negotiation, and the foundational importance of the act of differentiation. All of these concerns are far more apposite to, and fecund for, contemporary marketing communication than the sadly blinkered readings of cybernetic control theory that have typified the dominant post-War marketing orientations. It has become accepted usage to label the Wiener/Ashby, control-orientated school, *first-order* cybernetics and the observer-orientated school, *second-order* cybernetics, not reflecting any particular chronological precedence but rather indicating that second-order cybernetics concerns itself with the meta-analysis of cybernetic constructions. Second-order cybernetics has had a tremendous influence upon constructivist thinking (radical or otherwise) and can be seen as lending to it a number of tools that help to build "a theory of knowledge construction that successfully avoids both the absurdities of solipsism and the fatal contradictions of realism" (von Glasersfeld, 1996, p. 148) and, vitally, provide constructivism with the means to talk about communication. It is particularly in the work of Heinz von Foerster that second-order cybernetics has become defined and it is in von Foerster's notion of *eigenforms* that we might find the catalyst to synthesize the social and individual constructionist approaches to communication and interaction. What follows is a comparatively svelte approach[3] to outlining what a second-order cybernetic approach to a constructivist understanding of marketing communication might entail[4]. It takes the form of a slow spiraling-in toward the central concern of marketing communication, and accordingly begins out on what are the very edges of that topic but the very core of a constructivist approach.

"MY DEFINITION OF A BOOMBASTIC CONSTRUCTIVISM"

The patterns I construct from my perceptions constitute my reality. I am a pattern-maker, then. And all my pattern-making is rooted in the act of making *distinctions*. The patterns that I associate with feelings of pleasure, with comfort, with satisfaction—these are patterns that I seek to repeat in my perceptions. All the elements of my environment, from other people, trees, and computers to the wind, the stars, and moonlight are constructs that I have abstracted from my perceptual experience, that I have given stability to. The same is to be said for the elements of my 'self'—my body, my sense of interiority, my word-store.

Language is one of the ways in which I construct more of this environment, and it is the primary way in which society, the grouping(s) of others, seeks to pass on to me the ability to recognize certain stable patterns that they have distinguished. My interactions with others, my interactions with society, are further examples of the process of stabilization which typifies my personal construction of reality through the seeking of patterns in my perceptual experience. Language is able to "re-present" patterns of perceptual experience that are not necessarily present anymore and as such has a tremendous instrumental value in attempts to coordinate action between myself and others (and no doubt serves the same function for those others). However, because my use of language is built upon my personal constructs, any understanding between myself and others will be "a matter of fit rather than match" (von Glasersfeld, 1990, p. 36).

Language enables us to share constructions of reality but inevitably those constructions will never have exact equivalence. Interaction (through language but also through all other forms of perceptual experience) serves to negotiate (obviously with varying degrees of success) stable understandings. The viability of these negotiated understandings serves as the test of whether we and those we interact with have achieved an understanding of the language we use amongst ourselves and of the concepts we use it to share. Furthermore, when I speak, I speak of myself, of the realities that I have constructed (or that I have negotiated to share with others as far as inherent non-equivalence will allow), my 'self', of course, being also one of those constructed realities.

Each act of communication is an attempt to "re-present" a set of stable patterns that I have distinguished in my perceptual experience. While I am "anchored" in society (Poerksen, 2003, p. 22), and while social groupings are able to dominate my pattern-making ability through the force of their language (making me mistake "fit" for "match"), I am nevertheless ultimately responsible for my own reality, because I am responsible for my own perceptions. To focus on the social construction of realities to the exclusion of individual, personal construction is to be a midwife at a stillbirth.

My voice is the voice of my constructions, a listing of stable patterns that are viable to me. Many are viable to me because they appear to fit with constructions that others have, and through interaction they are often made to fit better, attaining greater stability. Sometimes, I realize that those words that I use with others to re-present patterns of perceptual experience that I have had do not fit very well at all the experience those others have had—and so I have discovered that my understanding of what those words re-present is obviously different. When I analyze the rhetoric of Philip Kotler, Chris Hackley, Barbara Stern, or any other voice, I am identifying patterns and constructing stabilities, just as, I am sure, their own words for themselves re-present the patterns they have observed and the stabilities they have consequently constructed. My reading/writing is my re-presenting construction; their readings/writings are their re-presenting construction. We might appear to share many constructions, or at least it seems we do because we use many of the same words (words like "rhetoric", "Internet", "interactivity", "marketing", "positioning"). Yet, in observing the constructions that others make, I am observing myself, my own pattern-making, my own distinction-making. For example, when I speak of "mainstream marketing theory" I am re-presenting a pattern of distinctions that I have made in my perceptual experience; some of those distinctions are marked out by others (say, in the words of Christopher Hackley), yet in distinguishing viability in them I construct them myself, I distinguish in them part of a pattern that must inevitably be different from the pattern they belong to for Christopher Hackley.

In observing, I make distinctions; in making distinctions, I construct. Much of my observation relates to social groups and social forces (much of my experience is experience of society), my education (formal and informal) represents the re-presentation by others of their own sets of distinctions and I find viability in repeating many of those distinctions. Many of those re-presentations of others' distinctions refer to areas of experience that I have not personally had—viability in such circumstances comes from whether behaving "as if" these re-presentations are patterns that I have distinguished results in my survival or thriving[5]. There are many of these 'social constructions' that, if I do indeed behave as if they were my observations, lead to my thriving. Yet, at the same time, each member of a social group that I belong to will understand such shared social constructions differently; again, there is only fit, not match. How can we say that all

Christians understand the Christianity that they profess in the same way? A radical constructivist would say that this, surely, cannot be the case. Each Christian is an individual observer, negotiating between the distinctions re-presented by others and the distinctions they have observed themselves. There are, consequently, as many different Christianities as there are Christians, as many different Marxisms as there are Marxists (let alone socialists), and as many different constructivisms as there are constructivists[6]. In all of these matrices of distinctions, I may observe 'core' dogmatic distinctions that, for me, appear to constitute the essential pattern of each one. Yet, in further interaction with others over time, I perceive that what I have taken to be the essential patterns are not the same patterns that others would prioritize, or that if we share, in labeling words, our distinctions of essential patterns, nevertheless the way that we understand those patterns is different.

My individual perceptual experience of the concept I use the word "Marxism" to refer to, is a complex, evolving, matrix of distinctions that is the result of my interactions with a large number of individuals and a large amount of media. My teachers, family members, friends, speakers I have listened to, interviews I have watched, books I have read, news I have seen, the numbing force of a police truncheon against my left arm—my conception of what Marxism is, the matrix of observations, of distinctions, that I am re-presenting when I use that word, is constructed from all of these things. And when I say "my teachers", it is an unfortunate artifact of this carrier of temporary stabilities that we call language that what for me re-presents very specific individuals, in very specific times and places, is distinguished as an amorphous social grouping by others ("ah, yes, teachers", you say, nodding your head) or, even more likely, leads others to re-present their own experiences of very different individuals at very different times and places.

Of course, amongst my list of 'perceptions leading to a viable pattern re-presented by "Marxism"' I have naturally included my personal experiences with mass media. My construction of "mass media", like that of "Marxism", is the result of my distinction of viable patterns in my perception. Some of these patterns are perceived in conversations with friends, colleagues and students, others are distinguished in my reading of works about the construction "mass media" as other individuals see it, and others are the result of my experience when watching TV, and DVDs, listening to the radio, surfing the Web, reading newspapers and magazines. Each one of these interactions has an effect upon the stabilization of the pattern "Marxism" for me, but each of those interactions is with an other that I have constructed. When I read a newspaper, I construct a pattern of distinctions around that newspaper that go to create a viable stability that I may call *The Daily Telegraph*, *Kıbrıs*, or *The Guardian*, and within that pattern are further individual voices that I construct relating to 'columnists', 'reporters', 'editors' re-presented by proper names. These patterns, as well as evolving over time, necessarily are different for me than they are for any other reader of the same newspapers—because I have created them from my own perceptual experience of the newspaper. The time of day that I habitually read the papers, the feeling of the newsprint against my fingers, the page layout, the opinions of my family and friends regarding the paper that I am reading, the types of words that I find on the page, the 'tone' and 'style' of different editorial voices, all of these perceptions can be distinguished as patterns by me because they relate to perceptions from my larger experience. In this way, *The Times* is a newspaper of compromise for me—my mother wishing to read *The Guardian*, my father *The Daily Telegraph*, they settled on *The Times* as the household paper. The compromise that was reached was a complex mixture of negotiation, harmony, and dissatisfaction (in my perception) and included the oft-repeated assertion that *The Times* reflected my father's political opinions more than my mother's. So, my experience of *The Times* as a "mass media" channel, and hence my distinction of the patterns that stabilize it, and so what I am re-presenting to myself when I use the title, is naturally going to be different from anyone else's.

So, this brings me on to the issue, essential for a consideration of interaction in marketing communication, of persuasion and influence. As I noted previously, language is a tool which enables me to, however crudely, align my perceived distinctions with those of others in order to bring about coordinated action. If I can discern a certain pattern in my perception and if I can cause an other to perceive a similar pattern, then we can agree to refer to it by the same words or phrases. I will remind you at this stage (because language has a way of quickly fogging this issue) that the patterns I am referring to are constructions. As von Foerster says,

> "these distinctions are not out there in the world, are not properties of things and objects but properties of our descriptions of the world. The objects there will forever remain a mystery but their descriptions reveal the properties of observers and speakers, whom we can get to know better in this way" (von Foerster & Poerksen, 2002, p. 17)

I would hold that persuasion means achieving agreement amongst others to propositions you have expressed, or as Perelman and Olbrechts-Tyteca have formulated it "the goal of all argumentation . . . is to create or increase the adherence of minds to the theses presented for their assent" (Perelman & Olbrechts-Tyteca, 1971, p. 45). From a constructivist perspective, I can only ever *observe* such adherence; I may distinguish certain patterns of perception that I will take (construct) as the adherence of others to the propositions that I have presented. How do I go about producing a change in my perception such that I would observe that an other, or group of others, are adhering to my propositions? What, in other words, might be a constructivist understanding of the process of persuasive communication?

The essence of persuasive communication is the attempt to try and make an individual or group of individuals act as if the pattern I have observed is also a pattern that they have observed. Action is an important factor here because unless there is some form of action (some behavior) I will not be able to observe any adherence to my construct in my audience. For my persuasive purposes, it is worthless if the others of my target group adopt my construction but never display behavior that would confirm it (and from a constructivist point of view, the only way I can construct an idea of what is in their minds is if I have some observable pattern to perceive). So, in communicating particular constructs to an audience, the issue of viability will be paramount. I must re-present the contextual patterns that have convinced me of the viability of the construct, so that the audience may distinguish its viability in the same way that I have. But, of course, when I re-present the series of contextual patterns of perceptions that I have distinguished as grounding the viability of a particular construct, I am re-presenting my own personal experience—experience that an audience does not have. As I have already mentioned, language provides us with the ability to re-present personal, individual experience to ourselves and others, but such re-presentation is necessarily re-presentation of perception, not reality. The audience observes my re-presentation of personal constructs and, because this is what we do as humans, they proceed to distinguish patterns within my words, my constructs and the way in which those constructs achieve patterns with the constructions of reality they each maintain. Viability becomes an issue of how closely my re-presented constructs accord (create patterns) with their existing realities. Certainly, this rendering of the persuasive process coincides very closely with the practical advice offered in classical rhetorical pedagogies—Aristotle's work on rhetoric constantly underlines the necessity of presenting your arguments in ways that remind the audience of their own beliefs about the world. A vivid example is provided when Aristotle is discussing the "great assistance" that the use of maxims can give to a speech:

> The maxim, as has been said, is a general assertion, and the listeners are delighted when a point is generalized which they happen to presuppose in the particular case ... [...] ... So one should guess at the sort of opinions that the audience happen already to have presupposed, and then speak in general about them. (Aristotle, 1991, *The Art of Rhetoric*, Book III, Ch. 2:21)

We persuade, then, through a consideration of the patterns distinguished by others. This consideration must in itself be based upon our perception of the patterns that others appear to communicate to us—the words and concepts that we may observe them using. We observe the distinctions of others and mark the patterns that develop between the words of others and the re-presentation of our distinctions to ourselves. This is where the key is, this reflexive element. The observer observing themselves. And this is where most traditions of Western rhetoric and all models of communication that marketing has entertained are blind.

The persistence of the transmission metaphor throughout Western considerations of communication and language means that it is difficult to understand constructions of communication that reject the idea of information being carried from a sender (or senders) to a receiver (or receivers). In other words, all of the communication models that I have dealt with in the first and second chapters, no matter how radical or revolutionary, presuppose that something (information, argumentation, emotion, text, subtext, etc.) is passed from one person (or a matrix of people) to another person (or matrix of audiences, be they passive or active). The radical constructivist approach to communication is to sidestep this assumption altogether. I can begin to outline this position by first turning to a passage by Humberto Maturana and Francisco Varela in their striking rejection of the "tube metaphor" of communication. They point out that because the common view of communication is that it involves something being "generated at a certain point" and then "carried by a conduit", we "usually speak of the 'information' contained in a picture, an object, or, more evidently, the printed word", thinking that "what is communicated is an integral part of that which travels in the tube" (Maturana & Varela, 1996, p. 196). However, Maturana and Varela assert that this metaphor is "basically false" because it assumes that "what happens to a system in an interaction is determined by the perturbing agent and not by its structural dynamics" (ibid.). For it is clear, they write, that:

> such is not the case with communication: each person says what he says or hears what he hears according to his own structural determination; saying does not ensure listening. .[. . .] . . . The phenomenon of communication depends on not what is transmitted, but on what happens to the person who receives it. And this is a very different matter from 'transmitting information'. (ibid.)

The meaning is not in the picture, then, it is brought about by me. I construct the meaning according to my own "structural determination". When we observe the distinctions that others appear to make, our observation is a creation. For the constructivist, in the classical rhetorical scenario of a standing speaker facing a sitting audience, it is not the case that the speaker transmits an argument that the audience deliberates upon and then either accepts or rejects; rather, each audience member constructs an understanding of what the speaker is saying, and each of those understandings will be dependent upon the individual experience of the individual audience member. Additionally, the speaker observes the "reaction" of the audience and constructs meanings for each cough, rustle, and murmur. Each human agent in the room is engaged in a continuous, never-ending creation of meaning that changes themselves. The speaker is changing, the audience members are changing, everyone is evolving and developing patterns that are stitched in to the larger complex of patterns that they each bring from their individual perceptual experience. Furthermore, feeding and sustaining this ongoing creation is the self-observation, the meta-level pattern-distinction of looping self-reference as each person present marks patterns in her own pattern-making. Surely, you might insist, at root this is still a case of transmission? The speaker must be transmitting something for each of those audience members to observe, after all? The constructivist would point out that, really, the transmission metaphor makes no sense, is of no use. For there is no 'thing' that is sent from one person to another, that is just a long-standing metaphorical conceit. After all, if each individual in the audience constructs a different meaning from her observation of the speaker, how can we speak of a single 'message' that is transmitted? How could we possibly point to this 'message'? Are we to privilege the speaker's idea of what meaning her speech contains? Yet, the speaker's understanding of the meaning of the speech changes as she delivers it, as she observes her own reaction to it, to the environment, and to the audience's reactions.

So, let me frame this now in marketing communication terms.

A product, service, or brand is a construction; it has reality as a construction in the minds of those who observe it. What might I be talking about, then, when I say "it"? The product, for example, is not just the physical object that I observe, it is the constantly changing matrix of observations that I distinguish and re-present to myself[7] as 'the product'; so, as an agent in a marcom setting, I might observe the product at a client presentation, setting its patterns against existing patterns from my experience, creating new patterns from those juxtapositions, and continually re-formatting, re-patterning in a self-referential, autopoietic loop (I might refer to this as 'thinking about', 'considering', or 'brainstorming' the product). At certain points, I will be asked by other individuals for my opinion and at those points I have to provide a snapshot of the matrix of patterns I have distinguished around 'the product'. People want stability, they want 'my idea', and I want 'their idea' and when we solicit these expressions we are actually requesting stability. In our own patterning we are always working toward stability, toward homeostasis—I want to know what the product means to me, what it might mean to the target audience, what can I do with it. This is the significance of our constructs; we make patterns in order to seek stability, consistency, and so viability. When the client asks me what I think about the product the client is expecting a construct that is stable—if I say one thing and then say the opposite at the next meeting, the client will be frustrated with the instability of my constructions. And, indeed, I would most probably be embarrassed, too (see Cialdini, 2001, for a soft social constructionist approach to why this might be so). My patterning is a part of a drive toward stability and as such I want stability in my 'reality', in my constructions, and in the same way I expect it in the communication of others' constructions. But, this is not possible. As I work through the stages of campaign design I am observing more—my observation, actually, can never stop. I have a conversation (an interaction) with an account planner who re-presents to me an aspect of her patterning of the product that she has constructed as the result of an incident in a focus group. Although the incident was small, it has stuck in her head (perhaps because it reminded her of something else) and it now possesses a strong influence in her construction of the product's brand. My observation of this leads me to a re-patterning, slight perhaps, but nevertheless my construct evolves. And so it continues for me and for all the others—when we interact we re-present dynamic patterning as temporary stabilities but the very process of interaction (of observation) increases the instability of the pattern, leads to change. The process of advertising campaign design, to continue with this particular marketing communication example, is one of multi-dimensional, continual, self-referential interaction. The large number of human agents involved at various moments in the process are observing each other (the constructs they distinguish as others) and themselves (the construct they distinguish as themselves); in observing they are continually creating, re-patterning. From one vantage point (and one particular observer), everyone might appear to be working toward a final, stabilized re-presentation of a communally-produced construction. Yet, that itself would just be a construction—each individual interactant constructs an ever-evolving stream of patterning that at any time is fixing itself into stability or dissolving in a new re-patterning. Even when presenting a consensus to a client, surely an obvious moment of stability in the construct, individual members of the agency team will have quite different matrices of observations and re-presentations that the 'consensus' is embedded within (and so the 'consensus' means a different thing to each member of the consenting group). The client, in observing the presentation by the agency, marks a pattern she usually re-presents with the constructions 'consensus', or 'agreement', or 'united front'. The agency team observe an impressed client. Yet, all interactants are continuing the process of observation as they part ways out of the conference room—each continues the constant looping of pattern-making and pattern-evolving and, although the print campaign executions have been approved, each individual is constructing 'the product' still, now in the light of an approving, happy client, now in the context of her own stabilized constructions of 'job security', 'one more for my book', or 'I still don't think we've got a handle on the target audience'.

Three weeks later, the first insertion of the ad appears in *Car & Driver*. There have already been two changes to the headline since the sit-down with the client—stability is a continuum, and the advertising manager's construction of 'the product', 'the agency', and 'the ad' are continually in evolution. The longer the final PDF sits on her computer desktop, the more she stares at it, the more she thinks the tone of that headline is just too smarmy, reminds her too much of that constant, tight grin on that account executive's face. Her construct of the target audience, which (no matter how much quant work she has) still largely depends on patterns she has discerned in her observations of her two brothers over the last 20 years, is losing its stability in the face of some poor reviews of competing products in the trade press. The *Car & Driver* ad appears, from one vantage point, to be a unified, confident presentation of a company's message about its product. But by the time it appears in print, everyone involved in its production has moved on through continual streams of patterning and re-patterning, constructing and re-constructing; they no longer 'understand' the ad in the same way they did when the final sign-offs came. If they see the presentation in the magazine (and many of the interactants will not, or only see it as an isolated tear sheet), each observes it embedded in a different matrix of distinctions. While everyone uses the same words and appears to use them to refer to the same things, the constructs that these words are associated with and the temporarily stabilized patterns of perceptions that are re-presented by the constructs are inevitably different from individual to individual.

Constructs like 'the client', 'the agency', 'the creatives', 'the message the ad gives', 'the target audience', 'the reach', or 'press reactions' are social constructs *embodied individually*. So, while the construct of 'the client' is part of a discourse of power and exchange, a discourse which has been developing for many hundreds of years, that discourse has its continual expression in the observations and patterns discerned by individual humans. Consider the different levels of what I might call 'resolution' to be discerned in the construction of 'the client': firstly (though I am not trying to imply any degree of precedence), there is the broad sense of 'client' as it used across a large range of service scenarios, someone that one does work for, someone upon whom the success of one's business enterprise is dependent whether you are an engineering consultant, a freelance web designer, an architect, or an account director in an advertising agency. In each different business context, however, the 'client' can be understood with more distinction, so that advertising agency personnel would be socialized to see the client within a particular discourse frame that might be rather different in its broad strokes to the way that personnel in an engineering consultancy might construct 'the client'. At a finer resolution, different ad agencies can try and inculcate different perceptions of 'the client' from the 'industry norm' (they might be working against dominant themes in the industry discourse or attempting to refine certain aspects of that discourse), perhaps even going so far as to encourage the use of other terms for the client across agency usage. At an even finer resolution, agency personnel will observe fundamental differences in the way that different clients behave, discuss, and reach consensus on the differences and create shared constructs accordingly (the easy client, the creepy client, the pushy client who always wants the logo bigger, etc). At the finest level of resolution there is the individual pattern-making that is the result of personal experience. Naturally, this finest level is interwoven with all the others yet it also colors the individual perception (and patterning) of all other resolutions.

Analyses of marketing issues from social constructionist perspectives focus almost entirely on the broader resolution levels of discourse, ignoring the finer, personal levels that inevitably are structurally coupled with them. There are a number of reasons for this, I think. The first has to do with the idea of the patterning of observations that is at the root of the radical constructivist position. Our perceptions are useful to us in so far as we can discern patterns in their flow. We search for patterns, we seek for stability across observations; we match and compare. To find similarity we must first make distinctions[8]. We are therefore drawn toward the creation of what, in common English usage, are called "generalizations". Since discourse began, the vast majority of Western research methodologies, whether quantitative or qualitative, have sought patterns in data sets. Patterning is an aggregation—the individual becomes a token for a construct that they can be observed to share with others. Market research (like most other research in other fields) thus seeks to perceive the wood rather than the trees. Social constructionist approaches point out that what might be considered a wood is only considered a wood because it looks like another wood everyone has always been talking about or because to call this grouping of trees a wood allows it be owned outright by a particular individual and thus sold at a profit. But still, no one wants to look at the trees as individual trees—how could we, what would be the purpose in that?

Marketing practitioners need to construct generalizations and, often, pay others to construct even more for them. They are expected by senior management to construct generalizations of data that can then be used to make decisions that will allow a business to survive and thrive. Whether they use statistical modeling in Excel sheets, familiarity with a product and representative customers over time, guided discussions and deep interviews with focus groups, or just plain 'gut-instinct', practitioners of marketing communication create constructions of their target audiences which are founded in the dynamic of aggregation—to make unmanageable individuals disappear in a manageable pattern. This process is simply one more instantiation of what the radical constructivist sees as the primary motif of the living being. What is interesting about current marketing theory and practice, however, is the extent to which mainstream voices are appearing to pull against this aggregation. Relationship Marketing, and the Service-Dominant Logic of Vargo and Lusch (2004) that has come to be seen as its intellectual handmaiden, use language and arguments that promote the construction of the consumer as an individual (Pepper & Rogers "one-to-one" [1999] marketing and Gummesson's [2008] "many-to-many") rather than as member of a segment, as involved in continuing relationships with firms (which implies the potential recognition of the dynamic nature of personal constructs), and as co-creators of value (which acknowledges the constructed nature of value and so potentially the constructed nature of all understandings in the marketing system). In other words, there are major elements in the current service-orientation which, at least on the surface, promise a refocusing upon the individual consumer as a creator and a concomitant rethinking of the firm's self-construction in the light of its relationship to the consumer's value creation. Marketing interactions are certainly being talked of in terms of dialog, continuous dynamic relationships and shared constructions—but, given the long history of marketing engagement with communication as the transmission of control signals, how far do such terms represent rhetorical strategies to engage with alternative discourses of interactivity while still remaining firmly entrenched within the first-order cybernetic paradigm? As the next chapters will show, there are strong tensions within contemporary marketing discourses between rhetorics of control or measurement and rhetorics of dialog and interactivity. While there are many assertions of the importance of the consumer creation of value, for example, attempts to contextualize such assertions within larger understandings of what such creation means for marketing communication and interaction have remained vague and unconvincing. A constructivist orientation to these issues offers a substantial framework with which to examine the connotations of these radical calls for re-structuring (or re-interpreting) the marketing enterprise around one-to-one interactivity.

Returning to the definition of interaction from Watzlawick, Bavelas, and Jackson that I presented earlier in this chapter, I would now like to expand upon it, whilst framing it within a more clearly marketing context, in the light of the constructivist orientation outlined above. If we start off with the understanding that interaction is a process in which "two or more communicants" are "defining the nature of their relationship" then we must first recognize that such a process is never-ending. A relationship can never be defined, in the sense of arriving at a finished definition, because all communicants involved in an interaction are necessarily changing in their own matrix of internal constructions. The notion of definition, however, carries with it the connotation of exploration, of trying to distinguish the boundaries around something. Or, in the terms I have been using, a stabilization. Communicants, therefore, are engaged in a continuous attempt to discern stability in the patterns of relationships they observe between each other. This implies within it the search for stable patterns in the observable language and behavior of those with whom we communicate. This process carries within itself the seeds of a strong tension, however. We seek to define, to stabilize, but due to our reflexivity, true stability is unattainable (even in our memories of those who have passed away—our constructions of them continue to change, if only to change form in the entropy of forgetting). Our ability to observe ourselves, our capacity for self-reference, determines that we (our constructions of ourselves) are never the same; in observing the way that I am thinking I change the way that I am thinking, in thinking about the way that I am thinking about an other I change the way in which I think about that other. Recursion guarantees change. To engage with the recursive nature of human communication, as Krippendorff (2009) points out, is to acknowledge that "understanding is *never finished*" (ibid., p. 78, emphasis in original). Interaction, in Krippendorff's terms, becomes "the recursive unfolding of communication constructions held by participants (including of each other)" (ibid.) and participants approach understanding when those unfoldings are "viable relative to each other" (ibid., p. 79)—but the recursive unfoldings and the intertwinings continue, the constructing never stops.

Having said all this, then, let me provide my own definition of interactivity:

> **Interactivity is the continual process between communicants of exploring the changing boundaries of the constructed understandings of themselves, of each other and of their own selves within those constructions of each other.**

From a marketing perspective how might such a definition be interpreted? Well, from the ground up it assumes complete equality between "communicants"; there is no sense in which the "producer" can have communicative control over the "consumer" or *vice versa*. The definition also implies that all communicants are creators, constructing understandings of each other and themselves. What happens to persuasion, then, or the "value proposition" (Vargo & Lusch, 2004) that will compel the consumer to choose a relationship with a particular brand? If interaction is premised upon continual creation, and so continual change, how can a persuasive message or proposition be understood? Earlier in this chapter, I discussed the way in which the dynamic nature of our constructions exists in tension with our search for stability and consistency in them, meaning that persuasive propositions are inevitably founded upon constructions of others that have become ossified, lifeless, and irrelevant due to the long production process, the large number of people that are involved in that process and the inadequate amount of interaction between the communicants. Krippendorff suggests that we think of language as providing us with the possibility to *co-ordinate* constructions between ourselves, rather than *share* them (Krippendorff, 2009, p. 83). In order to integrate this stance into a larger construction of marketing communication based upon my definition of interaction, I will first slightly reformulate the definition in more explicitly marketing terms, then sketch out some accompanying premises and explore some of their ramifications.

(a) Interactive marketing is the continual process in which stakeholders and potential stakeholders in a network of service relationships explore the changing boundaries of the constructed understandings of themselves, of each other, and of their own selves within those constructions of each other.

(b) Exploration of these changing boundaries does not originate with, nor reside within, any one particular stakeholder but is an integral property of any network of service relationships.

(c) As a part of such exploration, some stakeholders may attempt to co-ordinate their constructed understandings with those of other stakeholders.

(d) Such co-ordination occurs through the communication of static (re) presentations of constructions and the comparative adoption or rejection of elements of such static (re)presentations by stakeholders as viable within their own patterning or not.

(e) Co-ordinations between stakeholders are necessarily temporary due to the dynamic nature of the constructions and the recursive effects of stakeholders as observing systems observing their co-ordination.

(f) Co-ordinations between stakeholders lead to strengthened stakeholder viability, but such strengthenings only last as long as the co-ordinations between stakeholders.

(g) The drive toward the exploration of the changing boundaries of constructed understandings is rooted in the stakeholders' tendency towards stability in their constructions.

(h) The greatest threat to the process of co-ordination is posed by the stakeholders' tendency towards stability in their constructions.

(i) Aggregation of constructions is a function of the tendency toward stability.

(j) Any observer of the network is a stakeholder in the network.

The previous conjectures will form the basic structure of the model of interactive marketing communication that I will introduce in the final chapter of this book and it is there that I will argue in detail for their necessity, internal consistency, and applicability. Hopefully, having followed my explication of a constructivist approach to marketing interactivity in this chapter, the reader will recognize the reasoning informing most of these statements but for the sake of clarity there are a number of points that require some further explanation.

In premise (a), the first obvious change to my initial general definition of interactivity is the use of the word "stakeholder". As the constructivist paradigm asserts that all observers are necessarily creators it stands to reason that the use of such heavily-charged terms such as consumer and producer will lead to the assumption of unwarranted and unhelpful distinctions within a constructivist approach to interactive marketing. Furthermore, as we will see in Chapters 5 and 6 when I examine issues of customer co-production and the apparent convergence of consumption and production, there are a number of other marketing and critical perspectives that are uncomfortable with the divisions such language implies. At the same time, the creation of neologisms would threaten to make an already unfamiliar set of constructions far too alien to deserve the patience and goodwill of the reader. Consequently, I have settled upon the use of the word "stakeholder" to refer to anyone who has an interest in a particular network of service relationships. In that the word has become adopted into the mainstream marketing management lexicon it has the benefit of being familiar, although its use therein has become somewhat inexact and this stands as a disadvantage. The word "stakeholders" is often glossed as simply "audiences" (i.e., Smith & Taylor, 2004, p. 10), an understanding which for my purposes is close to useless because it implies a distinction between some form of producer, actor, or performer who presents to groups of receivers. Kotler and Keller make significant use of the term and understand it as referring to "various constituencies who have a critical interest in and impact on the company's performance" (taken from their description of the "stakeholder-performance scorecard", Kotler & Keller, 2006, p. 118). As is clear from the context of my premise (a), however, "stakeholders" in my construction of interactive marketing are not definable by their orientation to *the company* but rather to a network of service relationships. Additionally, the exact understanding of the phrase 'to have an interest in' remains crucial. So, I will propose a formal definition of a constructivist understanding of 'stakeholder' in the following terms: *a stakeholder is someone who engages in the construction of understandings regarding one or more aspects of a relationship.* This definition looks to Jonathan Potter's discussion of stake and interest in discourse analysis (Potter, 2005) but combines it with a recursive constructivist emphasis. Accordingly, when we construct an understanding of a relationship we place ourselves within that understanding—we therefore have an 'interest' in our construction of that understanding and that interest will also be distinct from (though it might be co-ordinated with) someone else's construction of their understanding of the relationship. We have the strongest interest in the understandings we construct in the sense that they constitute our world. Our interest in our constructions of the relationships we observe ourselves to be a part of will lead to us realizing that others will inevitably have similar interests in their constructions of those relationships; we will, as Krippendorff would point out, begin to realize that others will have constructions of the relationship that will include constructions of ourselves. Potter's focus on interest and stake is centered around the way in which the descriptions we create in our conversations are shot through with attempts to 'manage' stake, discounting it, calling it into question, pointing it out, excusing it, etc. From my perspective, what I would like to embed right at the heart of any consideration of interactivity in marketing is the idea that all individuals engaged in a service relationship (and that includes, naturally, academic observers of such relationships) have a 'stake' or 'interest' in it by virtue of the way in which they have placed a construction of themselves within their larger constructions of that relationship. The way in which they have placed themselves in such constructions (and the way in which they have placed constructions of others in those constructions) influences what Potter would recognize as the management of 'stake' in their discourse, namely the reflection of those positionings in the discourse of their descriptions.

The next construction that requires explanation is my usage of the phrase "network of service relationships". As I have already pointed out, it makes little sense within my understanding of interactivity for there to be a distinction between 'the firm' and then all the other communicants in a marketing system (suppliers, customers, etc.). The adoption of the sense of stakeholder that I have just argued for carries with it the idea that, instead of the firm being the center of a marketing system (where all the communicants distinct from the firm might be said to have a 'stake' in it), it simply becomes one of the stakeholders in the network of relationships that surround a particular service or complex of services. The focus of 'stake' or 'interest' has moved away from the firm and is instead located in the many diffuse constructions constituting the relationship. All individuals engaged in the construction of the relationship have a stake in regard to how they have positioned themselves in their construction of the relationship. The firm's stake is no more powerful, nor 'important', than any other stakeholder— apart from to itself. Of course, I am talking about 'the firm', or the firm as a stakeholder, but that is itself a collective construction which, at a finer resolution level, can be broken down (or, rather, constructed by the observer) as a co-ordination of many individual constructions (the ramifications of which I shall explore in the final chapter). So, the "network of service relationships" is a representation of an understanding in which marketing relationship come about as a result of the provision and use of services, and such provisions and uses can be thought of as occurring across a network of stakeholders. This aspect of my understanding of interactive marketing is superficially compatible with certain presentations of Relationship Marketing, particularly Evert Gummesson's (2008) approach to the service definition of marketing and his application of Castells's 'network society' trope. I will be examining the weaknesses in Gummesson's treatment of interactivity in Chapter 6 and I certainly would take issue with his uncritical use of Castells (see Lehmann et al., 2007, for constructivist critiques of the 'network society'). However, the basic premise of the Service-Dominant Logic as filtered through Gummesson's own services marketing position, namely that marketing concerns services in the sense of the "service given by whatever we purchase, irrespective of this being goods or services" (Gummesson, 2008, p. 10), has the potential to be (somewhat violently) bent to my will in providing the basis for a constructivist view of what is 'offered' or 'proposed' in a marketing relationship. The traditional distinction between goods and services collapses in a constructivist appreciation of the way in which each stakeholder constructs her own understanding of what a particular good or service is. In this sense, Vargo and Lusch's (2004) "value proposition" can be seen as a comparatively constructivist attempt to formulate the way in which stakeholders create understandings of value that can be radically different from each other (though, as I will show later, this constructivist stance is not maintained through the bulk of their S-D Logic presentation). Accordingly, I will define a service as: *the (re)presentation of a stakeholder's understanding of the value contained in the relationship between them and another stakeholder.* Appended to this definition, then, is the statement that such relationships are understood as occurring within a *network* of stakeholders, meaning that the constructions of self and others that inform the (re)presentations of a stakeholder's understanding of value in a particular relationship are connected in a dynamic, complex manner with the constructions of a multitude of others.

Premises (b) through (f) will be expanded upon in the final chapter. The tension evident between premises (g) and (h) is a basic feature of marketing and will be examined in detail in the next chapter's exploration of the rhetorics of measurement and dialog as evidenced in contemporary marketing discourses surrounding blogs, data mining, and the various viral/WOM/connected typologies. The final premise, (j), stands as a fundamental reminder of the position of the academic, marketing practitioner, or commentator *within* the system that they are constructing. Applying this to my own discourse, I need hardly state that the analysis, commentary, and model-building that is presented in this study are snapshot examples of my constructed understandings of the marketing relationships I perceive myself to be engaged in. The talking about marketing, and the talking about the talking about marketing (and recursively ever on), are, within the sense of my definition, part of interactive marketing. Academic authors are stakeholders in just the same way as everyone else in that they construct understandings of their relationships to the constructions of those others they are in service network relationships with and then seek co-ordination through the communication of static representations of such understandings. Granted, there would appear to be a further level of recursion involved in the construction of marketing theories, or the analysis of such theories, but the point is that, substantially, buying an iPod involves the same process of exploring and co-ordinating constructions of value in relationships that writing an article on Wroe Alderson or the ELM does.

Before I move on to detailed considerations of the place of interactivity in some contemporary marketing discourses I would like to finish this chapter by addressing the place of rhetoric within the understanding of interactivity and marketing that I have begun to outline previously. I have already made much use of a number of understandings of rhetoric and will continue to do so in the analysis ahead. My use of rhetorical analysis enables me to distinguish and group together certain aspects of a discourse, to aggregate them, and then identify them as representative of certain constructions that I observe as being present in that discourse. For example, I have already talked of rhetorics of control and, within the constructivist terms I have delineated in this chapter, these rhetorics of control are my constructions resulting from my observing and discerning particular patterns in certain discourses. My (re)presentation of these constructions contains my construction not just of these rhetorics but also of the authors who are apparently responsible for them and my understanding of what their intentions are. Additionally, my rhetorical analysis includes my own constructions of my self (and the ensuing recursive nesting that this implies). The suasive element in this system is to be found in the way that I attempt to represent my constructions in a way that will (hopefully) co-ordinate with yours, in the hope that my constructions, in being co-ordinated with yours, will be viable. But you, the reader, exist as a construction in my head and my understanding of your constructions, your understandings, is dependent (once again) on my observing and discerning patterns in a large number of discourses and relationships. You, my reader, are an aggregation of constructions in my head, just as I am to you. Yet the 'you' that I am speaking of can never, of course, be you. If I were writing these sentences in a forum on the Internet and addressing them to a specific person, I would not be able to disentangle you from the 'you' of my constructions. Even if you are standing right in front of me and conversing with me regarding the moral bankruptcy of self-referential marketing texts, 'you' are still an aggregation of constructions to me and my efforts to persuade you of the internal inconsistency of your argument will still revolve around me attempting to represent a series of constructions that will co-ordinate as closely as possible with those I observe you to have created. A conversation would allow me to re-evaluate my construction of you based upon the real-time observation of how co-ordinated my constructions are with yours. *Kairos* thus becomes an important element in the co-ordination of understandings between stakeholders—and a potential antidote to the static nature of representations of constructions (in whatever media). Yet, networking technologies like the Internet do not fundamentally change the constructed nature of our understandings of ourselves, each other and the worlds we live in. The next two chapters will examine some of the ways in which discourses of marketing theory, marketing practice, and information technology contain underlying metaphors and larger rhetorics regarding interactivity which are co-ordinated across the constructions of many diverse stakeholders. The final chapter will then aggregate my observations of these discourses and the constructivist approach to interactive marketing outlined previously into a more detailed and formal model.

4   The Rendition of the
Consumer's Voice

My exploration of the marketing discourse surrounding the interactive nature of the Internet has demonstrated that academic marketing theorists have been using the confluence of Web technologies, relationship management concerns, and increasing perceptions of marketing ineffectiveness to construct a rhetoric of salvation around the prospect of creating conversations with newly 'empowered' connected consumers. As I have shown, this rhetoric is heavily infused with assumptions of control (it is a rhetoric of management, after all) and the models of communication that are constructed as part of this rhetorical discourse betray their origins in transmission or conduit paradigms. This chapter moves away from the academic discussion of interaction and examines an area of more practitioner-orientated discourse generated by marketing professionals, consultants, and software developers. I hope to show that there are significant superficial differences between rhetorics of consumer interaction constructed by marketing academics and practitioners and that many of these differences can be located in the extent to which each discourse engages with the detail of technological implementations of interaction strategies. At a deeper level, however, I will demonstrate that practitioner and academic assumptions of control are identical. In arguing that current marketing practice's engagement with interactive technology is constructed around discourses of measurement, management, and control, I am echoing comments from an increasingly vocal set of observers who are noting that the emancipatory and egalitarian potentialities of the Internet are, for all the twittering, blogging, and Digging, not yet very apparent in practice.

The ostensible subject of this chapter is the discourse surrounding the use of data mining techniques in order to aggregate, analyze, and represent consumer opinion as part of RM- or CRM-inspired marketing communication efforts. The real motivation behind this part of the book, however, is to draw attention to the way in which the use of data mining technologies necessitates a constant encouragement of consumer talk and that, consequently, what appears to be a valorization of relationship-building dialog and co-creation works instead to de-individualize consumers and strip them of their voices. In other words, a disconnected aggregation is arising from a promotion (indeed, celebration) of individual connection. I will link (pattern) this paradoxical state-of-affairs to the self-stultifying foundation of Relationship Management upon assumptions of communicative control.

REPRESENTATION AND 'EMPOWERMENT'

In eschatological terms that we are by now quite familiar with, online marketer Paul Gillin has declared that the boom in use of "social media" that occurred in the "first few years of the millennium" is a "sea-change for marketers" (Gillin, 2007, p. xii). Gillin characterizes the essence of this development in the following way:

> Social media offers marketers a chance to break this gridlock and engage with their customers in a whole new way. The new discipline is coming to be known as 'conversational marketing'. It means creating a dialog with customers in which useful information is exchanged so that both parties benefit from the relationship. As trust builds, customers develop loyalty that makes them long-term partners, leading to a more lasting relationship. (Gillin, 2007, p. xiii)

It is not hard to see the basic tenets of RM at work in Gillin's rhetoric, here. Marketing relationships are built on trust which itself is founded upon mutually-beneficial exchange over time. Gillin explicitly links this exchange to the idea of conversation, which is presented to us as the guiding motif of this new marketing approach. Conversation, then, is framed as a mutually-beneficial exchange where I give you information that you want (or will find useful) and you do the same for me in return. It's a neat, bi-directional understanding of communication in which information is transmitted back and forth between agents who are both senders and receivers. Social media technologies, by which Gillin means blogs, podcasts, and social network sites (such as MySpace and Facebook) are presented as the environments in which these "conversations" occur. The 'traditional', Web 1.0 marketing formats of website banner ads and e-mail campaigns have already become ineffective: "Spam and list exhaustion are undermining e-mail marketing. . . . Web users ignore banner ads, except for the intrusive ones, which they despise" (ibid.). Although Gillin doesn't mention them, add-on scripts for *Firefox,* one of the most popular cross-platform browsers, enable large chunks of web-based advertising to be hidden from the user so that the surfing experience can be almost entirely free of advertising[1]. E-mail campaigns suffer from the increasing ubiquity and sophistication of spam filtering technologies as well as a general hardening of users' personal mailing habits in the light of experience and education. The "conversations" that Gillin is talking about, then, are occurring within Web 2.0 formats and the king of that format is the blog.

The blog is often described in terms of revolutionary empowerment and "associated with the key concept of equal participation and a higher degree of publicness" (Cammaerts, 2008, p. 360). A blog, by its very nature, "looks inward" (Rickman & Cosenza, 2007, p. 610) in that a blogger broadcasts her thoughts, feelings, and opinions to the online community. Consequently, the format celebrates individual voices as expressions of individual viewpoints as well as the sense of community that develops from the discussion of the views expressed by such individual voices. The extent to which 'amateur' blogs are influencing the status and production of 'professional' journalism is a point of continuing debate (see Beckett & Mansell, 2008, for recent coverage in the mainstream communications literature) but they have been credited with serving as a "training ground or mechanism in creating alternative communities of opposition" (Kulikova & Perlmutter, 2007, p. 31) and there is a general perception that blogs represent "participatory interactive media, allowing citizens to freely and openly engage in the public sphere, producing their own content and interacting with peers" (Cammaerts, 2008, p. 360). Yet, while journalism has been cautious in formally coupling itself with this new media (to the extent that their relationship can almost be said to be mistrustful and competitive, see Lowrey, 2006), marketing opinion leaders have tended to enthusiastically urge the adoption and integration of blogging formats into the communication mix as they have become more of a feature of the Internet in general. In part this positive response on behalf of marketers can be put down to the RM environment that had already swept across mainstream marketing management theory and practice (or, at least, practice-talk) in the 1990s.

Social networking technologies (across both the Web and mobile telephony) promise obvious advantages in any attempt to build relationships with prospects and customers and the blog format offers a degree of structure, consistency, and manageability that marks it out as a more recognizable, more familiar communication enterprise than other more superficially 'alien' formats like Flickr or Facebook. Indeed, certain aspects of the blog format are highly classical; one voice speaking to a crowd of people, haranguing them even, is a pattern absolutely central to the history of Western models of persuasion and rhetoric and the marketing communication forms that arise from them. Despite its bleeding-edge-of-technology context, blogging is a highly verbal form of communication and from a marcoms perspective can be seen as an opportunity to return to the golden age of reasoned, closely argued, sophisticated copy of the 1950s and 60s. Image-dominant marketing communication, while important for many segments of late 20th-century advertising practice, ironically sits uneasily on the multimedia Web, where text use typifies interactive discourse. Although 'viral' ad clips have found a strategic portal on YouTube and interactive Flash games and animations are significant elements in online integrated campaigns, marketing uses of image-dominant messages on the Web have remained closely huddled around the traditional forms of banner ads and film trailers. Interaction is still mainly a textual phenomenon on the web; clicking a word, ticking a text-labeled box, filling out a comment form, registering at a site, searching Google (even when searching for an image!) all are handled through an interface that is verbally-focused. Blogging is a constant symbolic confirmation of the primacy of verbal persuasion on the Internet. An examination of the different ways in which marketing is engaging with this observation provides us with the opportunity to differentiate many of the constructs that inform marcoms discourse in this area.

David Meerman Scott, a one-time VP of Marketing for NewsEdge Corporation and now a web marketing author and consultant, outlines three ways he thinks that blogs can be used for marketing:

1. To easily monitor what millions of people are saying about you, the market you sell into, your organization, and its products.
2. To participate in those conversations by commenting on other people's blogs.
3. To begin and to shape conversations by creating and writing your own blog. (Scott, 2007, p. 50)

We can see, then, that Scott unproblematically demarcates marketing uses of blogs into the three modes of monitoring, participating, and creating. There are a few points that are worth noting about this schema. Firstly, it is noticeable that the word "community" is entirely absent from this framing of practical marketing blog use; even the description of the monitoring mode speaks of "millions of people" rather than groups, groupings, or communities. This might be regarded as a consequence of the 'inwards looking' nature of the blogging enterprise, as already noted above. It is easy to see blogging as an entirely individualist activity and hence orientate one's involvement with it in an exclusively individualistic manner. However, the individual speaker, just as in any rhetorical system, is afforded power and influence through the engagement of the audience as individuals and as groupings. Secondly, a radical constructivist perspective would point out that the distinction between these three modes is, at root, illogical and unhelpful.

The act of monitoring, of observation, is necessarily an act of participation and creation. When we observe, we create patterns of stability in our observations and in re-presenting these patterns in our language and conceptualization we are participating in the environment that we are observing. Such a constructivist approach might appear to have very little connection with Scott's on-the-ground, sleeves-up style of 'practical' marketing advice discourse. After all, he is writing about three different activities that have quite different superficial appearances: reading blogs, commenting on blogs, and then setting one up and running it yourself. Many readers of blogs never use the commenting systems and many regular blog commentors never go away and set up their own blogs, so it might be argued that we are talking about three separate activities that, 'in reality', do not have to have anything to do with each other. The tension between these two perspectives arises from the different understanding of the key link between observation and creation. When I read a blog, I am commenting on it whether I publish those comments on the blog itself or not. I understand and interpret what I think the blogger has to say and so create a 'reading' of the blog. If I try to (partially) express this reading by using the commenting system, then my perception of the particular style and delivery dominant on the blog helps to shape my presentation of my reading; in other words my 'reading' is changed through my expression of it in a particular media. In order to not seem like a 'n00b' or 'troll' (and precipitate certain types of reactive counter-commenting) I will adopt particular rhetorical and stylistic tropes which unavoidably mutate the re-presentation of my comment. This is, perhaps, the logic informing the "read comment aloud" option on YouTube[2], where commentors have the chance to hear their typed comment read aloud back to them by the website before they hit the OK button. However, whether I publish or not, my reading creates. For Scott, however, fully trapped within the empiricist, objectivist paradigm, reading and creation are necessarily different. A company can "monitor" the blogosphere for mentions in the same way that they can trawl the traditional above-the-line media for "column inches" and coverage. Such observation is treated as 'data gathering' and framed within a particular technologist discourse that I wish to very carefully interrogate in this chapter. Before moving on to that examination, however, I wish to introduce some further voices in the construction of the discourse around marketing users of blogging.

In their chapter in Justin Kirby and Paul Marsden's collection, *Connected Marketing*, Corcoran, Marsden, Zorbach, and Röthlingshöfer advance a slightly different triumvirate of marketing uses of blogs. They argue that,

> whilst blog marketing is still in its early experimental phase, three distinct approaches appear to be emerging. First, marketers can seek endorsements (aka blogvertorials) on popular, opinion leading third-party blogs. Second, you can set up your own 'business blogs' (sometimes called brand blogs or corporate blogs) to directly or indirectly promote your product or brand. And thirdly, marketers can engage in the controversial practice of creating 'faux blogs': fake or false blogs of happy but imaginary clients, customers or consumers. (Corcoran et al., 2006, p. 149)

Both the 'monitoring' and 'participating' modes of Scott's schema are missing here, whilst the 'creating' mode has been expanded considerably. Corcoran et al.'s three "blog marketing solutions" are all active attempts to influence communities of readers through supplying news, previews, and samples to influential bloggers (who will subsequently generate the persuasive copy themselves) or through the building and writing of self-promotional blogs. *Joining in* the blogging process as commentors is not something that Corcoran et al. even raise as a possibility. There is a definite difference in tone and attitude between the two positions, then. Some of this might be put down to the fact that, as quoted above, blog marketing is in its "early experimental phase" and to expect consistency from its theoreticians and practitioners is unreasonable. However, I would suggest that there is something more interesting to be observed in the difference between the two approaches. Other than a very short chapter by Pete Snyder, the contributions to Kirby and Marsden's *Connected Marketing* avoid any substantial coverage of data gathering, text mining, or other observational strategies for taking advantage of what people say on the Web. Monitoring is most definitely not a buzz word in their presentations of buzz marketing. Indeed, for Scott, while "monitoring" is one of the three basic modes of web-based marketing, in the end he has very little to say about it, 2 pages out of a 275-page book. Additionally, Gillin's study, which is entirely devoted to evangelizing the power of blogging across different marketing communication contexts, has no specific chapter devoted to the "monitoring" mode; his basic contention is that the blog is a voice of influence upon consumers and consumer communities and should be understood and used as such. When he does address the prospect of creating a corporate blog specifically in order to generate user comments, the way he frames the terms of such an operation is indicative of a very human-level *listening*, rather than a data-driven *monitoring*:

> Blogs, discussion boards and other forms of interactive media are the most cost-effective customer feedback mechanism ever invented. You won't get a representative sampling of customers but you will get your most passionate customers. The number-one best reason in the world to blog is to engage in a conversation with people who care about your company and products. (Gillin, 2007, p. 84)

Gillin, then, sees corporate blogging as a way to "engage in a conversation with people" but also as a "customer feedback mechanism"; in other words, his choice of descriptors demonstrates a tension between the contexts of one-to-one human communication and mechanized systemics. This tension is endemic across all manifestations of marketing management and, as I have shown in earlier chapters, is part of the legacy of the Shannon/Wiener communication as control model. In the case of these voices from the discourse of early 21st century web marketing, however, this tension can be observed to have strong connections to the struggle between two different forms of discourse in marketing communication: One generated around the idea of "data" and the other generated around "conversation". I would suggest that what we see in the difference between Scott's approach and that of the other voices here is that in the former we can see, temporarily, a slippage from one discourse in to the other. Scott's two page (and these are *short* pages) exposition of the monitoring mode starts off with, appropriately, a quote from a blog entry by Glenn Fannick, "text mining and media measurement expert at Dow Jones":

> "Organizations use blogs to measure what's going on with their stakeholders and to understand corporate reputation. Reputation management is important, and media measurement is a key part of what PR people do. Companies are already measuring what's going on in the media; now they need to also measure what's going on with blogs." (Glenn Fannick, quoted in Scott, 2007, p. 51)

"Measuring" and "monitoring" are words which carry associations of empirical, objective observation of external, verifiable data, data that can be quantified and so compared. This rhetoric is in stark distinction to the language of "conversation", "dialog", "participation", and even the PR terminology of "maintaining good relations" and offering "compelling, constantly updated content" (Corcoran et al., 2006, p. 150) that can be seen in the writing of Gillin, Corcoran et al., and, most of the time, in Scott himself. It is almost as if the rhetoric of conversation and co-creation dominates these practitioner-generated discourses, only occasionally slipping to reveal another rhetoric of objective measurement. My metaphor here speaks of masks but masks are consciously adopted and so perhaps it might be better to say that the rhetoric of measurement *leaks* across into the dominant usage.

The tension between rhetorics of measurement and dialog in discourses of web marketing can be regarded as an expression of larger professional and academic tensions. Central to this cluster of conflicting rhetorics is the problematic, aggravating place that data mining technologies have played, and are still playing, in the juncture between Relationship Marketing/Customer Relationship Management theories and web practice. As Scott's use of Glenn Fannick's voice indicates, there is a very clear sense in which some corporate agents "use" blogs not to communicate with or build communities of consumers and customers, but instead to watch them, monitor them, measure them. This use of blogs can be traced back to the technological implementation of CRM principles in the 1990s where a variety of statistical algorithms began to be implemented in the development of software applications designed to monitor large-scale consumer-consumer and consumer-business interactions and analyze patterns detected in them. These software implementations, often referred to as data mining or text mining applications, all have in common the one element of "machine learning"— meaning that the software crunches a truly vast amount of inputted data (whether that be RSS feeds from blogs, forum postings, user comments, logged conversations on customer care lines, etc.) and outputs the patterns that its algorithms have generated. In other words, there is no human 'monitoring'. The central tension that surrounds this approach is beautifully exemplified in the following summary by Scott:

> Text mining technologies extract content from millions of blogs so you
> can read what people are saying. (Scott, 2007, p. 51)

This sentence portrays the software as simply (and rather mysteriously) helping the marketer read the unfeasibly large amount of commentary on the Internet. But the marketer never 'reads' that content; the value of text mining software is precisely that it means the marketer never has to directly read anything other than the output of the program which, as I have already intimated, is designed to present patterns in the content, not the actual content itself. Scott's characterization of the text mining process avoids a technical description of the part that machine learning plays in the marketing analysis of blogs in favor of a distinctly more 'human-centered' explanation. Scott continues with a further quote from Fannick's blog that uses a far more mechanistic metaphor. Speaking of the need for technology to deal with the "unprecedented amount of unsolicited comments and market intelligence available on blogs", Fannick describes it as "a unique way to tap into the mind of the marketplace" (quoted in Scott, 2007, p. 52). Here, although "tap" can carry agricultural associations (tapping a tree for rubber, for example) as well as domestic ones (tapping the water pipe) its primary association in this instance has to be the wire tap, a way of secretly listening in on people's conversations (I would also note the conduit metaphor of communication that underlies this usage). Although Fannick uses a technological metaphor here, however, he is still mirroring the framing that Scott demonstrates—implying that the marketer uses the technology to listen in on actual conversations, whereas, again, text mining is designed to make such practices completely unnecessary. So, both Scott and Fannick use language to construct a telling of text mining that softly negates its mechanistic, aggregating, abstracting processes, while positioning it as a way of listening in on conversations, thus emphasizing the human at the expense of the procedural. This is, I would hold, simply a more engaged version of what Corcoran et al. and Gillin are doing in ignoring the influence of text mining in blog marketing: a concerted attempt to excise machine learning elements from the discourse of Web 2.0 marcoms.

The next section approaches this tension between discourses of monitoring and participation from the opposite side, by examining the rhetorics of those involved in the development and implementation of text mining technologies. I will then return to a more in-depth reading of those rhetorics of participation and creation that we have seen in the discourse of web marketing professionals and opinion leaders.

SERVER-SIDE PERCEPTION

Ngai's (2005) academic literature review of journal articles on Customer Relationship Management indicates that over the main period of CRM growth, most academic articles have either taken the form of general survey and conceptual overviews or they have specifically targeted Information Technology and Information Systems issues (software tools and systems, data mining, and knowledge management). This patterning can be read as a manifestation of the way in which CRM has led to a lot of very general talk and a smaller amount of very specific engagement with the technology designed to implement CRM approaches. This pattern within CRM discourse is even evident in two of the principle definitions that Ngai chooses to demonstrate the lack of consensus regarding the exact nature of the field; R.S. Swift's contention that CRM is an "enterprise approach to understanding and influencing customer behavior through meaningful communications in order to improve customer acquisition, customer retention, customer loyalty, and customer profitability" and J. W. Kincaid's view that it is "the strategic use of information, processes, technology, and people to manage the customer's relationship with your company (Marketing, Sales, Services, and Support) across the whole customer life cycle" (both quoted in Ngai, 2005, p. 583). Swift's forefronting of "meaningful communications" sidelines technological and process aspects of the field, presenting CRM as generating meaningful content rather than simply trying to find meaning in customer communication (and so subtly favoring creation over analysis). Kincaid, on the other hand, talks of the "use" of information and technology to "manage" a one-sided relationship—producing a definition that emphasizes the informatic exploitation of the customer.

The implementation of CRM systems in companies will naturally tend to follow a two-stage process that reflects the dichotomy in the definitions and attitudes seen above. First, an organization will consider the general merits and characteristics of a CRM approach. At this stage the marketing department might well be dominant in the discourse, perhaps backed up by external consultancies. Secondly, if the organization chooses to pursue a CRM re-orientation, the technological implementation of the CRM system will become the primary focus and the IT department (and IT experts in the solution provider) will tend to become more dominant in the resulting discourse. "Creating a CRM solution for most companies is generally a matter of complex integration of hardware, software and applications" (Bose, 2002, p. 90), and so IT personnel, consultants, and solution developers have come to play a crucial part in the evolution of CRM in the Web 2.0 world. They are also, therefore, significant contributors to the discourse streams that surround the integration of CRM and the information produced in and around blogs, forums, and all other forms of conversation accessible on the Internet. Although CRM understandings of "customer" can be very wide and include "vendors, channel partners or virtually any group or individual that requires information from the organization" (ibid., p. 89), most implementations of the approach tend to focus upon the traditional 'consumer' as the object of analysis and projected relationship building. These consumers have been making increasing use of the

Internet to communicate with and talk about those companies and brands that they are engaged with and consequently CRM implementations have moved away from the limited internal points of data collection prevalent in the 1980s and 1990s (customer call logs, warranty information, etc.) and embraced the vast ocean of customer talk that the Web is home to. The motivation behind the collection and analysis of such customer information is often put in terms similar to the following explanation by Anne-Marie Scarisbrick-Hauser, of the Silvertrain Consulting Group in Ohio:

> Making a connection with the customer is one of the vital components to creating a successful customer relationship. To create and maintain this connectivity, a readily accessible and timely flow of data related to the customer's behavior, preferences, perceived needs, beliefs, and attitudes must be gathered and maintained in a centralized location. (Scarisbrick-Hauser, 2007, p. 115)

A centralized database, fed by a continuous flow of data, is seen as a way of "connecting" with the customer because it offers the possibility to apply analytical processes which can be used to profile the individual. But profiles are aggregates, patterns discerned in the volume of data that can be statistically applied to individuals now interpreted as part of a grouping. Scarisbrick-Hauser's use of the trope of connectivity is telling here: The organization connects to the consumer as one component of a mechanical or electrical system connects to another. Surely, connection implies communication—but what type of communication? The cyborgization of the customer through the use of such metaphors is a constant feature of marketing analytic rhetoric but it must be remembered that, as I have shown in earlier chapters, this is all part and parcel of the strong influence of the Shannon/Wiener model throughout marketing management discourses of theory and practice.

The fundamental tension between rhetorics of monitoring (which include seeing the consumer as a data set and the customer/company relationship as a conduit-suffused, cyborg system) and rhetorics of conversation (where dialog is built and meaning is co-created between two equal partners) can be approached as an inevitable result of the paradox that lies at the heart of CRM. The idea that there can be a possibility of 'managing' a relationship with a customer is founded upon the assumption that relationships are about control. Yet CRM has evolved in response to the observation that organizations suffer from a lack of "a true understanding of the needs and preferences of customers" (Shaw et al., 2001, p. 128) and therefore are doomed to lose them unless they adopt a "wholehearted commitment and philosophy dedicated to knowing each consumer and treating each one as the company's complete focus" (Pitta, 1998, p. 472). Martin Evans has written convincingly of what he terms the "relational oxymoron" at the center of the RM/CRM approach, one aspect of which is that it "implicitly means the management of customers when true relational interaction should be mutually beneficial" (Evans, 2003, p. 665). So, 'getting to know' the customer, building a conversational relationship with them, establishing a dialog, all of these instances of the rhetoric of conversation, this sparkling array of espoused motivations that feed the evolution of CRM, are locked in a strange, vice-like, symbiotic death grip with the urge to spy on, listen in on, extract, mine, aggregate, and profile as much consumer data as it is computationally possible to process.

Sometimes, the struggle between the two rhetorics is more apparent than others. A recent editorial article in the *European Journal of Marketing* was devoted to the implications of the increasingly bravura emphasis being put on what I am calling the rhetoric of monitoring. The authors, Nick Lee and Gordon Greenley, were moved to comment on this issue by their own reading of an editorial celebrating the dominance of data by Chris Anderson in *Wired* magazine. Anderson called for a move away from theories of human behavior, telling his readers to "forget taxonomy, ontology and psychology". Anderson continued:

> Who knows why people do what they do? The point is they do it, and we can track and measure it with unprecedented fidelity. With enough data, the numbers speak for themselves. (Quoted in Lee & Greenley, 2008, p. 1141)

Citing recent comments by Peter Norvig, research director of Google, Anderson takes the line that now we have so much of it, data is all we need to predict behavior. Naturally, given the *EJM*'s catholic and theory-friendly policy, Lee and Greenley quickly conclude that "no matter how sophisticated the data analysis tools get, or how gigantic the longitudinal data sets become, data without theory remains noise" (ibid., p. 1142). Such sentiments are all very encouraging at the level of academic discourse in a liberal, inter-disciplinary forum such as the *EJM*, but they sidestep the significance of two such powerful opinion leaders pronouncing on the death of, not just theory, but inquiry. Furthermore, the tail-end of their editorial points to a far more defensive motivation than the quick dismissal displayed in its opening suggests, as it develops into a commentary on a number of strands across marketing education, marketing academia, marketing publishing, and marketing practice which all display trends toward valorizing data sets over inquiry. They note that, given the stratospheric prices paid by businesses for data mining applications and the emphasis on predictive output that such software carries, "the why is only important if it is needed to better predict the what" in such "pragmatic situations" (ibid., p. 1144) and, inevitably, marketing education and marketing publishing will follow the lead of such an industry trend. Their position, ultimately, comes down to the assertion that data without theory cannot be said to constitute scientific knowledge, whereas theory without data is an inseparable step of the scientific method, which is not just the search for a predictive algorithm but the exploration of why and how such an algorithm might work. That the authors feel the need to argue for such a position in the editorial of a major marketing journal is indicative of the strength of the rhetoric of monitoring in both current marketing practice and theory.

Companies, of course, do not go about collecting data on consumers and other stakeholders simply to bundle it all away in a database and forget about it. The monitoring is performed in order to gather data for analysis and that analysis is, unavoidably, informed by theoretical positions. Lee and Greenley's editorial characterizes the marketing uses of data mining as bereft of theory and inquiry. But the act of collection is always informed by theoretical perspectives—although these perspectives might not match those of Lee and Greenley. The construction of a database is dependent upon initial assumptions of what types of information need to be collected and retained, how they should be organized and presented and how they might be processed. A database therefore reflects a model of how the designer patterns her observations. Naturally, as with an advertising message, there is not just one designer; a team may develop the database, perhaps using pre-existing applications (which reflect their own developers' perception patterning) and a number of voices from the client (marketing department, customer services, IT, etc.) will have to be integrated. The resulting database represents a theory of the relationship between customers or consumers and the various elements of the organization's system. Perhaps none of the designers involved would use the word 'theory' to describe what the database represents, and maybe none of them would say that they were 'doing theory' when they work on its construction—but that doesn't detract from the observation that they are building models of how they think their 'world' works.

Once the shape in which the data will be gathered and categorized has been decided upon, analysis can be performed on it. All analytical techniques are built upon theoretical models, reflecting particular interpretive perspectives and paradigms. The choice of analytical approach and the implications it has for the theoretical framing of the data might often be subsumed within larger, mundane operational concerns, habits, and rituals but, again, this does not mean that such implications do not exist. Now, if what Lee and Greenley really mean is that there is a lack of reflexivity in the theoretical assumptions informing a lot of marketing analytics, then that might well be the case—critically examining the epistemological paradigms underlying hierarchical clustering algorithms does not often get done in data mining studies. But then there are also a lot assumptions that hardly ever get examined in critical, interpretive marketing work (the voices of which demonstrate their own ideological, philosophical, and observational footings).

In order to put Lee and Greenley's fears into some context we need to look more closely at the discourse that does exist around the implementations of data mining. This allows us to now return to our original topic of the marketing use of information derived from the monitoring of blogging and to examine the rhetoric of those individuals and groupings who are instrumental in the development of data mining software.

In her 2001 study, "Data, data everywhere—and not a byte of use?", Julie Abbotts remarks on the frightening observation, drawn from her investigation into 40 respondents from companies across the UK, that "in around a third of the companies surveyed", "the marketing department did not even own the data" collected in the name of CRM (Abbotts, 2001, p. 186). In other words, the databases designed to collect customer information were not administered and overseen by the marketing department who should be making use of it. Additionally, Abbotts found that "there was little or no personal customer data held by the majority of the companies surveyed" (ibid.), meaning that most of the information on the database was of a simple demographic nature—and therefore of very limited use in any CRM program. William Hauser, writing 6 years later, paints a similar picture, commenting that "marketers have been lax or slow to thoroughly embrace the marketing analytics component of the research process" (Hauser, 2007, p. 39). A significant component in this, he reasons, is that marketers have tended to keep themselves distant form the actual nuts and bolts of the analytical component of the data mining process, preferring to allow other departments, such as IT, to concern themselves with the development and exercising of the statistical skills necessary to interpret the databases. Marketers, Hauser comments, are under "the misguided impression that technology will do all of the work for them" (ibid.). Such observations tend to reflect the tension I have already been delineating between rhetorics of dialog and rhetorics of monitoring within the discourse of CRM. These tensions are manifested in differentiations of expertise between what Wang and Wang (2008) call "business insiders" (those management personnel, such as marketers, who have a deep knowledge of the company's goals and strategies and whose rationale for using analytics is "to improve the business performance of her or his organization") and "data miners" (experts in data mining who understand the needs of the company but are "not directly responsible for business actions", Wang & Wang, 2008, p. 625). The interaction between these two fields of expertise and orientations provides much of the fascinating interference pattern evident in the CRM discourse (and that discourse covers the gamut of marketing approaches and implementations of the 'idea' as well as the various data mining, business intelligence, and knowledge management engagements with it).

To examine the rhetoric of the "data miners" I will be principally interacting with two sources that might broadly be described as text books. In the same way that I have used Kotler and Keller's text to stand as a token for mainstream marketing discourse, I will be letting Spangler and Kreulen's (2008) *Mining the Talk* and Toby Segaran's (2007) *Programming Collective Intelligence* act as representatives of mainstream discourse on data mining techniques. Both texts are written from the point of view of software developers very much involved in the building of data analysis solutions for corporate clients. The ostensible aim of Segaran's book is to demonstrate to readers how to implement the most effective (and non-proprietary) algorithms that will enable them to get data from websites and then analyze and understand that data. In that he states that his book is designed to teach them "how to write smarter programs" (Segaran, 2007, p. xv), and that most of the examples throughout the book are written in the Python programming language, Segaran's readers are clearly assumed to be software developers. Spangler and Kreulen both work for the Research Division at IBM, and specialize in text mining and data analysis. Their book is written for the more general reader, in the sense of "business professionals who have data management or analysis responsibility or needs" (Spangler & Kreulen, 2008, p. xvii). It would seem that the audience for the two books might therefore be split between the "business insider" (Spangler & Kreulen) and "data miner" (Segaran), although both sets of authors would fall under the rubric of "data miners" themselves.

Segaran's text takes advantage of the way in which many large companies whose business is focused on Internet services (like Kayak, Twitter, del.icio. us, eBay, Facebook, etc.) make it easy to interface with their information by making available what are called Application Programming Interfaces (APIs). An API is a protocol that allows a program to access data straight from the website in a form that is easily machine-readable (for example, in CSV or XML format). APIs mean that a developer can create a separate program that can rely entirely on large volumes of data streamed in directly from, say, del.icio.us, without the user having to personally connect, log on to and query that site. The program can then analyze the data using whatever algorithms the programmer has implemented and the user has chosen. In addition to the freely available APIs, RSS feeds provide a way to extract raw data from the vast ocean of blogs (often referred to nowadays as the blogosphere) on the Web. An RSS (Really Simple Syndication) feed "is a simple XML document that contains information about the blog and all its entries" (Segaran, 2007, p. 31) and is accessible by a simple URL, just like any other web page. Using RSS feeds, a developer can siphon the data present in a blog (including the continually updating entries and comments) into a program and, once more, submit it to algorithms that can provide insight into the patterns and relationships in the text of that blog.

Instead of using the accepted term 'data mining' to describe what is done when applying such algorithms to these, potentially, very large datasets, Segaran talks of "collective intelligence". The use of this term suggests a careful distinction between certain uses of the same technology, or perhaps at an effort to distance his work from that of others. The motivation, or significance, is a little cryptic, however. For Segaran, "collective intelligence" is concerned with "building new conclusions from independent contributors" (Segaran, 2007, p. 2), and he provides two examples in order to illustrate the very different ways in which collective intelligence can be used: Wikipedia and

Google. While both sites use the combined thoughts of a very large amount of people, one to create a continually expanding and updating community encyclopedia and the other to provide page rankings for web sites based upon how many other sites link to them, Wikipedia "explicitly invites users of the site to contribute" whereas Google "extracts the important information from what web-content creators do on their own sites and uses it to generate scores for its users" (ibid., p. 3). The software used by Wikipedia, as Segaran notes, is not designed to really *do* anything to the information generated by users, it does not analyze it or use machine learning techniques to derive insight from it. At Google, however, the algorithm enshrined in its software is the whole point of its business—how Google analyzes the data of the Web is the source of its competitive edge. Segaran's collective intelligence terminology allows him to include Wikipedia as well as Google within his purview. And yet, his book is predominantly about the use of statistical algorithms on data sets that have been extracted from Web users *without their knowledge*. While, of course, the readers and users of all the blogs and sites that he integrates into his code examples have originally contributed their thoughts deliberately, they have no knowledge when the data they have generated is used, via RSS-trawling and the API interfaces, in order to provide the developer or end-user of a 'collective intelligence' application with insight into whatever area they are trying to investigate. Segaran's framing of this situation is telling; while speaking of the various ways in which people use the Internet, (to shop, to be entertained, to do research, to create their own content on their own web sites, etc.) he concludes,

> All of this behavior can be monitored and used to derive information without ever having to interrupt the user's intentions by asking him questions. (ibid., p. 2)

We don't have to bother the user, in other words. He or she may go about their normal business on the Internet, while we quietly track them, listen to them, monitor them. Now, Segaran's point is that the insights that the techniques of collective intelligence can bring to us, although arrived at through the analysis of data from many unknowing individuals, is not related to any one of the individuals directly. Collective intelligence is presented as a creative act in that it produces new information that individual users, *qua* individuals, do not own. The knowledge that can be generated from such techniques is presented as emergent knowledge, only available from the observation point of the collective data and simply not existing at the level of the individual. Consequently, extracting raw data from users without their explicit consent is not problematic for Segaran. Rather, he distinguishes between "explicitly" collected data, where the user is openly asked to provide information, and "casually collected" data where the user's online behavior is surreptitiously monitored. The use of the word "casual" here is remarkable for its euphemistic bravura.

The marketing applications of Segaran's text are multiple. Although a few of the coding examples covered in the book have only a very tangential relationship to traditional marketing concerns (using genetic programming techniques to construct an artificial intelligence competitor for an online game, or the use of linear classifiers to compute the best matches on a dating site), all of the algorithms and most of the examples have some form of implication for the marketing practitioner. For example, the discussion of clustering uses the social network website Zebo (www.zebo.com) to illustrate how different clustering algorithms can be used to find interesting correlations between products that users of the site have declared they would like to buy or find desirable. Interestingly, Segaran notes that the Zebo example would be of obvious interest to both advertisers and social critics! Significantly, the dataset for this coding example is not generated through an API for Zebo, but is instead imported into the program by using the search engine embedded in the website's homepage, a feature included by its designers to make the site more convenient and ergonomic for their users but which is here used to automatically "scrape" a large amount of information from the site's database. Segaran also uses clustering to analyze word frequencies across a dataset of blogs, demonstrating how it is possible to use hierarchical clustering to determine thematic or stylistic groupings amongst them, a procedure that can obviously be applied to the sophisticated monitoring of online chatter around brands, product categories and trends.

Spangler and Kreulen's approach is quite different from that of many of the data mining textbooks on the market in that they do not set out to cover a large range of different algorithms and methodologies, in order to provide a well-stocked toolbox for the knowledge worker. Instead, their book is devoted to the explication of one particular technique that they have been instrumental in developing at IBM. This puts their content in a curious position, because the book in one sense can be seen as a piece of marketing communication for the data mining services offered by the authors' company. Indeed, readers are encouraged to download a free demo version of one of the "wonderful tools" developed at IBM to take advantage of the methodology discussed by the authors (Spangler & Kreulen, 2008, p. xviii) and are also warned that if they try and produce their own software based upon that methodology, they "really should discuss this with suitable representatives from IBM business development" (ibid., p. xix). Precisely for these reasons, however, the book provides a powerful window into the nature of the "data miner's" discourse when speaking to the "business insider", illustrating how the subject is framed in business case terms.

Spangler and Kreulen begin by talking up talk. The opening four paragraphs describe the myriad ways in which "people are talking about your business everyday" (ibid., p. 1), and the overall tone seems to be chosen to induce as much paranoia as possible in the "business insider" reader. Each paragraph covers a particular group of talkers: first customers, then competitors, and finally employees. As the various ways that each group can talk about the reader's business are enumerated ("they are writing emails to you, posting blogs about you, and discussing you endlessly in public forum" (ibid.), etc.), each paragraph ends with the question, "Are you listening?" in a beautiful example of what the ancient Greek rhetors would call *epanaphora*. Finally, just when they've got any self-respecting "business insider" quivering like a naked mole-rat surrounded by a pack of hungry hyenas, they whisper; "all of this talk is going on out there now, even as you read these pages" (ibid.). The payoff is that Spangler and Kreulen are going to tell us how to listen to this talk and "turn it into valuable business insights" (ibid., p. 1). Much of the book evinces the standard CRM rhetoric that we have become quite familiar with, although there are certain emphases that differentiate its marketing perspective. For example, although much of the study revolves around ways to mine the talk generated by customers, Spengler and Kreulen do devote a number of chapters to analyzing the text produced by employees and other stakeholders. In the end, though, there is no doubt that the principle trope is one of "constant attention and monitoring". All sources of talk about the organization need to be listened in on because they represent "ongoing interactions and relationships that need to be understood and leveraged" (ibid., p. 8). Needless to say, the *leveraging* of a relationship reflects the standard CRM control rhetoric in which relationships are managed for specific marketing purposes.

If we keep our focus on customers and examine how Spangler and Kreulen approach the mining of their data we can see that there are two principle lines of attack. The first revolves around what they term "customer interaction" which means the collection and analysis of what they term "unstructured information" each time a customer interacts with the extended company system. For example, customer calls to a customer care line or interaction with a computerized Helpdesk application can provide a large amount of "unstructured information" in the form of the descriptions that customers volunteer of the issues they are having or their experiences with the product, as well as the words used by the company representative when attempting to resolve those issues. This information can be clustered in order to produce insights into which issues are common, exactly how and where the customer relationship process breaks down, which employees can be considered more effective than others, what emerging issues look like they are going to be more important in the future, and so on. The second line of attack is to be found in what Spangler and Kreulen call "mining the Voice of the Customer (VoC)" (ibid., p. 71). This term is used to describe seeking "to hear what customers are saying about our company outside of" their "business interactions" with the company (ibid.). In other words, we mine the Voice of the Customer when we listen in on what they are saying about us when they are not talking directly to us. The language that Spangler and Kreulen use to describe this has interesting associations. They say that the "trick" of VoC mining is to realize that customers are constantly talking about us in many different places and what we have to do is to "tap into this multi-threaded stream of consciousness" (ibid.). Once more we are presented with a use of this word "tap" but this time the stream of data that is being bled (a distinctly more biological and alarming metaphor, I grant you) for significant information is portrayed in quasi-mystical terms. The clear implications of the phrasing are that the vast, dynamic ocean of communication that exists on the Web is one stream, one consciousness built up from, emergent from, the multitude of voices that thread in and out of each other. This weaving of thread, of course, reminds us of the overarching metaphor of the *Web*. It is almost as if, by listening in on our customers, we are sensing the central vibration of the Web itself. In that much of the research that feeds into data mining originates in the fields of machine learning and artificial intelligence, and bearing in mind Spangler and Kreulen's proffered identities as researchers in these areas, it is perhaps not too surprising to find hints in their work of the secular mysticism that is a marginal part of such discourses. The idea that the increasing size and complexity of the Web may lead to an emergent consciousness is one that has fascinated and entertained many computer scientists and programmers. It is often interwoven with notions of the Singularity popularized by Ray Kurzweil and the diaspora elements of what used to be called the Extropian community. After all, the Internet is a global network of computers that currently contains a healthy portion of all the knowledge collected by mankind; it's superficial similarity to a gigantic 'brain', therefore, inevitably raises the possibility that 'it' might evolve consciousness. This trope is all the more reasonable to those who have been acculturated to discourses which make much use of the rhetoric of emergent properties, such as those arising from general systems theory, systems dynamics, systems engineering, and even certain strands of biology[3]. One way of interpreting Spangler and Kreulen's implementation of the Web as consciousness trope is to point out that it de-individualizes the voices that they will be mining. Customers who willfully approach the organization and enter into a communication relationship with it are consciously offering information to it. However, those consumers who are talking about the organization behind its back, as it were, are most definitely not volunteering information to it. While it might be argued that communication on the Web is carried out in the public domain, one tends to not appreciate just how public one's discourse can be. Consumers who make comments about Nike footwear on a blog about running generally tend to consider that the communicative domain is constituted by the blog author (who they might be directing their comments to) or other readers of that particular blog (who they might know quite well if they are regular contributors to debate on that site). I have been quite surprised, for example, to find that an email I posted to a technical discussion group in 1998 (and which I haven't been a member of for at least 8 years) is still around on the Internet, popping up when certain search words are keyed into Google. The archives for the group are stored in nicely searchable html format on the organization's main web server—and, consequently, my small email is still publicly present as an information-giving voice on the Internet. Spangler and Kreulen's rhetorical encapsulation of such personal voices within a "multi-threaded stream of consciousness" abstracts away any sense of individual ownership. Our voices are merely "threads", we should not imagine them as ours—rather, the stream of consciousness that is the Web belongs to all of us.

For a text that is at its outset so very much concerned with asserting the intellectual property rights of its authors and sponsoring corporate entity, the careful maneuvering of consumers' voices into a zone of amorphous, anonymous, collective consciousness is very telling. Data mining is not about individuals, it is about investigating groupings and patterns in large anonymous data sets. When a data mining application scrapes my comments on a blog into its database, it is not trying to investigate me personally as an individual. The algorithmic processes that my voice gets submitted to only make sense, are only worthwhile, when my voice is one amongst hundreds or thousands. This is the central reason why matters of personal privacy are almost never raised in the marketing data mining literature[4]; individuals are not the focus, it's the pattern that matters. Even when analysis is used to produce recommendations for individual customers (as on Amazon.com) such recommendations simply reflect the way that particular customer's browsing and purchasing habits fit them into a cluster. The individual only exists in so far as she can be subsumed into a crowd. Such customization is, in essence, still an act of aggregation.

For Spangler and Kreulen, monitoring Internet "chatter" (ibid., p. 88) is a matter of "tapping" into the "stream of consciousness" of the Web, listening out for particular query terms so that the appropriate software can then create little "snippets" (ibid., p. 78) of text (say the sentences in which a key word appears) that can be sorted into taxonomies for analysis. They very persuasively use a number of examples to demonstrate the way in which such a methodology can be used to "get some idea" (ibid.) of how a company may be perceived by a self-selecting (and thus non-representative) sample of consumers on the Web. The technique outlined in *Mining the Talk* means that the "data miners" are able to present the "business insiders" with both visual representations of data and also listings of the "snippets" that have been scraped into the dataset. Regarding such occasions, Spangler and Kreulen make the following observation:

> Often we find in these presentations that it is the quotes from actual customers that are far more compelling and persuasive than any graph or chart can be. It's almost as if the customers have joined the meeting, adding their own opinions to the mix. (ibid., p. 80)

Once again we come to a portrayal of the tension between the rhetoric of monitoring and the rhetoric of conversation. Although the purpose of the text is to promote a proprietary data mining system, the quote above demonstrates the dominating power in "business insider" discourse of the trope of customer dialog. Marketing analytics strip consumers of their identity and yet at the same time are bound up with the urge toward engagement in one-to-one conversation with individuated consumer voices. It is not just the "business insiders" at Spangler and Kreulen's presentations that display this ambivalence. The discourse of data miners themselves, particularly when in contexts that might be termed mixed company (i.e., they are talking to an audience of business insiders and other data miners), is suffused with references to conversational schemes. Summarizing their VoC mining results, for example, Spangler and Kreulen conclude with these words:

> More often than not, our customers really want us to serve them better. They are telling us how to do it, if only we would listen. (ibid., p. 91)

Considering that this passage refers to the use of what Segaran would call "casual" data, the statement is strangely surreal. Effectively, what the authors are saying is that when consumers are talking amongst themselves (and therefore choosing not to interact with the company directly) they are actually trying to tell the company something. And then, even more curiously, the implication seems to be that when this is happening the company is somehow choosing not to listen.

Segaran's text is largely built upon the rhetoric of monitoring, giving little sight of conversational tropes or dialogical urges. Spangler and Kruelen, however, exhibit far more of the rhetoric of conversation as well as displaying an unwillingness to overbalance their language with objectifications of consumers, although this does lead them to construct some curious ways of justifying the appropriation of customers' voices. The discourse of marketing analytic uses of web based consumer commentary can be observed to display increasing tension between the two rhetorics of monitoring and conversation the further that discourse is orientated toward a mixed audience of "business insiders" and "data miners". Data mining does not have to use Web-derived information and much of its implementation over the past 20 years has focused on what Spangler and Kreulen have called "customer interaction", the data stored through the largely automated recording of customer transactions. Such data mining practices have been intimately connected with the rise of RM and CRM and the rhetoric displayed in the discourses surrounding them appropriately mirror the central conceit of such marketing orientations, namely, that information leads to relationship building. A good example of such a perspective is provided by Berry and Linoff (2004) who inform the reader that,

> A customer-centric organization maintains a learning relationship with its customers. Every interaction with a customer is an opportunity for learning, an opportunity that can be seized when there is good

communication between data miners and the various customer-facing groups within the company. (Berry & Linoff, 2004, p. 520)

It is noticeable here that communication occurs between the data miners and in-house agents whereas interaction happens between the customer and the organization. Additionally, the characterization of the relationship between customer and organization as a "learning relationship" implies a deeply one-sided approach to the driving force behind it. The relationship is there so that the organization can learn from the customer—for whom the benefit is unclear. As we have seen at the opening of this chapter, however, there are many marketers who are calling out for a more direct, conversational engagement with the consumer and who are highlighting the Internet as the medium which can facilitate this. Scott and Gillin are both part of a discourse which seeks to frame blogging as a useful and practical marketing tool. However, as we have seen, there are clear tensions in this discourse that have links to the wider context of how data mining has been used in the cause of CRM.

Scott and Gillin both promote the marketing use of blogging to aid in creating relationships with consumers; they are therefore both examples (one might even say, constructions) of the wider RM and CRM discourses that fetishize 'relationships' as the key to successful marketing. As RM theory has found its implementation in CRM practice the understanding of what a 'relationship' might mean has become more and more mediated through technology, particularly in the use of data mining to analyze the information collected from customer transactions. And as the Web has evolved and consumer talk has mushroomed, CRM thinking has naturally followed consumers into these new discursive zones leading marketers to devote considerable effort to shoehorning CRM rhetoric into their understanding of social networking sites and the blogosphere. As much previous CRM practice has revolved around data mining customer transactions, so the attendant rhetoric of monitoring has found itself reproduced in CRM engagement with the Internet, while at the same time the obvious topology of a talk-focused Web has seen the growth of a marketing rhetoric of conversation which seeks to imitate, or even join, the patterns of open dialog that appear to typify online communication habits. As the work of Segaran and Spangler and Kreulen exemplify the interface between data mining and the Web, and so rhetorics of monitoring and conversation, is a fluid, if tense, one. There is a sense that when facing the business insider, the data miner is careful to give priority to the rhetoric of conversation, whereas when talking amongst themselves the rhetoric of monitoring dominates. A similar dynamic is evidenced in D. M. Scott's open acknowledgement of the *power* of blog mining but total marginalization of it throughout the majority of his book.

In order to examine the rich implications of this tension between rhetoric of monitoring and conversation, I will now move back toward an examination of how marketers like Gillin, Scott, and Corocoran et al. construct theories of relationship building and conversation around the active commenting on and creation of blogs and forums.

Scott states that when he mentions a company on his own blog his comment only ever gets linked or replied to by that company "about 20% of the time" (Scott, 2007, p. 60). He concludes from this experience that only this percentage of companies actually monitor what people are saying about them on the Web. As we have seen, such a conclusion ignores the possibility that Scott's blog is being automatically monitored by companies for data mining purposes using those types of approaches outlined by Segaran and Spangler and Kreulen. For Scott, though, the oversight is symbolic of a far more personal, human approach to interaction with the blogosphere. If you are not actually reading the blog, then you are not really monitoring it because the purpose of reading it is to be able to react immediately with a communication action. A blog entry about your company or its product requires some form of blog-related response from you—whether that is a comment posted to the original blog or your own blog entry with a link back to the parent article. Software can help immensely in alerting a company to web chatter about its brand, products, or services (Ben Hedrington's 'spy' application mentioned in chapter one is a good example of how this works), but for a new set of voices in marketing the automation stops there. The conversation that needs to exist between bloggers, blog readers, blog commentors, and companies is something, they reason, that needs to be created personally. The knowledge that Gillin, Scott, and the practitioners (and occasional theorists) of connected marketing seek to convey in their discourses is a set of writing and protocol techniques that they promote as effective tools in creating communication relationships with consumers who are enthusiastic, active, vocal, and online, and so replacing "marketing monologue with marketing dialogue" (Corcoran et al., 2006, p. 155). The technological aspects of blog marketing are rarely covered in any great detail by those writers promoting it. This is because blogging, unlike web site design, for example, needs almost no technical background or training. It is facilitated by "easy-to-use, low-cost blogging software" so the amount of monetary investment it requires can be *very* low (although the investment in terms of time needed for writing and responding may be considerable depending on how seriously a company takes the blog). Consequently, the focus for blog marketers is on how to generate dialog rather than on involved technical explanations or complex metrics. Indeed, Gillin's language in the extract below demonstrates a disdain of marketing analytics that makes Lee and Greenley's discomfort appear quite mild by comparison. In describing how the new approach of what he calls "conversation marketing" requires a very "different set of skills" from those traditionally fostered in marketing, Gillin declares:

> It means throwing out the spreadsheets and mailing lists. It means ditching terms like "reach", "frequency", "impressions" and "click-through-rates". It means understanding who your customers are, who influences them and how to engage with those influencers. It means exchanging information, not delivering a message. (Gillin, 2007, p. xiv)

This is almost the mirror reversal of the quote from Chris Anderson that Lee and Greenley start their editorial with. It amounts to a call for the abandonment of metric-led marketing communication on the Web and for the embracing of a conversational model of influence. The ways in which these conversations are meant to be conducted, however, provide us with a somewhat paradoxical situation. Blog marketing, buzz marketing, connected marketing, conversation marketing—whatever the terms is, it is noticeable what it is not. It is *not* Relationship Marketing or Customer Relationship Management. One certainly gets the impression from the general *lack* of reference to RM in these Young Turk marketing paradigms that the Relationship Marketing approach has failed, or has simply become irrelevant. Certainly, the feeling might be mutual—the 2008, 3rd edition of Gummesson's *Total Relationship Marketing* makes no attempt to discuss the significance or possible marketing use of blogging or social network sites on the Web, despite an expanded section on Relationship Number 12, the e-relationship. Similarly, Peppers and Rogers (1999) maintain a very narrow focus on forms of "customer interaction" data mining in their coverage of the one-to-one use of community knowledge. One possible interpretation of this silence in blog marketing discourse regarding the influence of RM themes is that it is the natural slighting of an established voice by an upstart element wishing to disassociate itself from the outmoded fashions of a previous generation. Another meaning might be that the silence represents an embarrassment—perhaps an embarrassment at the failure of RM to deliver on its promises of dialog and co-creation. Whatever stance one might adopt on the relationship between blog marketing or connected marketing and the legacy of RM/CRM, the confused, uncomfortable hole that exists in both discourses makes the paradox at the heart of blog marketing even more noticeable. For, despite the rhetoric of conversation and dialog that we meet in all the voices attached to the promotion of the blog marketing revolution, it soon becomes apparent that the trope at the heart of the paradigm remains control.

The attraction of blogging for marketers is that it appears to offer an access point to credible voices talking to enthusiastic consumers (whether they are consumers of music product, sports product, hi-tech gadgets, mapping software, whatever). As Schuyler Brown, co-creative director for Buzz@Euro RSCG agency, writes "blogs are built on buzz, and they build buzz" so "by targeting blog owners, marketers are simply engaging in a specialized form of influencer marketing" (Brown, 2006, p. 217). Importantly, blogs are understood to be valuable both by consumers and marketers because they "are perceived to be independent" (ibid., p. 216). The apparent absence of commercial interest means that the readers of a blog on, say, the latest mobile phones are likely to treat the blogger's opinions on a new handset as unbiased reporting rather than a sponsored piece of marketing communication. However, the very success of a blog due to its perceived independent position is likely to render it more and more connected with commercial interests. As Cammaerts (2008) has pointed out, while the Internet was founded upon a "nonprofit philosophy", "market forces have established themselves as the hegemonic paradigm of the medium" (ibid., p. 363). A successful blogger will find themselves courted by larger blogging networks (often owned by even larger traditional media conglomerates) as well as all manner of companies that wish to gift them with their latest products and promotional trinkets. Indeed, as a blog gets more successful, more widely read and relied upon for the latest news regarding its specialized area, so the blogger will be grateful for more and more favored (controlled) access to pre-release products and insider gossip from industry sources. Even without overt evidence of what has been called "blogola" (ibid., p. 362) readers can become highly suspicious of the commercial ties on sites that they themselves have been regular visitors to. For example, despite continued denials from the blogging team, accusations of editorial bias toward Apple products (particularly the iPhone) are common in the comments left on the gadget blog, *www.engadget.com*. Contributing to the murky waters are a number of well-discussed cases of "blogola" such as the incentives offered to a number of bloggers to promote the new Dr Pepper milk drink, Raging Cow (Corcoran et al., 2006) and promotion trips organized for entertainment bloggers by Warner Bros (Cammaerts, 2008). Even when done transparently, the use of existing blogs for promotional purposes is fraught with difficulties. Nokia is often held up as an example of a successful exponent of this approach (Corcoran et al., 2006; Gillin, 2007), particularly the work done on its behalf for the N series of phones by Andy Abramson, of the Comunicano PR agency in California. The key to Abramson's success was in remaining as hands-off as possible, providing carefully picked bloggers with informative review packs and product samples and then letting them get on with it. This is a difficult prospect for many brands to envisage, however. The surrender of control that it implies goes against the central paradigm that I have been arguing informs mainstream marketing management's understanding of communication.

Laying your brand open to the unfiltered, uncensored vagaries of enthusiast journalism is not quite what most marketing professionals imagine when they discuss Web 2.0 opportunities. The occasional examples of large companies taking the plunge still tend to raise eyebrows. Frito-Lay's recent deal, brokered by Federated Media, for seven high profile blogs to produce unsupervised, unapproved content under the Cheetos banner was reported in *Advertising Age* by being bracketed with commentary and data that highlighted how contradictory the move was to industry common sense. Michael Learmonth (2009) noted at the beginning of his piece on the *Cheetos* blog buy that "mass marketers have generally taken a wary stance toward blogs, but Frito-Lay isn't just embracing bloggers, it's letting them define their brand". This amazed tone is then backed up in the final paragraph of the article by figures from a 2008 Collective Media survey of advertising executives and their clients which show that "39% said blogs were on their 'do-not-buy' lists for digital campaigns compared with 73% for user-generated video and 27% for social media". What is perhaps even more indicative of the uncomfortable relationship between blogger and brand in this instance (or perhaps the trade media depiction of this relationship) is the way in which writers on one of the blogs, the influential technology and geek site Boing Boing (*boingboing.net*, which started out as a print fanzine and regularly ranks at the top of Technorati's blog listings), were portrayed in the news piece as if they really had no idea what to do with the opportunity. Boing Boing editor, Xeni Jardin, in order to be as transparent as possible to her readers, blogged both her reasons for accepting the sponsorship and the terms of the deal (though not the financial details). As part of her defense (what else could such preemptive argumentation really be?), Jardin explained how the only substantial brief she received from Cheetos was "Don't be mean". Boing Boing's final answer as to how to handle this opportunity was effectively to shift it off-site by commissioning an independent digital arts collective to come up with a series of web videos set in a fictitious soviet-style republic. This almost seems like the blog is trying to 'wash its hands' of the commercial taint, openly signaling to its readers that the editorial content remains untouched by Frito-Lay (even though the brand did not require control or approval of content before release). Additionally, I would point out that the resulting web videos are very tame and feature the product in a very traditional advertising manner (big picture of, and lots of focus on, the product) using an almost embarrassing amount of 'borrowed interest'. Here, the result, at least in terms of the Boing Boing section of the deal, looks like something that is almost as un-blog as it is possible to be. Jardin's post accompanying the first (of 6) web videos contains a number of statements that (perhaps purposefully) complicate the situation. Jardin's introductory paragraphs run as follows:

> First things first: The Boing Boing Video episode above is a paid ad for Cheetos. It contains subliminal messages. For real. It is also a security bulletin produced 50 years ago in the future by the citizens of Soviet Unterzoegersdorf, regarding the detection of a package containing mysterious, orange cheesy particles, presumed to be American in origin.
>
> Normally we'd just run this ad alongside our editorial content, but I love it and there's a complicated story behind it, so we're running it on its own. Now, allow me to explain further. Warning, I am about to get all meta on your ass. (Jardin, 2009)

The reference to 'getting all meta' is a signal that Jardin's explanation will be stepping out of the usual discourse frame, leveling up or chunking up (depending on whether you prefer gaming or NLP references) in order to talk about the circumstances behind the video rather than the content of the video itself. It is also a reference to the fact that Jardin is going to talk about details relating to the financial model of the Boing Boing site and this has the potential to break the frame of editorial separation from advertising (a frame that is a rhetorical hold over from traditional above-the-line media and which has always had the status of what William Gibson might call a "consensual hallucination"). Jardin's prepares the way for the Frito-Lay story by pointing out that the site "relies upon sponsorships to do all the weird, unfettered, freespeechy" content that readers visit the blog for. While this sponsorship usually takes the form of commercial messages (videos, banner ads, etc.) that are kept to the margins of the screen and are therefore spatially separated from the 'content' which runs down the center, in the case of the Frito-Lay deal the web video was included in the editorial content section. Jardin's blog entry picks up on something that was (strangely) absent form the *Advertising Age* coverage, namely the presence of what appear to be 'subliminal' images of Cheetos in the video. A large number of commentors on the blog entry pointed out that the images are on screen for too long to really be called subliminal, as a message cannot by definition be subliminal if you immediately notice it. This would appear to be a case of both the video makers (monochrom of Austria) and Boing Boing being ironic, or again, "meta". The Cheetos message is made to appear so blatantly an advertising artifact that it includes even that most notorious of advertising devices, the subliminal frame, though, as it is a "meta" statement, the frame has to be made as obvious as possible (and so lose its alleged nefarious power).

The majority of Jardin's blog entry is actually devoted to telling the story of how the Boing Boing team tried to deliver some packs of Cheetos to the videographers in Austria. This makes for much comedy regarding European border and customs staff and, of course, much use of the product name and chatter regarding its packaging. And, importantly, is all very "meta". So, given the fact that Frito-Lay got pretty much what it wanted, which was a high-profile, tech savvy blog entry about its target product, while exerting almost no control over the content or style of the editorial message (and thus appearing very in-tune with the ideology of a blog which has been vociferous in its promotion of Creative Commons usage policies and free speech on the Internet), how might the interactive nature of this piece of marketing communication be discussed? We might consider that there are a number of interactive relationships on display. With no particular priority, we might identify the following relationships: between Frito-Lay and Federated Media, Federated Media and the Boing Boing editorial team (blog writers and house artists), Frito-Lay and the Boing Boing team, Frito-Lay and the commentors on the blog, and Boing Boing and the blog commentors. As I have pointed out earlier, it must not be forgotten that there are many readers who are not regular commentors or who might not comment on this particular story (though they will be commenting to themselves and perhaps those around them). What we might characterize as the 'business relationships' above (involving Frito-Lay, Federated Media, and the Boing Boing editorial team) are not in any real sense different to the types of relationship that might exist between any brand, a sponsorship agency, and a sports team or celebrity. They are interactive relationships in the non-marketing-revolutionary sense, the sense that everyone would expect them to be interactive—negotiations are undertaken, opinions are traded, concerns allayed, deals struck. The 'revolutionary' interactivity that blogs are said to offer by the likes of Gillin, Scott, Brown, and Corocoran et al., is to be found in the relationships between Boing Boing and its commentors and those same commentors and Frito-Lay. The nature of the discourse generated in this instance is instructive and it is therefore worth taking a little time to plot out some of the interactions that occur in the comments section.

The first thing that needs to be pointed out is that Boing Boing operates a moderated commenting system on its blog pages. This moderation system is not predominantly software-powered but rather relies on the heuristics of designated "Community Managers", in this instance Teresa Nielsen Hayden (who has the help of two assistant moderators). The responsibility of the moderator is to read through the comments as they are sent to the site and then delete those that are considered to be unhelpful to the creation of meaningful dialog around the blog entry. Full deletion of a comment is common but the moderator also has the option to "disemvowel" the text making it difficult but not impossible to understand or to delete certain parts of the comment (such as an inappropriate external link). Comment moderation was instituted on the site in March 2008 for three main reasons as described in the moderation FAQ (which, in a perfect example of "meta" behavior, has generated over 1,500 comments at the time of writing). Firstly, as Hayden puts it, "every general-interest online forum that's worth reading has some kind of moderation system in force" (Hayden, 2009). Secondly, the previous non-moderated commenting system "went so septic that it had to be shut down". Finally, in common with all other high-traffic blogs, it "attracts non-automated scams" and therefore needs the flexibility and fuzziness of human reasoning, rather than a computational algorithm, in order to try and combat such threats to its readers. So, to return to the topic at hand, at the end of her Frito-Lay entry, Jardin writes "flame me in the comments if you disagree", only to have one poster point out that they are indeed trying to do so but his comments keep on getting pulled down. Hayden is a significant voice in the comments section, explaining her moderation policy in general and for this particular story, replying (often with a with a strong dose of sarcasm) to various posters who express unease or dissatisfaction with the Frito-Lay deal. Jardin, too, contributes to the discussion, providing meta-commentary on her own blog entry, defending the monochrom video, and chatting about Cheetos with posters. One of her first posts in the comments section is to reply to a reader who has voiced serious concern that Boing Boing has apparently supported the use of subliminal advertising—Jardin flatly states "I was joking". This comment inevitably loops all the way back to her original blog entry at the top of the screen where the phrase "For real", while initially appearing to emphasize the validity of her claim (and hence rhetorically flagging her honesty in this minefield of commercial influence), is now shown to be a marker for irony. Which, naturally, brings into question how much of the rest of her blog (and posted replies in the comments) should be taken ironically? Hayden drops a remark in one of her comments that indicates she has been very busy cleaning up fallout regarding the subliminal issue, writing that,

> you would not believe how many self-righteous, anonymous comments we're getting from people who (a.) think subliminal advertising has more than a marginal effect, and then only on people who were already inclined to want something of that sort; and (b.) think those briefly-seen pictures of Cheetos in the video qualify as "subliminal".

Frito-Lay, as we are told constantly by all concerned in the deal, had no control over content or direction and yet Cheetos is linked negatively here in the minds of an 'unbelievable' (to extrapolate from Hayden's description) number of readers with one of the most manipulative of all alleged marketing communications strategies (as the popular writings of Wilson Bryan Key would have it; i.e., Key, 1974). The dialogs that are played out in the comment section here are not between Frito-Lay and the readers but rather between the readers and the bloggers who, having agreed to the deal and (perhaps even more importantly) committed to an artistic interpretation of that deal, find that they are now the voice of Frito-Lay in the sense of defending the commercial message from allegations of manipulation, poor execution and the irresponsible promotion of foods of zero nutritional value. Neither Frito-Lay nor Federated Media have to step in and field the flack, instead this task falls to the bloggers who (theoretically) know best how to talk to and deal with their regular audience. The 'interactive' marketing communication that is on display here is typified, therefore, by tropes of distancing and elision. While the comments section does have a few posts talking positively about their own perceptions of Cheetos as a brand the majority of comments are split between debating whether Boing Boing has sold out. Talking down the product (in a variety of ways ranging from mentioning the alleged poor work practices of Frito-Lay's parent company Pepsi-Co., to simply unfavorable remarks regarding the color, healthfulness or naturalness of Cheetos or their connection with drug subculture practices). Toward the end of the 111 comments that had been posted by my last visit, the "interaction" had meandered off into a discussion of various recipes made from highly processed foodstuffs and a mildly competitive run of comments attempting to use the most Lovecraftian vocabulary possible. In other words, the conversation that Frito-Lay's blog buy inspired on Boing Boing ended up generating little chatter about the good side of Cheetos and quite a large amount of talk about how bad it was for the blog and how unnatural and unpleasant the product is. Not one of the posted comments, however, addressed Frito-Lay directly—they were either aimed at Boing Boing in general or various specific bloggers and posters. There *were* conversations about the product but those conversations were overwhelmingly either mixed (in the sense of being neutral about the product but negative about Boing Boing's deal) or negative. Can it be said that readers were constructing dialogs *with* the product (or brand)? Certainly, all readers who explicitly addressed the presence of Cheetos or Frito-Lay displayed in their discourse a construction of the product and/or the brand. It is clear that many of those constructions are radically different from each other, while some exhibit strong common aspects; a series of comments riffing on the theme of Cheetos as favored "munchies" for drug takers, for example, demonstrates that for some posters this is a shared characteristic of their construction of Cheetos. Indeed, it is difficult not to remark upon the importance of performance in blog posting. Comment posters are often performing for each other in a deeply *kairotic* manner, responding to insults, challenges, expressions of disbelief and incomprehension as well as sparring with the moderator (and assistant moderators) in ways that best display their wit, argumentation skills, superior knowledge, or experience or even rhetorical command of insult. This performance aspect of posting is most spectacularly demonstrated by the *Cheetos Sestina* written by one poster, MGFARRELLY, as a comeback to Hayden's ruling that further posts on the sell-out theme will only be accepted "if they're couched in formal verse". Cheetos and Frito-Lay, at least within the context of this particular piece of marketing communication, have no possibility of joining such a conversation. They are completely divorced from the *kairotic* moment of the blog; they have no voice, formal or informal in the comment thread. Instead, Jardin and Hayden accept (or are forced into, or find themselves taking on) the role of surrogates—so that when some early posters make critical remarks concerning Cheetos they respond with sarcasm (or, in blog terminology, "snark"), although this becomes somewhat tempered as the thread evolves. Now, Frito-Lay *could* have placed a PR 'soldier' in to the fray—either as an overt employee responding to comments or as a covert "sock-puppet" (though both options might have been forbidden by the terms of the sponsorship agreement). However, certainly no overt representative is present and if one of the posters in the thread is a covert agent for Frito-Lay, she is certainly not shilling for her employers in any obvious manner. Interaction in the sense of *kairotic* conversational engagement between representatives of the brand/product and prospects or customers is not apparent. What can be said to be apparent in the Boing Boing blog buy is 'buzz' or 'word of mouth'—people talking about the product or brand. They are talking about it, and indirectly about its relationship to the blog that they read, because the brand has managed to place itself within editorial space: No one would be posting comments if the video has been confined to the generally understood commercial margins of the screen. In order to attract attention, avoid ad-blocking scripts, and generate conversation between readers and comment posters Frito-Lay created a deal that was guaranteed to produce heated debate due to is transgression of current ethical blog norms. By giving the blog almost complete freedom in how the "Cheetos Boredom Busters" were executed it guarantees that the blog editors will identify strongly with the results of their own artistic and strategic decisions and therefore feel the need to defend them on the site. Frito-Lay also shifts any possible outrage away from itself and on to the blog team. And it generates buzz in the comments section. But, as carefully planned as it *might* have been (and this is simply my reading of my set of observations), one has to ask was it worth it?

If we view the Frito-Lay/Boing Boing community relationship not from the perspective of a *kairotic interaction* but rather as an instantiation of a control system, perhaps we might achieve more insight into the communication system that underlies this context. Frito-Lay is trying to achieve a highly mediated form of communication with the blog readers in order to control the nature of their personal constructions of Cheetos. If it tries to institute a direct communication relationship with the audience it might feel that the brand will suffer as a consequence of the general apathy and cynicism toward advertising messages that has become a theme haunting marketing discourse around the demographic of young, technologically-literate, Americans. If the blog delivers the message in its own way, on its own terms, then the readers will pay attention to a voice that they trust. Frito-Lay is essentially saying: 'OK, we give up, we've got nothing, there's no way we can talk to these people and get them to listen to us'. It is abnegating interaction, in fact. The blog buy is a way of stepping up the control resolution; traditional direct means are too clumsy to reach this sensitive audience so far better to place something in between to gently interface with them in a language they understand. And, it is not the case that Frito-Lay is using the blog to 'translate' its message into geek speak. Frito-Lay is giving a meta-level message to the Boing Boing team (find a way to promote Cheetos as a boredom buster) and then letting them construct the detail of the message, the fine-grained resolution. So, where is the feedback? How does Frito-Lay measure the success of its new control system? The obvious metrics for a blog reside in the numbers of comments posted, the number of external links to the blog post, and the number of page views. A quick look at the number of comments posted already outlines a narrative of increasing disinterest. At the time of writing this, Boing Boing has released the second of its monochrom-produced videos and that has garnered only 46 comments compared to the 111 for the first video. The 46 posts for the second installment reflect pretty much the same mix of opinions as the first. So, if the generation of online conversation about the brand is a goal, then at the moment it looks like the system is not working. While the *Advertising Age* coverage can be counted as part of the buzz surrounding the blog buy, the very different demographics courted by the blogs and the trade paper would tend to imply that it is not the type of conversational input that would be considered optimal by the brand.

What the Frito-Lay deal illustrates is a turning away from conversation—an elliptical, tangential attitude toward communication that appears to be in accordance with RM and connected marketing rhetoric of interaction with target audiences and conversation generation but in the details of the discourse displays a rejection of contact, a willful muteness. As the *Advertising Age* piece summarizes it, "Frito-Lay representatives were not available for an interview" (Learmonth, 2009). Indeed, the Boing Boing team can be seen as *over*communicating in order to fill the silence. The voice of Frito-Lay is so powerfully absent that Jardin has to become ventriloquist, constructing a voice for them so that she can create a dialog that can be displayed before her readers to speak for the free and easy attitude the brand is supposed to have had toward the creative brief:

> . . . the only editorial guidance we received was pretty much: don't be mean (don't do anything involving Cheetos that would make someone cry, particularly kittens), and avoid anything having to do with sex, violence and drugs. While they did not specify this, I also figured Nazis, pedophiles, 4chan (see previous), or Hugo Chavez (eye-roll) would be bad news. (Jardin, 2009)

So, Jardin even feels the need to fill in the gaps in her interaction with Frito-Lay. The apparent absence of a corporate voice might be interpreted as a necessary strategic elision in order to avoid annoying ad-weary readers with blatant commercialism. After all, if the blog writer is playing the part of a brand ambassador, the president generally doesn't send the ambassador to speak and then join in the conversation over her shoulder. This would just be unwelcome, unhelpful kibitzing. But Boing Boing are not brand ambassadors nor even have they been hired as brand advocates—they have been maneuvered into a role where they are the advocates for their own business and aesthetic decisions which have become entangled with Cheetos.

The use of blogs as mediators between brands and commercially suspicious consumers tends to function on a highly non-interactive level. This is not to say that there is no interaction going on; as I have pointed out there are many variations of traditional business interactions that are clearly part of the discourse generated from such relationships. Rather, the interactions between consumers and the brand are kept to a very abstract minimum—existing constructs of Cheetos (many of them negative) are exchanged between comment posters, and when anger or annoyance is expressed by posters it is only directly expressed toward Boing Boing *not* the brand. This might seem like a win-win situation for Frito-Lay, who avoid being the direct target of frustration and displeasure and instead manage to control the generation of online conversation around the brand name. But what

Bradley Ferguson calls "black buzz" (Ferguson, 2006, p. 185), or the negative impact on a business that bad word-of-mouth can bring, would be an obvious issue here. Yes, posters are clearly having conversations revolving around their constructions of the brand, yet those constructions in most cases do not reflect positively on Cheetos. Is this, then, an example of a brave brand battling against the culture of corporate control of communication only to be hoisted by its own petard? I would contend that the lack of communication from Frito-Lay and the passing of the interactive onus entirely on to the blog demonstrate the urge to create discourse but not be part of it which in turn suggests a misunderstanding of what a relationship is. I will take up these points in the following chapters. Now, having examined the still-beating heart of blog sponsorship, I will move on to a consideration of interaction in corporate blogging.

A company has the option, just like any individual, to produce its own blog or even a stable of blogs representing different departments or interests within the company. This is often called 'corporate blogging' and can be a large part of a company's online presence or only a very small element in its Web communications strategy. Interaction within a corporate blogspace takes the same form as it would in any other blog context, namely, in the comments section. Many corporate blogs, however, do not have comments sections precisely because they encourage a level of interaction that the bloggers or their corporate superiors are not comfortable with. Unfortunately, as Gillin points out, "in blog culture, commenting is considered an essential part of the conversation" (Gillin, 2007, p. 25). According to this logic, if you turn comments off, or don't even build them into the blog, you are effectively saying to the reader, 'I don't want to talk with you'. A moderation system like that operated by Boing Boing takes up a large amount of someone's time to manage and therefore raises the cost of the blog significantly. There are moderation systems (like the one operating at the Slashdot computer news forum, www.slashdot.org) which are entirely run on a volunteer, no fee basis by the readers of the site. But such models are unlikely to be considered by corporations already skittish about allowing too much public access to the construction of their corporate image. Because, in the end, a corporate blog is there to help build a particular construction in readers' minds regarding the company. The strategic assumption behind the corporate blog is that if the organization demonstrates that it is seriously concerned with providing consumers with up to date information on its products, services, plans, and motivations then the consumer will receive the impression that this organization is one they can build a relationship with. Obviously, I've deliberately couched this last sentence in terms redolent of the transmission model because, after all, that *is* the model informing such logic; you use your (blog) behavior to transmit a message to the audience, who after simplistically decoding it, receives it loud and clear.

Corporate blogs might, on the surface, offer certain opportunities to radicalize and challenge the transmission assumptions that have beset marketing communication for so long. Because the blog format is based upon the idea of a personal voice it forces a company to personalize its marketing communication, giving voice to actual personnel rather than siphoning a nameless, unidentifiable (and so personality-free) message stream. A rich example of this approach is the blogging culture developed at Sun Microsystems. Sun is a key player in the growth of the technologies that have given us both Web 1.0 and Web 2.0, being responsible for (amongst many other things) the development of the Java programming language (which is central to the creation of many cross-platform applications running on the Web), the Solaris operating system (a flavor of Unix used on many corporate servers), and has recently bought the rights to the MySQL database (which powers a majority of the heaviest traffic web sites in the world). Sun hosts a large number of employee blogs at its dedicated site, blogs.sun.com, and has made blogging an integral part of its corporate web presence (with links to various employee blogs from key home pages in the large corporate web megasite).

Sun's emphasis on blogging is a reflection of its move toward a business based more and more on open source solutions. An open source application is one whose entire source code is available freely to the public. Consequently, if you release an application as open source you cannot easily charge money for it because someone else will be willing to give the application to you for free. The business model for enterprises developing open source systems tends to focus around the selling of support; you get the product for free but you have to pay for support and training from the developers of the software. Because the source code is freely available anyone can change it or add to it or just open it up and have a look around to find out how it works. Making your applications open source is therefore seen (and is presented as such by organizations who have decided to follow this approach) as something that represents a giving back, or contributing, to the general community of software developers and users. Blogging at Sun can be framed, therefore, as part of the (financially) vital effort to build communities around Sun products and services. Sun blogs, particularly those maintained by the more high-profile project leaders and senior management, serve to build relationships with consumers through the demonstration of openness and passion for the brand. The chief blogger at Sun is surely Jonathan Schwartz, the CEO, who writes Jonathan's Blog (located at blogs.sun.com/jonathan/). Schwartz's blog talks about the type of things that one would expect a CEO to want to talk about—financial results, news about recent deals Sun has formalized, new product releases, commentary on industry trends and issues. The blog home page is typical in its reversed diary format and each entry carries a hyperlink at the bottom that takes the reader to the comments posted in reaction to that particular story. While Schwartz's blog certainly doesn't generate the number of comments that sites like Engadget or Boing Boing or Gawker might, it is not unusual for his entries to garner between 30 and 40 comments and sometimes even over 60. Importantly, the comments are not completely sanitized—many of Schwartz's blog entries generate expressions of skepticism, criticism, and sometimes just downright weirdness. Despite the fact that much of Schwartz's language is quite formal, a strong sense of the personal emerges from his discourse in large part due to his constant defense and explication of the open source model that Sun has been following under his leadership. In some ways the comments, while interesting to read, are superfluous because Schwartz is continually engaged with an implied reader who represents the unconvinced investor or customer. There is a palpable sense of engagement not just with the products and services that Sun produces but with the issues behind his leadership choices and the vision he has of both the company's future and the future of computing. Even though some of his blog entries are simply re-prints of memos and reports that he has transmitted already through the corporate intranet, the opening up of these internal documents serves to strengthen the apparent commitment to transparency that is a key element in Schwartz's vision of Sun management.

In comparison to Jonathan's Blog at Sun, Bob Langert's blog, Open to Discussion, at the McDonald's Corporate Social Responsibility web site, exhibits a much more low-key engagement both with actual comment posters and any implied reader. Langert is a vice president at McDonald's and the figurehead of its social responsibility program. The blog is referenced by Scott (2007) as a good example of the corporate blog, being "well-written and updated frequently" and feeling "authentic" (ibid., p. 58). Langert often uses personal anecdotes to make points and this has the effect of leavening his otherwise rather dull style and of giving a sense of an actual person (rather than a committee of PR writers) behind the blog. Comments are solicited at Open Discussion but there is very little evidence of that type of reader engagement, with most blog entries generating only one or two comments and some none at all. The implied reader in Langert's entries seems to possess a quite hazy identity. There is little passion on display, the predominant style being one of grandfatherly, down home reasonableness. Social issues that impact upon McDonald's are talked about with gently evasive strategies that try hard not to say anything too inflammatory while attempting to quietly point attention away from McDonald's as a source of blame. A good example is the entry for October 23rd 2008, entitled "What my little league days say to me about the root causes behind obesity" (Langert, 2008). While mentioning recent moves by some U.S. cities to ban McDonald's restaurants from certain at-risk areas and New York's ruling that fast food outlets must post calorie information on their menus, Langert tucks them away late in the entry and introduces them with the words: "Today, I am reading about cities like Los Angeles planning to impose a moratorium on fast food restaurants . . ." (ibid.). The implication here is that Bob Langert, VP for Social Responsibility at McDonalds, is reading about these direct attacks on his company in the newspapers—as if it's just some strange small news story happening in some out of the way little locale, rather than a serious attack on McDonalds' national corporate image. Furthermore, Langert does not enthusiastically spring to the defense of his company; instead he draws the lesson from his own healthy childhood that "the old ways are still the best ways", meaning that the way to beat the obesity epidemic is by making sure our children get plenty of exercise, plenty of vegetables, and no snacks. The entry reads like a dialog with himself, a rumination—its very title suggesting a closed in, self-contained conversation. It has attracted precisely one comment, made a week or so after the original post, that with a gentleness of tone mirroring Langert's own seeks to make the case that McDonald's own meals might not be reflecting the ideals expressed in the main blog. Obviously posted comments do not necessarily reflect the number of readers but, in terms of the voice offered to consumers, this forum for discussing McDonald's part in an issue of major importance to the U.S. public (if the coverage it receives in the mainstream media is any indication) does not seem to provoke much engagement. Talking to yourself is, admittedly, a form of interaction—one that is recognized in the theory of the implied reader. But it is not the revolutionary form of interaction that Web 2.0 is supposed to be offering us.

Google's official blog (googleblog.blogspot.com) has no place for comments. The interactive nature of the enterprise is therefore quite traditional, in the sense that it offers no more access to the consumer's voice than would a traditional print magazine or newspaper. The site, however, has very high traffic, generally placing in the top 10 of Technorati's global blog rankings for "authority". Authority is a metric based upon how many other sites link to a particular blog and is often seen as a measure of popularity or influence. Certainly, we might see "authority" as an analogue of reputation: Being linked to is a form of quotation and when many other blogs include a link through to one of your stories that is an indication that what your blog has said is being quoted, or talked about, by other people. In fact, "authority" is the Web's way of talking about "column inches". Google's official blog site attracts so many column inches because its content is carefully written, and usually contains breaking news about new Google services. Many people rely on such services as part of their business model on the Web (bidding for ad words, using Google Analytics to track site traffic and bounce rates, etc.) and therefore the latest information from Google's technical staff is important to their competitive edge. The Google blog is not a personal blog in the way that Jonathan Schwartz's and Bob Langert's are; it does not represent the thoughts and advice of one particular person but rather a constant carousel of Google technicians and scientists. It depicts the organization as a community of voices, then, although because commenting is not part of the site's design that community cannot be questioned or publicly engaged with. It is entirely possible that blogs and websites that link to various entries on the Google blog are actually commenting upon, discussing, analyzing, and otherwise building a conversation around those entries. Such a pattern might be thought to facilitate a reader community, rather in the way that a book club amongst friends is a framework for the conversational sharing of interpretations and readings. Having said this, one of the problems with such linking practices is that those commenting on blog entries that consist of a link back to, say, the Google blog, have little reason to follow the link and read the original post. Instead, commentors might read a brief summary provided by the linking blog and then weigh in with an opinion on that summary, rather than one based on a reading of the original article. Such practices are so common that they have become part of the culture at certain sites. Slashdot comment threads, for example, can often become a conversation between those who have read the original article and those who have not but are quite content to give their opinion anyway (although the accepted Web slang, *slashdotted*, referring to when a site has so much sudden traffic due to a link on Slashdot that its server folds, is an indication that a large chunk of readers do indeed check out the original articles).

The pattern I am trying to delineate here is the very subtle nature of the interaction present across a number of different types of corporate blog. For Sun, McDonald's, and Google, blogging serves marketing communication purposes. Even though I might interpret their motivations differently, they all have in common a broadcast approach. One individual, or one company, talking to many. Although commenting might be facilitated on two of the sites, there is little in the way of conversational engagement or dialog between blogger and commentor. Certainly one cannot see the *development* of a communication relationship over a series of exchanges.

Interaction is, in the end, low down on the priority list of the corporate blog format. Instead, the blog is there to help in the construction of a persuasive discourse that 'transmits' authority, competence, confidence, and care for the customer. From such a perspective, the technical ability to comment on a blog entry becomes a rhetorical strategy that persuades readers that they have been given a means to voice their opinion to senior management. Even if few readers take the opportunity to voice their opinion (as with the Langert blog), the company nevertheless is seen to be providing it. A management-monitored space for customers to blow off steam or enthuse about a brand can be a valuable company asset. In Sun's case, the Jonathan Schwartz blog sometimes has the feel of what a programmer might call a "sandbox", namely a safely bounded development space on your computer system where you can experiment with code without putting the larger system at risk. In his blog entry for November 12, 2008, for example, Schwartz wrote about some of his plans to get Sun through the global financial crisis. In a long blog post there were two issues which raised great discussion amongst the 67 comments posted; the first was the prospect that a new deal with Microsoft would mean that everyone installing Java would be confronted with offers for Microsoft sponsored add-on software, while the second was the announcement that OpenOffice (Sun's free office suite) was also going to experience a similar 'integration' with sponsoring businesses and brands. The comments section generated a number of posts which congratulated Schwartz on his plans and approved of his vision but also saw a significant amount of negative opinion regarding the prospect of more ads and annoying 'bloatware' being tied into what should be a simple software installation. Many commentors protested at the prospect of ads being somehow forced into their OpenOffice documents. And three separate developers from Romania complained that they couldn't gain access to the Sun servers in order to download Java software anyway. Schwartz, or his deputies did respond to all three of these issues. A comment was posted toward the end of the thread by Wes Adams from Sun Microsystems addressing the three Romanians by name, apologizing for the inconvenience and informing them that the problem was now fixed (which was then confirmed by one of the original posters in the comment that followed it). Schwartz himself posted an update to his blog entry which appears to be a direct response to the anxieties expressed in the comments. It reads:

> Update: I should've clarified, above: users without any interest in toolbars can simply decline the offer during install—and receive their Java update without any sponsored software. (Schwartz, 2008a)

The opening phrase inescapably implies that Schwartz's initial published entry is lacking in clarity on this point. This admission is not something needed to have been done and in normal PR writing would have been avoided; there are, after all, a large number of ways to provide further clarity on an issue without admitting that you weren't clear enough in the first place. This is, perhaps, one of the problems with corporate blogs that really are written by executives (rather than a team of ghost writers)—the nuanced implications of their phrasings might be lower down on their communication priorities compared to those of a battle-hardened public relations copywriter. It is the same type of risk that occurs when an executive goes off-script at a press conference or during an interview with any media. Admission of fault, even if that admission is not fully intended, can also go a long way to demonstrate 'character', or what students of rhetoric would call *ethos*, and as such has a long-standing tradition as a rhetorical strategy. Schwartz uses another blog entry, posted a couple of weeks later on November 26, 2008, to address the comments to the November 12th entry complaining about the prospect of adding ads into the OpenOffice suite. In a very small font at the end of the November 26th entry, he adds the following aside:

> (And with apologies to the OpenOffice community—we are not going to be inserting ads into OpenOffice.org—we're creating partnerships to brand and promote StarOffice, and the cloud we're developing behind it). (Schwartz , 2008b)

This appears to be signaling a direct change of policy as a result of reactions to the previously announced plan to place adverts in OpenOffice. So, in a blog interaction between the CEO blogger and those posters who expressed dismay at the prospect of an overly commercialized OpenOffice, we seem to be seeing depicted a quick change of company policy as a result of consumer community feedback. StarOffice, which is the version of OpenOffice that is branded and distributed by Sun (as opposed to the community-maintained version) *will* be subject to branding partnerships but Sun will not touch the OpenOffice.org version. The comment is visually presented as an aside in the sense that it is in a micro-font and parenthesized—Schwartz is not addressing his entire audience here, only those who are from the open source community in general and the OpenOffice.org community in particular.

Schwarz's blog, then, enables him to announce plans, garner feedback, revise those plans, and then generate goodwill from making the whole process quick and open. A dialog does seem to be happening here and the Web does seem to be facilitating it. Sun's blogging policy, publicly available at www.sun.com/communities/guidelines.jsp, is perfectly in tune with Gillin's advice regarding a liberal attitude toward the management of staff blogging, summed up in the sentence, "Put a set of guidelines in place and let people go" (Gillin, 2007, p. 101). In keeping with much of the customer-facing discourse we have seen regarding marketing communication on the Internet, the anonymous policy author notes that the goal of blogging at Sun, "isn't to get everyone at Sun contributing online, it's to become part of the industry conversation" (Sun Microsystems, 2008). As some of the apparent interaction on Schwartz's blog demonstrates, the "rhetoric of conversation" can sometimes manifest itself in displays of feedback generation that influence senior level policy change. Due to the ease with which blogs can be run and the speed with which content can be posted, consumer feedback can be generated very quickly in comparison to more traditional methods (surveys, reader response to print articles, etc.), and management can be seen to be responding to it with equal alacrity. But, as the language that I am now using demonstrates, the communication model behind the corporate blog is still one based upon the control paradigm. A blog entry transmits a position on how to reach a goal, readers post comments on that position enabling the blogger to measure the success of its reception, the blogger can then alter the position to achieve maximum success of the goal. The goal here, though, must always be the satisfaction of the blog commentors. The reference signal for the feedback loop is maximum comment approval, however that might be determined by the blogger—perhaps 60% positive commentary, perhaps only 20% negative comments, or perhaps no comments on the entry at all. In any event, the blog becomes primarily not a process of communication but a process of control—changing output until the correct input from the feedback is received. Those who post comments to blogs are self-selecting and not necessarily representative of the wider reading audience; they might be genuinely concerned to communicate their opinion to the blogger or they might be more concerned with the performative function of posting a comment (and the same can be said of the blogger, too). From the corporate bloggers point of view, though, blogging has a marketing communication function above all else. Necessarily, the comments on such blogs will become part of a "rhetoric of measurement" even as their elicitation is couched in the "rhetoric of conversation". The simple cybernetic system that has been the unifying trope behind all approaches to marketing communication since its inception is engraved into the very heart of its uses of blogging. Comments on blogs provide an easily accessible, easy to point to, easy to measure feedback device that helps to reinforce the communication as control paradigm. At a meta level, the existence of such blogs can be used to transmit a message of honesty and transparency that is built upon the transmission assumption of rhetorical *ethos*.

The feature that makes blogs so apparently "interactive", namely the comments system, is the feature that ironically ties them so tightly to the mainstream marketing conception of interaction as cybernetic control. The intense allure of measurement, of analyzing the approach toward a goal, is made so easy by the blog format that it would take a great will to break away from such assumptions and build communities of conversations that are not powered by "rhetorics of monitoring". The use of "faux blogs" (fake blogs that purport to be by private individuals who are actually fronting for a brand, TV show or other marketing force) is a perfect illustration of how the marketing communication approach to blogs is still based upon an instrumentalist, conduit-obsessed perspective. A "faux blog" is designed with the strategic intention of producing particular effects in the audience through the transmission of carefully considered, fake messages. High profile instances of this practice, such as Edelman's work for Wal-Mart (Cammaerts, 2008), Wieden and Kennedy's campaign for the ESPON NFL Football 2K4 game, and McDonald's Lincoln fry blog (Corcoran et al., 2007), are primarily designed to promote buzz through an appeal to the *ethos* of the apparently non-sponsored 'consumer'. If the blogger appears to be an unconnected amateur with no financial benefit to exposure, her enthusiasm for the brand or the product will be interpreted as genuine and so the message that they are transmitting will be persuasive. The logic here is, of course, exactly the same as that informing the use of customer testimonials in print advertising. The faux blog, however, because it does not have to identify itself as a paid promotion can erase the cynicism that can be read into the advertising presentation of effusive customer support. The Web makes these attempts at misrepresentation much easier to spread through the practices of hyperlinking, embedding, and 'Digging'; so it might appear as if communities are instantly formed around such sites and that these communities of talk represent a wonderfully interactive manifestation of the democratizing of the entertainment industry. It is the users of the Internet who decide, after all, what will be talked about, what will be found worthy of linking and forwarding. The importance of evolutionary rhetoric in marketing's construction of online communities will be examined in Chapter 5, but for this discussion of blogging, I would like to underline the severely stilted approach to communication that current marketing practice and theory evince in their engagement with the blogosphere. The faux blog, the corporate blog and the sponsored blog are all premised upon a first-order cybernetic model of communication as the transmission of control messages in order to achieve a goal. Ongoing, evolving conversation that has the capacity to change everyone (including the blogger) is not what the marketing use of the form is about. Even when Jonathan Schwartz apparently changes policy, or re-frames his policy descriptions, according to feedback from comment posters, this is because the target of that particular discourse is not actual policy creation but the formulation of policy presentation. Schwartz uses the blog to affect the influencers and evangelists that are interested in following the thoughts of Sun's CEO. The readers of the blog will be people who are interested in Sun's broad future rather than just the details of a specific product (there are many other blogs on the Sun site devoted to highly technical aspects of the hardware and software systems the company produces). Those readers who comment will tend to be those who are habitually keen to express their opinions—they might be thought of, then, as the halfway stage in a word-of-mouth campaign, they are the opinion-givers. They are going to give their opinion not just to Jonathan Schwartz but to all those around them (colleagues, customers, clients). Schwartz's goal is the goodwill of these influencers, if he can get them on his side, then the larger community will follow. Encouraging such individuals to express their thoughts to the CEO of the company 'transmits' an *ethos* of openness and honesty, as does the apparent willingness to change course on certain policy matters or admit mistakes as a result of posted comments from such readers. From one perspective this looks like the readers are controlling company policy, but this is only a tenable position if you think that the blog is primarily about policy creation. If, on the other hand, one considers that the goal of the blog is the generation of goodwill amongst those in a position to be evangelists for Sun, then the admission of mistakes in explanation and the apparent backpedaling on the issue of incorporating advertising into OpenOffice.org can be constructed into a pattern of control signals designed to bring about the attainment of that goodwill.

Blogs, like all forms of discourse, are part of a process of reality creation. The canonical blog format, which consists of a 'parent' entry followed by comment threads discussing that entry, structurally sets the blogger's entry apart from, and above, the comments that feed off it. The blog entry is thus afforded the position of 'parent' text: All comments are in one way or another marginalia (to use a book-bound term) to the first entry. The parent blog entry sets the terms of the discourse that is generated in the comments—even in reacting against it, comments are marked by it. The blog entry creates a discourse space by making the initial distinctions of language, theme, reference, and tone. Comments are framed by these distinctions and so enter into a relationship with them (adopting them, rejecting them, playing with them, but always mindful of them). It is the nature of these distinctions that make certain blogs popular. Furthermore, as Gurak and Antonijevic (2008) have pointed out, a blog is a "communicative event" not a "written object", meaning that the diary format it is based upon "integrates a person's (fictional or real) experiences in a chronological narrative" (ibid., p. 65). They see the blog as "a twofold communicative event", the first being a continuous event of "writing oneself" and the second being the event of "rewriting oneself" by interaction with the comments. Developing this argument from a constructivist perspective, this would mean that bloggers construct their reality in their blog entries and then re-construct that reality in their interaction with the comments. Interacting with comments provides blog discourse with a process of re-creation, re-construction, whereby the blogger is involved in a continual revising and re-building of understandings. This is an attractive view of the genre, in that it characterizes it by an emphasis on growth through interaction—the blogger 'grows' and the community 'grows' through the mutual exchange of communication. Gurak and Antonijevic locate this unique potential of blogs in the observation that they "are *both* private and public" (ibid., emphasis in original) constructions of private experience and personal understandings are publicly expressed by being broadcast to a (largely anonymous) community where they are then revised, defended, and contextualized by being compared to the private experiences and understandings of others. For Gurak and Antonijevic, the goal of this process is to aid in the active creation of an identity; the blogger writes the blog to construct themselves. How can the marketing use of blogs, though, be said to fit into this scenario? After all, if a blog is created in order to have a particular effect on the readers, then this is a very different motivation than creating a blog to create oneself. In other words, the model of communication as transmitted control that informs marketing communication does not feature the sender in a continuous state of reflexive evolution. The sender remains the same. Indeed, the sender *has* to remain the same in order for the persuasive message to have any marketing purpose. If, through interaction with blog comments, the marketing blogger changes the substance of her discourse, changes her construction of reality, then the principle observation that readers will have of the brand the blogger represents is that it is in flux, inchoate, amorphous. And who wants that in a brand? The brand must be recognizable, it must stand for the same thing this week that it did last week. Stability, as I have argued in Chapter 3, is something we are constantly searching for in the patterns we create from our observations. Although generalized blogging can be framed as some form of interactive *bildungsroman, marketing* blogging cannot follow the features of such a genre while still being true to the basic principles informing marketing management's conception of communication. In marketing, communication serves the purpose of changing the consumer's attitudes and behavior. Communication cannot be considered as a process that produces a symbiotic relationship of change in both marketer and consumer without it slipping outside the carefully drawn boundaries of marketing's control paradigm. Change, when traditionally dealt with by marketing communication, needs to deny that it is happening by acting as if the new state of affairs was always the case. Most successful repositionings have hinged not on communicating how the new position is a natural evolution from the old one but rather by either acting as if the old position was never there or positioning the new branding as a revolution against the previous one. Marlboro and Lucozade, to name two obvious examples, did not achieve widespread recognition for their repositionings because their advertising displayed a reflexive conversation concerning their previous brand images; rather, both brands managed to utterly negate their previous images by never mentioning them (Lury, 2001). Attempts to deal with the new brand attributes by recalling to the minds of consumers the old brand attributes are inevitably going to paint the re-branding in a suspicious and murky half-light. When the diet orange soda Fanta Light faired poorly in U.K. markets a re-branding of the product in the summer of 2005 as Fanta Z was accompanied by a U.K. advertising campaign by London agency Mother that specifically focused on the idea that Fanta Light tasted terrible. The TV spot showed an assortment of consumers spitting out the old Fanta Light with the new Fanta Z heroically growing from the crushed remains of a Light can. While the knowing, ironic tone was designed to strike a chord with a young, media-literate demographic, it's rhetorical strategy was just another variation on the appeal to *ethos*—because I am honest about the failings of my previous product you can trust me when I talk about this 'new' one. Even when change is openly addressed in marketing communication, then, its purpose is the transmission of a rhetorical trope which will have a particular effect on the consumer.

In a medium such as the blog, which is so ostensibly centered around the recording of personal development, marketing communication will have a deeply paradoxical place. The marketing message is fetishized into a highly stable construction by those professionals responsible for its creation and deployment which means that the irritation and growth that occurs at the interface between public and private and between blogger and commenting readers cannot be countenanced. The marketing blog must present a stable discourse or risk losing the foundations on which its communications are premised. It is perhaps telling in this context that accusations of rigidity over the Boing Boing editorial position regarding the Frito-Lay deal began to be made in the comments section to the second Cheetos video. The integration of a marketing vector into the blogging format will inevitably create tensions and paradoxes around the need for control and stability.

If the marketing blog is a still-born, contradiction-filled chimera it is only so because its communication paradigm necessitates a discourse at odds with the very format. The rhetoric of conversation played out in marketing theory drives the practical adoption of this king of the talk format, yet marketing is most comfortable in its embrace (or death grip) with the technology of the Web when the rhetoric of conversation is subsumed under the rhetoric of measurement. The evolution of data mining from its application to customer transactions toward a more pervasive and continuous monitoring and analysis of Internet talk about the brand betrays the real understanding of conversation that online marketing is currently comfortable with. For the growing marketing emphasis is not on *having* a conversation with consumers but on *listening in* on their conversations. The one marketing use of blogging that none of the authors involved in cheerleading the format talk about is its surreptitious part in *encouraging* talk, talk that can be made use of. In short, Web 2.0 technologies are not predominantly useful for what they can allow marketers to do in terms of initiating conversations themselves but rather for how they can be used to generate more talk between prospects and customers. People will talk about the things they own, the movies they see, the fast food they eat, the cars they want to drive. Take a trip over to www.bevnet.com and read the exchanges on the message boards and you will find the most intense enthusiasm expressed for all manner of non-alcoholic beverages by posters who spend their time and money searching out the latest flavors and brand extensions. The site itself is a beverage industry site, a fairly traditional B2B, trade news on the Web concoction, but the message boards are full of enthusiasts not professionals. Listening in on, rather than engaging with, this sort of conversation is the real business of Web 2.0. The sort of data mining that we have seen discussed earlier in this chapter by Segaran and Spangler and Kreulen is designed to work on the sorts of large amounts of continuously generated, informal conversation that typify blogs, microblogs, and social networking sites. The more people are given the spaces and tools to talk, the more raw data that can be processed by such procedures. The sites that enable this blooming of chatter are also careful to provide the APIs that give developers the access to this horde of voices.

Faced with a medium and context that engenders severe tensions within its basic communication model, marketing retreats into a quantitative scopophilia. The approach to interaction that the traditional marketing communication mindset will feel most comfortable with on the Web is one based upon the facilitation, the subtle encouragement, of chatter that the brand itself does not have to take part in. One of the clear benefits of such an approach is that nothing much has to change. If the goal of marketing's interface with the consumer on the Web is to promote the generation of talk, then there is precious little onus to radically alter the marketing communication model. The consumer is stimulated to talk (through the provision of appropriate online spaces and through the traditional seeding methods of advertising, product placement, sponsorship, and public relations), is made to feel perhaps that if they are not talking (about something, about anything) then they are not really *present*. The resulting bloom of chatter is monitored, measured, mined by all who wish to trace the semantic connections and patterns that fluoresce around particular key words, brand names, locations, or even images (with the slow dawn of effective tagging practices). The more mobile phone use can be lead away from (legally difficult to monitor) voice and text services and toward the wide-open vistas of marketing-accessible online communication (forum posting, internet chat variations, microblogging) then the more complete becomes the reach. When two friends use their iPhones to twitter, every word they tap is accessible. An increasingly common phenomenon at conferences and physical meetings frequented by the digerati is the twittering of the audience at a presentation. As the speaker, you might think that you are the sole voice commanding attention but instead there are whole multi-threaded layers of conversation going on as you are speaking; your words are being microblogged as they happen, with large sections of the audience following not just you but the bloggers' reaction to you. Truly a challenge for any modern rhetor (whispering you can hear, twittering is invisible to you up there on the podium with your mobile unwisely tucked away in your pocket), but an example of the perfect opportunity the mobile online blooming of constant talk presents marketing. If you are outside the conference hall, listening in, you don't need to know what the presentation is about (we've forgotten about the speaker, already) because you have electrodes inserted into the minds of the audience, you are wire tapping their language, their moods.

This sort of scenario is increasingly being pitched by marketers who see the integration of mobile phones and the Web as the perfect evolutionary playground for the data mining systems originally developed for the implementation of old-school CRM. The gathering of geolocation data which most modern mobile handsets allow means that the tensions between rhetorics of measurement and conversation will only increase in the near future. GPS data from a mobile user can be integrated with the mining of GPS-tagged microblogging conversations in order to monitor what clusterings occur in the talk of those passing through certain locations. While such systems can again be used to give the impression of a more 'personalized', 'timely', and 'targeted' interaction with marketing messages the core procedures involved are built upon the avoidance of conversation and the promotion of constant monitoring. Marketing use of machine learning algorithms implies aggregation and not individuation, so while the theoretical discourses of RM and CRM blithely mouth the importance of the segment of one, the practical implementation of these orientations is evolving further and further toward an automated simulation of individual interaction powered by the increasing sophistication of computationally-derived generalizations.

Within the context of the control model of communication that beats at the heart of contemporary marketing management, the more consumers integrate their geolocation and online conversation, the more easily and effectively their voices may be articulated into the feedback system of marketing discourse. The sponsorship (both literal and metaphorical) of customer-created content, open Web forums for informal communication (blogs, micro-blogs, forums, etc.) and all other activities which aid or result in consumers generating more talk, serves the larger marketing management agenda expressed in the rhetoric of measurement which dominates the technological arm of current mainstream theory and practice. The ramification of this situation for marketing discourse is that we may witness a twofold dynamic of apparent moves toward conversational engagement with the consumer betrayed at the same time by a turning away from direct conversational interaction and an immersion in the language of automated aggregation. It might be appealing to characterize this as indicative of a trend in marketing discourse to turn away from the human and move toward the machine, perhaps initiated by a frustration with the inability to reach key demographics through traditional methods but such a depiction would completely avoid the more obvious sources for this paradoxical dynamic. In Chapter 6 I will be deconstructing the re-presentation of relationship that RM/CRM approaches have been built around in order to demonstrate just how much of a force it has been in the utterly paradoxical marketing discourse of conversational interaction that this chapter has been concerned with. Before this, however, we need to consider another vital component in contemporary marketing understandings of interaction—the viral metaphor.

5 Customer Communities and the Grammar of Control

THE VIRAL TURN

While the implementation of CRM systems has foregrounded marketing's coupling with data generation and analysis, there has been another discourse stream with similar connections into scientific constructions of knowledge that has co-existed with, and even at times buttressed, the rhetorics of conversation and measurement. Viral marketing (and its rhizome-like manifestations in buzz marketing, word-of-mouth marketing, and connected marketing) has had a profound influence on both the rhetoric of online marketing and the argumentative structures that are used to pitch and defend certain popular assumptions informing marketing attempts to theorize and engage with consumer communities. The central metaphor behind viral marketing, that an idea is like a virus in the way that it can spread exponentially across a population, is highly seductive to the mainstream marketing communications paradigm that indexes its evolution on finding ever more effective techniques to capture the minds of consumers. In its borrowing of medical terminology, viral marketing possesses the rhetorical glamour of science as well as echoing the headline-grabbing natural power of uncontrollable epidemics.

One work, more than any other, has served to consolidate the viral theme in the minds of marketing practitioners, and that is Seth Godin's (2000) *Unleashing the Idea Virus*. In this chapter I will be examining the way in which Godin's handling of the viral metaphor constructs a very particular model of consumer interaction, a model that has gone on to be influential in the larger marketing communication trend toward word-of-mouth, or buzz, strategies. Additionally, I will be investigating the way in which the early academic discourse around the science of memetics feeds into marketing constructions of online influence.

The re-presentation of ideas as viruses of the mind is generally traced back to Richard Dawkins's 1976 book, *The Selfish Gene*. Dawkins's theory was that the gene should be regarded as the essential unit of natural selection and the bodies (i.e., you and I) that contain the genes were best thought of as "survival machines" that helped to ensure their continual generation. His vivid portrayal of a gene leaping "from body to body down the generations, manipulating body after body in its own way and for its own ends, abandoning a succession of mortal bodies before they sink in senility and death" (Dawkins, 2006, p. 34) is indicative both of the descriptive flair that Dawkins brings to his subject matter and of the way in which he chose to rhetorically personify the gene and afford it a form of agency almost gothic in nature. While most of *The Selfish Gene* is concerned with Dawkin's depiction of the gene's story as he sees it, a small section late in the book proposes a view of culture that has proved perhaps more influential, if not also far more nebulous. After having argued the case for understanding the gene as a replicator unit which uses 'us' as a means to survival and dominance, Dawkins famously postulates the existence of "a new kind of replicator" which has "emerged on this very planet" (ibid., p. 192). He is speaking of a replicator of cultural units, what he dubs a *meme* (adapted from the Greek *mimeme*, to imitate). In an often quoted passage he lists some specimens of this new form of cultural replicator:

> Examples of memes are tunes, ideas, catch-phrases, clothes fashions, ways of making pots or of building arches. Just as genes propagate themselves in the gene pool by leaping from body to body via sperm or eggs, so memes propagate themselves in the meme pool by leaping from brain to brain via a process which, in the broad sense, can be called imitation. (ibid., p. 192)

The theory that ideas contained in human culture developed and spread in ways that were highly analogous to Darwinian natural selection was in itself not new (see Durham, 1991, for an overview), but Dawkins's depiction of the meme as a selfish replicator which 'leaps' from brain to brain was a significant conceptual (and rhetorical) difference. Although Dawkins provided little elaboration of exactly how memes could be contained in brains, how they could be empirically examined, compared, or measured, nevertheless he had himself produced (or expressed) a meme of considerable fitness. During the late 1980s and 1990s the discussion and development of rigorous memetic theories was taken up by an enthusiastic cadre of young scholars, amongst them mathematicians, social scientists, philosophers, anthropologists, and economists. Many of those actively researching this area gravitated toward the forum and information hub of the *Principia Cybernetica* online project (http://www.pespmc1.vub.ac.be), overseen by Francis Heylighen using servers at the Free University of Brussels. In 1997 the *Journal of Memetics—Evolutionary Models of Information Transmission* (JoM—EMIT) was established online (http://cfpm.org/jom-emit) and continued to publish a wide variety of scholarly articles relating to the areas of memetics, cultural selection, and, increasingly, social contagion theory until its hiatus in 2005. Those who make themselves familiar with the nine volumes of the *JoM* will appreciate that the field of memetics has been the recipient of much effort to bring the scientific method to bear upon its core concepts. Unavoidable, however, is the observation that much of that effort led to disillusion and frustration. Even in the second volume, the difficulties of establishing a new discipline based upon what was effectively just a powerful metaphor were being discussed in an article by Derek Gatherer (Gatherer, 1998) entitled, 'Why the Thought Contagion Metaphor is Retarding the Progress of Memetics'. At the same time that academic research into memetics was reaching its peak, the viral metaphor was vectoring into the field of marketing. Seth Godin, through a series of *Fast Company* articles, a free online book, a website, and an actual pay-for-a dead-tree version of the ebook, loudly and enthusiastically promoted the marketing application of the idea that "moves and grows and infects everyone it touches " (Godin, 2000, p. 13). Dawkins does get a mention, halfway through the book, and it's worth looking quickly at just how Godin carries this off:

> Richard Dawkins, a brilliant evolutionary theorist, had his own word for the phenomenon I'm calling ideaviruses: memes. He pointed out that a meme was like a living organism, surviving not in the real world, but in our world of ideas. (Godin, 2000, p. 94)

Then, two paragraphs further down:

> One of the behaviors noticed by Dawkins and practiced by anyone who markets with ideaviruses is that memes follow a vector. (ibid.)

These two mentions of Dawkins are beautifully handled, as one would expect from a popular marketing guru. There is no sense of precedence for Dawkins here, instead Godin positions himself and Dawkins as working on the same approach but in different disciplines. Furthermore, the second quotation implies that marketing practitioners using "ideaviruses" have been doing something naturally that Dawkins has only 'noticed'. Of course, the not-so-subtle favoring of practice over theory that Godin's words carry is typical of both practitioner and mainstream academic marketing paradigms (Hackley, 2001; Hunt, 2002). There is no bibliographic information for readers to follow up on the *meme* reference and Dawkins is not mentioned in the final acknowledgments section (which is written as a form of 'further reading and exploration' list). Ironically, it is difficult to feel discomfort at what appears to be a lack of due recognition for Dawkins when Godin himself encourages readers to "STEAL THIS IDEA!" and freely distribute as many copies of the ebook as they wish—incidentally replicating Abbie Hoffman's (1971) own "Steal This Book" meme. Furthermore, if Dawkins is correct in his characterization of the *meme*, replicating ideas have to look out for themselves, for there is little logic in claiming ownership of them, just as it would be absurd for a human to claim ownership of her genes if those genes are in fact the evolutionary unit using our bodies as "survival machines". Nevertheless, Godin's occlusion of the lineage of the ideavirus meme speaks of a curious discomfort with providing the roots of his re-presentation with an 'academic', 'scientific' foundation. By the time he gets around to mentioning Dawkins, the reader is already deeply immersed within Godin's own framing and the introduction of the possibility of a 'scientific' context has far less impact. There is also the possibility that Godin purposely attempts to downplay the connection between ideaviruses and Dawkins because of the latter's profile as a militant and public atheist intent on convincing all and sundry of the impoverishing effect of religious belief. In many sections of the U.S. market, connecting your new marketing idea with such a position might threaten its "smoothness" (to use Godin's own terminology) and adoption. Certainly, the almost complete absence of anything but a quick nod to the academic history of memetics in Godin's text is illustrative of the general way in which the promotion of viral marketing has tended to avoid engagement with the existing memetic literature. Not all of this subtle exclusion of discourse can be linked back to Godin's early texts. Indeed, it is quite striking that considering the existence in the memetic literature of a rather substantial body of work dealing with the quantitative modeling of memetic transmission almost none of it is referenced in marketing examinations of the viral theme. Furthermore, while there is barely any interaction with the 'scientific' research on such memetic models, viral marketing literature also does not examine the metaphorical nature of the infection trope. Instead, the idea as virus equation is taken as established fact with little need for further theoretical inquiry. Godin knows how the ideavirus works and that is what he is going to tell us—the biblical certainty of it all is what makes his package so appealing. Compared to so much of the scholarly work on the development of memetics, which is full of scholarly things like doubt, hypotheses, modeling, testing, and re-formulation, Godin's discourse frames the rules of memetics as if they were written on stone and universally accepted. This unquestioning attitude toward the 'idea as virus' construct has become the norm in the general viral marketing discourse that has evolved over the past 10 years. The reason for the 'smooth', wholesale adoption of the viral meme becomes apparent when one begins to examine the nature of interaction within the viral marketing model.

Godin's description of the basic ideavirus concept is as follows:

> What's an ideavirus? It's a big idea that runs amok across the target audience. It's a fashionable idea that propagates through a section of the population, teaching and changing and influencing everyone it touches. And in our rapidly/instantly changing world, the art and science of building, launching and profiting from ideaviruses is the next frontier. (Godin, 2000, p. 14)

The marketer, then, is depicted as someone who 'builds' an idea in order to 'launch' it at a population (the guided missile metaphor is clearly being invoked here) and then sits back and reaps the profits. The ideavirus is transmitted through the target population successfully due to its effective design by the marketer. If you follow the design rules outlined by Godin then your ideavirus will be primed and targeted with the right characteristics to exponentially "run amok" across the intended population. There is a chain-like interaction described here, soaked in the medical terminology of infection and viewable as an impressive integration of a variety of Krippendorff's typology of major communication metaphors (Krippendorff, 1993): the container metaphor, the control metaphor, the transmission metaphor, and the war metaphor, all now synergized by the infection metaphor. Viral marketing is all about interaction in that it focuses on how to get a message to spread from one person to another—yet the construction of interaction that it is founded upon is simplistic and one-dimensional. Indeed, I would contend that the use of the medical metaphor of infection in this area of marketing ironically encourages an imitation of worst-practice doctor–patient relationships. The viral marketer, although building a message that is designed to be passed on through consumer interaction, is encouraged to remove herself as far as possible away from the actual process of interaction; her concern is solely with the design of something that can take advantage of interaction rather than actually engaging *in* such interactions. In Godin's scheme, the only really important interaction that marketers have to concern themselves with is the initial communication relationship with the "sneezers", those people in the "hive" (a self-organized grouping of consumers) who are either most likely to talk about anything to anyone else in the group (the "promiscuous sneezers") or who are listened to by the rest of the group because their opinion is trusted (the "powerful sneezers"). It is the "sneezers" who will do the real job of marketing a product to the "hive". The nature of the interactions that Godin recommends for the two types of sneezers betrays a considerable amount concerning the assumptions underlying these communication relationships. The promiscuous sneezers, while not as trusted by the hive because their integrity is called into question by their past liberality of favor, can be used effectively in a campaign if the marketer can recruit enough of them. Godin is quite open concerning how such recruitment is to be achieved: "basically, we're paying folks enough to corrupt them into spreading ideas in exchange for cash" (ibid., p. 42). Powerful sneezers, on the other hand, achieve their trusted position in the hive by not being so free with their recommendation, so cash inducements (or the gamut of equivalents that traditional PR has evolved over many years of practice) do not have quite the same effect on them. Both the powerful sneezer and the marketer want their strong reputation within the hive to remain and therefore need to tread carefully in setting up any deal that may reflect badly upon the sneezer's apparent neutrality or objectivity. Godin's answer to the paradoxical marketing position of powerful sneezers (each time a marketer uses them their reputation in the hive falls) is refreshingly simple: Pay them more. You need to turn a powerful sneezer (who is jealous of her reputation and will thus protect it from damage by open association with marketing opportunities) into a promiscuous sneezer by offering the "right inducement" (ibid., p. 46). Using the example of the headhunting website Referrals.com, Godin points out that although someone might not recommend a job to her friend or colleague for a paltry $10 or $20, for $4,000 she might well bite the bullet. This is the essence of Godin's perspective on interaction with this valued customer resource: the discourse of inducements, favors, payments, gifts, benefits, and bribes. From a simple financial point of view, however, Godin's logic is hard to deny—for the money a brand might spend on a traditional "interruption" advertising campaign its can afford to give its powerful sneezers some very substantial inducements. Godin, both in his earlier *Permission Marketing* (2002 [1999]) and in *Unleashing the Ideavirus*, is very outspoken in his condemnation of the use of traditional advertising strategies in the contemporary marketplace; business, he writes, "can no longer survive by interrupting strangers with a message they don't want to hear, about a product they've never heard of, using methods that annoy them" (Godin, 2000, p. 24). Consequently, from a marketing strategy perspective, Godin's inducement approach to the spreading of ideaviruses to sneezers is framed within an explicit alternative: Either use interruption marketing and go bankrupt or switch to his two-stage model of viral and permission marketing and stand at least a fighting chance.

Other authors coming after Godin have tended to be far less dismissive of traditional advertising tools, presenting viral marketing as an appropriate option in certain circumstances and often as part of broader, integrated campaigns. Consequently, there has been far less emphasis on the need to arrange substantial inducements for sneezers. A good example of this more integrated approach is that taken by Russell Goldsmith (2002) in his *Viral Marketing: Get Your Audience To Do Your Marketing For You*. Although Goldsmith talks about advertising clutter, consumer mistrust of traditional marketing techniques, and the difficulty of reaching key demographics in the contemporary marketplace, his position is that viral marketing has a "place firmly set within the marketing mix" (Goldsmith, 2002, p. 5) and "just because viral marketing happens to be the latest buzzword, it does not mean that it is appropriate to every marketing campaign" (ibid., p. 16). Unlike Godin, therefore, Goldsmith's rhetoric is evolutionary not revolutionary. He is careful to deflate claims that viral marketing is something completely new to the marketing workspace, pointing out that, in the end, it is "simply word-of-mouth marketing via a digital platform" (ibid., p. 3). One of viral marketing's key advantages for Goldsmith is that it offers far cheaper production and media costs when compared to other, more traditional, elements of the marketing communications mix. Where Godin's rhetoric revels in the extended medical metaphor with its "sneezers" and "vectors", Goldsmith forgoes any use of such discourse outside of the core term "viral". For example, when describing the way in which key individuals can be seen to act as opinion leaders within groups (Godin's sneezers) Goldsmith relies heavily upon the terminology and language used in Burson-Marstella's "e-fluentials" report which is noticeable for its conservative, quantitatively-framed, agency-anchored discourse of "positive experiences", "sources", "opinions", "research before purchase", "gaining information", and "brands that they can trust" (ibid., p. 23). The use that Goldsmith makes of quantitative survey results is also significant when compared to Godin's dramatic but uncredited, unsourced, and unlabeled illustrative graphs (Godin, 2000, p. 32).

Goldsmith's presentation of viral marketing, like Godin's, cannot escape the interaction that is at the core of the theory. The bulk of his text is concerned with examining the reasons that people give for passing messages on to others, the logic being that if we can understand what motivates such behavior then marketers will be able to take advantage of it to produce emails, games, and videos that will 'go viral'. Goldsmith's own survey (conducted for the book using the online site tickbox.com) found that humor, product recommendation, and the chance to win a competition were the three most common reasons for forwarding an email or SMS text message.

The implication of the viral marketing model that Goldsmith presents is that interaction between consumers is based around a simple stimulus-response coupling; if a message is funny enough then the response will be to share it with friends and colleagues. The marketer's concern is therefore with the construction of amusing or entertaining messages that will take advantage of such a response. However, an amusing message doesn't sell anything. It is the outer disguise that facilitates the spread of the message but conceals the real marketing payload. Goldsmith argues that by passing on the message to someone else, the consumer "does your marketing for you" (Goldsmith, 2002, p. 2), reinforcing the idea that the viral message contains something which will do the 'marketing work' even when the distribution system is out of the marketer's hands. It remains unclear, though, how the marketing payload and the outer viral casing are meant to work together. There is a conceptual gap between the stages of a consumer being amused or entertained by a message and then being influenced by its marketing payload. Goldsmith's examples, liberally sprinkled through his book, do not make this aspect of the model any clearer. The centerpiece of these is the AdultShop.com campaign created around its viral video, *Big Boy Briefs*, in July 2001, which serves to illustrate Goldsmith's point that "sex is a key motivator" (ibid., p. 7) in online message forwarding. Unfortunately, sex failed to appear as an influencing factor in Goldsmith's own survey of forwarding habits, evidence, perhaps, of unwillingness by even anonymous respondents to admit to such practices and yet one more indicator that quantitative market research methods suffer from some serious drawbacks. Indeed, Goldsmith quotes Amanda Cooper, head of marketing for the company, who suggests that it is precisely this reticence on behalf of the consumer that makes viral marketing particularly appropriate for AdultShop.com:

> "Viral marketing works well for AdultShop.com as the majority of people are more comfortable forwarding something humorous which is adult in nature online rather than admitting they were on our website or talking about it". (Amanda Cooper, quoted in Goldsmith, 2002, p. 80)

The *Big Boy Briefs* viral video (depicting the empowering effects of some comical pump-up underwear) contained a clickable weblink in the final frame that directed viewers on to a specifically designed landing page at the AdultShop.com site. Here, the marketing purpose of the video is to engender enough curiosity for the site through associating it with a fun attitude toward sex that viewers will want to take the next step of clicking on the link, as well as sending the video (or a link to it) on to friends. The problem with the AdultShop.com story is that it muddies the waters concerning the relationship between the marketing purpose of viral messages and the traditional advertising and PR that surrounds them. Importantly, the campaign did not consist only of a release of the viral video into the churning, hostile environment of the World Wide Web. Goldsmith is quite open in relaying the considerable integrated forces marshaled for the campaign: direct emails to the 30,000 strong customer database, web banner advertising, and emailing of the entire video to "friends and colleagues who expressed an interest" (ibid., p. 83). On top of this, and perhaps most telling of all, is the fact that the video was picked up by an assortment of international television shows that specialize in the airing of funny and bizarre ads and clips. The fact that the video was clearly amusing enough to garner such coverage speaks of its successful viral design, and certainly demonstrates the impressive saving in media buys that such pick-ups by television represent. But in the end, the "viral" campaign was driven by TV coverage (using traditional one-to-many broadcast models), traditional interruption advertising, and direct mail. Discussion of the actual viral spread of the video over the Web is conspicuous by its absence in Goldsmith's text.

Two other illustrations of the use of forwarding strategies, both using software solutions provided by U.S. company MindArrow, are given prominent space by Goldsmith. MindArrow (the transmission/injection metaphor implied by the company name is telling) has developed an application suite that enables marketers to place videos in emails that can be viewed without the need for particular media plug-ins or codecs to exist on the client-side. Marketers can therefore send rich, multimedia emails with sound, video, hyperlinks, and, importantly, tagging scripts that allow records to be generated of who clicked on what link, viewed what video, and who forwarded anything on. The two illustrations of this technology in action were a campaign directed at promoting a Britney Spears's single and a business-to-business emailing by Oracle advertising an e-business seminar series. Goldsmith provides no evidence for the success of the campaigns, simply quoting the company's statement that its MindArrow software registers a "27% pass-along or 'viral' effect" (ibid., p. 93). Which raises the question again of what the exact nature of the marketing use of the viral principle is. If the message is 'passed-along' is it ever interacted with? In the medical paradigm, a virus both infects a biological system so that it may grow within that system and is (unwittingly) 'passed along' by that system to others. But in a marketing paradigm if all that ever happens is that the virus is continually passed on from one person to another all that the marketer can be sure of is that there has been a vector of infection. Attention is focused away from whether the infected person actually gets sick or exhibits any symptoms. Yet (to continue the metaphor), making people sick is what the marketer needs to do. Essentially, viral marketing has reduced interaction to the consideration of an extended chain of transmission, a form of jerry-built broadcast where the medium is the entertainment-consuming masses. Even then, the detail provided in Goldsmiths AdultShop.com example implies that at their most 'successful', viral campaigns need to be incubated with the nurturing warmth of traditional advertising formats.

Both Goldsmith and Godin produce texts that are in thrall to the trope of exponential growth. The possibility that ideas can be spread across large target groups without outrageous media buys is a highly seductive construction yet the substance of their viral marketing discourse revolves around the repetitive use of powerful metaphors of growth and infection which are not fully theorized or explicated. The apparent successes of certain early examples of the viral paradigm have tended to have an overbearing effect upon the shape of the developing viral marketing discourse, acting as a canonical set of references which serve as discourse-sanctioned historical 'proof' of the viability of the approach. The iconic Hotmail narrative which is enthusiastically referenced by both Godin and Goldsmith (and is re-told in many instances of viral marketing promotion) is typical of this canon. Many writers start with the Hotmail story because it appears to be one of the most certain sources for the origin of the "viral marketing" phrase and easily lends itself to being framed as quantifiable proof of the success of the method. Justin Kirby provides a succinct version of the tale when he writes that Hotmail:

> "simply added a short line of promotional text to the bottom of very email message sent via their service, clocking up 12 million sing-ups within 18 months from a marketing spend of US$500 000". (Kirby, 2006, p. 90)

In a rather ambiguous section of their viral marketing literature review, Cruz and Fill (2008) comment on the popularity of "the Hotmail story", noting that it has "achieved nothing short of a worldwide plague" (ibid., p. 746), although it is unclear whether the plague they are referring to is the story or the use of Hotmail. Paul Marsden describes it as "the campaign that put *viral marketing* on the map and that helped Hotmail become the leading personal web-based email service provider", noting that its success hinged on "turning users of the service into brand advocates" (Marsden, 2006a, p. xxi). As Godin and many other commentators point out, it was one of the venture capitalists associated with Hotmail, Steve Juverstson, who "coined the term 'viral marketing' to describe the way the service grew" (Godin, 2000, p. 55). Like any good foundation narrative, however, there is room for a little individualizing contention and a number of authors, while still acknowledging the Hotmail campaign as the first major proof of concept, locate the point of absolute origin in different competing events. Goldsmith, for example, cites Justin Kirby's U.K. student union campaign against government grant cuts of 1994 which Kirby himself says he was inspired by his reading of Douglas Rushkoff's *Media Virus* text (which itself is heavily influenced by Dawkins' description of memetics, see Rushkoff, 1996). Elsewhere, Kirby has identified a 1989 *PCUser* magazine article as containing the "earliest known use of the term 'viral marketing'" (Kirby, 2006, p. 89). The Hotmail story generally exhibits an almost fetishistic hold over the discourse. One of the obvious features that makes the story so iconic is the impressive growth statistics involved: Numbers like 12 million sign-ups in 18 months are guaranteed to get anyone's attention and will inevitably be rhetorically used to justify the paradigm. But beyond the numbers, the Hotmail tale is the model trope for the viral approach because it illustrates the simplicity of the 'pass-along' dynamic. The single sentence hyperlink ('Get your free email at Hotmail') contained as a P.S. at the end of all emails sent from Hotmail appears to strongly imitate the (medical) virus by being a message within an unwitting container. Users of Hotmail are not generally conscious of the marketing hyperlink; they are focused on generating the content of their message and making sure that it gets sent. The Hotmail server adds the marketing message at the end of their text, just like a virus being passed on through blood, mucus, or any other biological medium. The Hotmail marketing message benefits from its association with a friend or acquaintance of the user, in a similar way that the virus benefits from its association with a carrier (and as Dawkins' selfish gene benefits from its survival machine). Furthermore, a Hotmail user is unlikely to send emails to just one person, but will instead communicate with many people. This is what makes the Hotmail story so persuasive as a rhetorical example—it demonstrates how the act of communication can make someone an *unwitting* source of infection. You do not wish to pass on a virus to someone else, you do it accidentally because you are not aware that your actions result in the infection of others. The Hotmail hyperlink piggy-backs onto your email message without your knowledge. You do not deliberately pass it along. From this perspective, the Hotmail story, while holding a canonical place in the foundation narrative of viral marketing, is actually highly *atypical* of common viral marketing theory and practice. All the other examples provided by Godin, Goldsmith, Marsden, Kirby, et al. are characterized by the attempt to engineer the conscious, deliberate passing along of a message. Consequently, the collections of 'viral marketing rules' that one finds endemic in the literature are all concerned with how to make your viral message entertaining, useful, easy to forward, attractive to the target audience, etc. None of these concerns are actually applicable to the Hotmail story because no one is *choosing* to send on the Hotmail hyperlink. A good example of the general unwillingness to accept this fundamental difference is provided by Dennis Pitta's article examining the viral strategy behind gydget.com (Pitta, 2008). Pitta follows Godin's lead in emphasizing the medical metaphor when defining viral marketing:

> In medical terms, viruses propagate by finding a susceptible host, and quietly replicating until they reach a critical mass to overwhelm the host. [. . .]. The critical element is that viruses do not provide their own resources for growth. They use the host's resources to multiply and in the right environment, they can grow exponentially. [. . .]. In marketing, the viral model takes the form of using a host and its resources to fuel the potential for exponential growth in a message's exposure and influence. Like viruses, such strategies take advantage of rapid multiplication to transmit a message to thousands. (ibid., p. 281)

Pitta appears to be suggesting here that a viral marketing scenario includes a host, the host's resources, and a message. It is the message which will "influence" and be transmitted to "thousands" and, therefore, we can say that Pitta sees the passing on of the marketing message to be the essence of viral marketing. Indeed, his definition of viral marketing is that it "describes any strategy that encourages individuals to pass on a marketing message to others" (ibid.). On this basis, gydget.com is built upon a convincing viral strategy—small software widgets (in the form of graphic windows depicting news and content for particular bands, sports teams, actors, etc.) which are offered freely to fans who can then upload them onto their own MySpace pages, blogs, and other social network sites for free. The windows offer a number of tabbed viewing choices (tour dates, music videos, match results, etc.) and also contain a button that viewers can click in order to load that gydget on to their own site or blog. A fan can thus act as an information source for her favorite act or team, relaying centrally-controlled content. The gydget system is particularly well integrated into MySpace (taking good advantage of the available API) and is able to reward those users who place the gydget on their pages by featuring them within the window as "friends" (a powerful incentive if you are a fan of the subject of the gydget). Pitta notes that political campaigns made good use of the technology during the 2008 U.S. presidential election, using them to provide "supporters with a way to show their affinity with the candidates" and adding that "anyone who clicked on a gydget became a voluntary target for information and promotion" (ibid., p. 282).

In his explanation of how gydget.com works, Pitta states that it followed the model of Hotmail, "one of the classic examples of viral marketing" (ibid.). Yet, as I have pointed out above, the Hotmail story characterizes the viral metaphor quite differently, in so far as the hyperlink to sign up for an account is a subtle, piggy-backing one that the user is not voluntarily and consciously displaying. Microsoft, who now owns the Hotmail service, continue the original tradition with their tag lines advertising their own communication services (Windows Live, at the time of writing) added to the bottom of outgoing emails. Blackberry and Apple phones, somewhat similarly, have used the original Hotmail model to include a "sent from my Blackberry" or "sent from my iPhone" auto-signature whenever users email from the integral mailing software on these mobiles (though in both of these cases the signature is visible to the user while they are composing their email and can be relatively easily deleted or substituted for a user-created one). The Hotmail model operates in a fundamentally different way to the straight implementation of digital word-of-mouth that gydget.com exemplifies. When I write an email from a Hotmail account I cannot see the tag that the service places at the end of my mail; the service uses my communication habits to spread knowledge about itself. My email message acts as the "host" and the Windows Live hyperlink is the virus that insinuates itself within my message and feeds off its familiarity or trustworthiness to the addressee. However, the gydget is voluntarily added by the consumer to their own website. Furthermore, the consumer is quite aware of how the gydget works and what content the various buttons and links lead to because they themselves have already experienced using it (their satisfaction with this content is, after all, one of the reasons they will have chosen to place it in their own page). The "host", presumably, is the user's web page and the virus is the gydget. But, if this is the case, the logic of the viral metaphor immediately breaks down. Nothing is being 'quietly replicated'. The gydget is designed to attract attention to itself and persuade the surfer to 'take it home'—it's a cute puppy not a virus. Another possibility is that the gydget window on the fan's web page is the "host" and the virus is the marketing message it contains, in other words, persuasive content. This, however, is not a supportable interpretation because, once more, the whole gydget ecosystem works transparently, in the clear light of day. The gydget contains content that the fan *wants* to know about and is happy to broadcast. In fact, the communication model that informs this enterprise can be thought of as broadcast relay with no barrier to entry, or sponsored syndication of news for enthusiasts. Strangely, the model is almost anti-viral in its longer term implications in that the gydget only makes sense if there are people who do not have access to the information that it broadcasts. If everyone has a gydget for the same band, then no one is going to need the information that the gydget provides on other people's pages.

The point of the above analysis is not to make a case for what might be the 'correct' use of the term 'viral marketing'. We create the realities we inhabit through our use of language. Consequently, when someone uses the term 'viral marketing' it reflects something of the way that she is constructing her world. My interest here is in the examination of the different ways the virus metaphor is used rhetorically within marketing discourses and how those uses, those constructing re-presentations, reveal the models of communicative interaction informing them. The viral metaphor predicates a way of observing customer communities as networks of carriers. Godin's choice of the word "hive" is striking in this respect in that it links the viral metaphor with the metaphor of the apiary. The aspect of the life of bees that Godin's metaphor carries over into the discussion of customer communities is the way in which these insects are noted for their communication habits, the bee dance through which a successful explorer can inform the rest of its hive of the whereabouts of newly discovered pollen sources. The bee hive is a closely organized social group with clearly defined castes and roles—and popular human discourse concerning the place of communication in the hive is centered around the trope of dance patterns performed by individuals broadcasting targeting information to the mass of the group. In other words, the way we tend to talk about bee communication in the hive is firmly rooted in our own transmission metaphors for our own communication. Communication in the bee hive is utilized as an illustrative parallel for word-of-mouth in human groups and implies that messages are transmitted by one person to a number of people within a group, and this message can then be relayed (through exact imitation) to others until the whole hive is cognizant of the location of the new target. The connection to the viral metaphor lies in the trope of message replication; the virus replicates itself, infecting an exponentially growing group of hosts just as the message danced by the bees spreads across the hive. Yet, there is a substantive difference between the two metaphors that is elided in the subtle rhetorical coupling of the two figurations in Godin's discourse. The bees *dance* a message, the virus *is* the message. The difference lies in the framing of *agency*. As I have shown above, there is a discomfort amongst viral marketing writers (of both the academic and popular persuasion) with the relationship between message, host, and virus. Using the virus as a metaphor for a marketing message implies that the viral message is inserted within an unwitting host who passes it along by accident. In such a scenario the host is unaware that they have been recruited by the virus. In the hive metaphor, however, the bee is very much a conscious propagator of information—and in marketing terms, therefore, the consumer would be a willing brand advocate, relaying the marketing message to groups who may then further the spread of that message through imitation of the brand advocate's discourse. The Hotmail story falls into the logic of the viral metaphor, while most other viral marketing campaigns (like, for example, those implemented through gydget.com) follow the logic of the hive communication metaphor. Essentially, word-of-mouth marketing is more instructively and logically compared to the communication system of the bee hive than it is to the growth of an infecting virus. Why, then, has the virus metaphor had more 'stickiness'? One of the obvious reasons is its comparative attractiveness to the marketing population: Thinking of your prospects as vanguard bees who are going to dance your message across their hive is more of a difficult sell than the image of the viral marketer hunched over the test tubes in the marketing lab preparing a devious little bug that once unleashed upon the population will spread into an epidemic all under its own steam. The viral metaphor promises the advantage of control—you will design the virus and it will go and behave in the way that you have designed it to. The patterns danced by the bees, of course, are *out* of your control: Once you have exposed them to the first dance, its possible evolution via the vagaries of human imitation cannot be managed by you. The viral metaphor, then, imagines control squarely in the hands of the marketer, who positions herself as the designer of the course of infection, perfecting the message until it can be released to patient zero and do its creator's bidding. Godin's mixed metaphor blending of the "hive" and the "sneezers" manifests the desire to have the best of both illustrative parallels. His discourse constructs an understanding of digital word-of-mouth that places agency firmly in the hands of the marketer, outlining the customer as a passive patient succumbing to the virulent marketing message. Communities, for Godin, are groups of pattern imitators (the hive) but, in a rhetorical move that decreases the model's vulnerability to (even random) mutation of the pattern, Godin's hive members are not sketched as imitators but rather as infected (passive) victims of the sneezers.

To call a campaign an example of viral marketing is a strategic, rhetorical decision. When a marketing practitioner does so during a pitch to a client, or when a marketing academic does so in an article for a refereed scholarly journal, they are choosing to adopt the metaphor for a rhetorical purpose. The finding that most practitioners appear to define viral marketing as being the online version of Word-of-Mouth marketing (Cruz & Fill, 2008, p. 749) means that the choice to refer to it in discourse as *viral* rather than WoM indicates a motivation to differentiate viral practices from other, non-digital versions of the same approach. Given that I have argued that the use of the viral metaphor reflects a discourse paradigm of control and management, it might be fair to say that the rhetorical choice to adopt the phrase into one's discourse reflects a positioning of the digital communities as controllable by the marketer. In other words, some form of terminological differentiation is needed to rhetorically stress the marketer's ability to control something that otherwise appears to resist control. Online customer communities represent a challenge to the marketing management paradigm because they demonstrate how self-organized groupings can develop around the sharing of opinion and information concerning product categories, brands, or related issues. The marketing management paradigm is one based upon assumptions of control, but emergent online communities either resist marketing control or have evolved in order to discuss issues outside a marketing frame (for example, as enthusiasts, fans, or expert users). The trope of apocalyptic crisis that has been haunting marketing discourse recently has many sources (as the essays in Brown, Bell, & Carson, 1998, suggest), but one of the most consistent manifestations of the figure is connected with the fear that consumer use of the Internet is in some way threatening to disconnect marketing practitioners from prospects and customers. Word-of-mouth within online communities can render highly expensive and minutely managed marketing campaigns impotent. Kylie Jarrett (2003) summarizes the source of the fear in the following way:

> Social networks can be used to quickly disseminate negative and potentially damaging information. Thus, despite often intense loyalty to a brand, the interrelationship and camaraderie of consumption community members can lead them to be quick to organize and challenge a company's practice deemed inappropriate or counter to consumer desire. (Jarrett, 2003, p. 338)

The rhetorical power of viral marketing lies in its seductive ability to *over*power the empowered online consumer. It is no accident that Goldsmith, for example, devotes a large section of his opening chapter to reproducing the long email exchange between "Jonah Peretti" and the Nike iD sales representative office. The emails, detailing Peretti's attempts to get Nike to stitch the word "SWEATSHOP" on to his sneakers as part of the iD personalization process, are described by Goldsmith as "potentially extremely damaging to Nike" (Goldsmith, 2002, p. 6). The reprinting of the email exchange takes up five complete pages of Goldsmith's short book. Furthermore, this example of online campaigning against a major corporation is showcased before any case study of viral marketing has even been mentioned. The argumentative logic is clear: Marketers and managers need to listen to what Goldsmith has to say because word-of-mouth on the Internet has the potential to cause great harm to their business. Accordingly, viral marketing is a counterstrike, a rhetorical attempt to regain control and dominate communication within the marketspace. Rhetorical, because the construction of the viral trope is based upon the power of metaphor to sway the judgment of clients, agencies, and marketers themselves. For the seductive power of the viral metaphor is not just something that is used to convince the client that this marketing lark still has potency in the face of the Facebook generation, but it is also, vitally, a tool of *self*-conviction, promoting the mythos of continued control within the ranks of marketing management practitioners and theoreticians.

To illustrate the way in which practitioner and theoretician collude in the construction of this matrix of affirmations, I would like to work through a case study published in a peer-reviewed, academic journal, the *Journal of Interactive Marketing*, examining strategies implemented in the early viral marketing efforts of the Web service Plaxo (Kalyanam, McIntyre, & Masonis, 2007). I should initially point out that one of the paper's co-authors, J. Todd Masonis, is founder and vice-president at Plaxo Inc., while the other two authors are academics at Santa Clara University. This coupling of academic and practitioner voices can be considered a key to producing a "less fragmented understanding" of marketing experience (to adapt Stephanie O'Donohoe's judgment of this trend in advertising research, O'Donohoe, 1998, p. 214). It does also, however, point to a way in which practitioners and academics can mutually support each other's discourses.

Plaxo can be thought of as a form of contact database aggregator. It aids users in updating the contact details of everyone contained across their (often multiple) digital address books. So, for instance, it can help me aggregate all of my Outlook, Hotmail, and Gmail contacts and make sure that they have my very latest details. The Plaxo service automates the rather laborious task of emailing everyone in my different address book databases and informing them of my current contact details and asking them to supply their own. The service has obvious benefits in a highly dynamic business environment where people might be changing their employers, work details, and home addresses frequently and yet need to keep in touch with, and available to, a large network of past colleagues, associates, friends, and acquaintances. In their opening paragraph, Kalyanam et al. state that the Plaxo experience

> shows how continuous adaptive experimentation focused on a viral marketing concept generated a tight feedback loop with its customers. This practice enabled the company to go beyond a tipping point of customer adoption into spiraling growth. (Kalyanam et al., 2007, p. 73)

The integration of disparate terminologies and discourse frames demonstrated in this passage is typical of the way in which the viral marketing metaphor is spliced into marketing discourse. "Adaptive experimentation", the authors note, is a term usually used to designate the process by which management decisions are continually tested for their efficacy upon the market. In its adoption of the term "adaptive", of course, it references the mechanism of Darwinian evolution by natural selection (see Darwin, 1985, p. 114, for the original context) which in turn leads us on to the biological/medical frame of the viral metaphor. Interwoven into the evolutionary rhetoric is the figure of the feedback loop (the 'tightness' of which is necessarily moot), invoking the cybernetic paradigm of control (and its biological/mechanistic origins). Finally, the authors clearly reference Malcolm Gladwell's (2002) "tipping point" trope which is itself based upon a metaphorical instantiation of the dynamics of epidemics. "Spiraling growth", as a metaphorical construction, refers to yet another 'natural' pattern of increase, namely the vortex (or, perhaps more likely, the thermal-following rise of birds). The passage quoted above, then, can be seen to contain metaphors constructed predominantly from natural vehicles or scientific disciplines which analyze natural systems. The metaphors speak of the human harnessing of the natural power of exponential growth. The use of the 'adaptive' frame confers a sense of evolutionary law to such harnessing; it is noticeable that the authors suggest that adaptive experimentation 'generates' a feedback loop, implying that the adaptive orientation produces or causes the growth of a feedback loop, whereas the adaptive experimentation methodology is premised upon the initial construction of reliable feedback loops (there can be no experimentation without the establishment of the means of observation and measurement). The overall effect of this opening paragraph is to rhetorically indicate that the case study will display an evolutionarily inevitable mastery of natural forces of exponential growth.

Kalyanam et al. continue by sketching the course of the first viral marketing campaign for the product which, while initially successful, resulted in some problematic consumer reactions. The point that I would like to pick up on regarding this section of exposition is the way in which it sets up the expectations of a critique of viral marketing while actually reinforcing its basic claims. The authors open with a declaration that viral marketing is a "seductive concept" (ibid.) which appears to set up the possibility that marketers might be being attracted to an idea which has little substance and only surface glamour. Defining the strategy as an "Internet adaptation" of word-of-mouth, the authors refer back to their referencing of "adaptive experimentation" in the introduction. Agency is, once more, a rhetorical issue in this construction; Kalyanam et al. cast the Internet as the source of the adaptation (rather than a human or group of humans), strengthening the evolutionary frame of their discourse and underlining the natural power of the viral strategy. They move on to make ritual obeisance to the Hotmail story and the increasing use of viral marketing by Fortune 500 companies but then appear to put a damper on everything by stating that "most viral efforts are likely to fail" because (and they appear to quote Gladwell although the reference is missing from the article's bibliography) they fail "to reach a point of 'internal combustion'". Again, the mixing of metaphors strengthens the connotations of human mastery of natural forces and further implies that the authors will be able to supply us with the specifications to achieve this dominance for ourselves. Indeed, this is more explicitly offered in the authors' claim that, on being faced with a troubling decrease in membership uptake, Plaxo implemented a "viral growth equation concept" that enabled them to dramatically recover from this downturn. Once more underlining the application of evolutionary theory to the management of their viral strategy, Kalyanam et al. comment that the use of "experimentation and natural selection" had a positive impact upon the rate of viral growth. Interestingly, they describe this as a "highly reasoned" approach, a comment which connects the metaphors of evolution and biological growth with a characterization of human logic and rationality, and so once more suggests the human intellectual domination of natural forces. Evolution is not a process that we are part of but rather it is an algorithm that we may *direct* or, to use a more apposite term, *manage*.

The Plaxo case study addresses two separate challenges to the success of the company's viral marketing strategy. The first is the decline in sign-ups that followed the initial growth spurt and the second is the result of Plaxo's solution to this decrease in demand which produced the desired target of 5,000 new members a day but, as a by-product, began to foster online suspicions that the company was responsible for privacy invasions and spam messaging. The authors choose to represent this second problem in a telling way; they write that Plaxo's growth had become "like the myth of the Ebola virus". The authors compare Plaxo's growth with that of Ebola because that virus is apparently so deadly that it threatens its own survival by killing off all available hosts. The choice of the word "myth" here is startling, particularly given that Kalyanam et al. then later refer to this pattern of Ebola epidemics in entirely factual terms (Kalyanam et al., 2007, p, 81). In this context, writing of the Ebola 'myth' carries its own memetic connotations—our popular knowledge of the course of Ebola infections is inculcated in us through our attention to mass media coverage relaying bizarre and horrific stories from far away places. Ebola is a virus but it is also a meme. When Kalyanam et al. refer to the "myth of the Ebola virus" they are reminding us of the constructed nature of our knowledge of 'Ebola', the way in which such constructions are relayed via media, and also the far-reaching influence of the 'virus' metaphor. It is an almost entirely isolated moment of reflexivity in the article, however, and, as I have already noted, effectively recanted in the later stages of the paper where the self-destructive virulence of Ebola is afforded full reality status. Perhaps this instance of reflexivity is an unintentional slip or an artifact of earlier, more critical, framings present in the collaborative work (even solo scholarly articles being palimpsests of many drafts that reflect the history of the text's journey toward final editorial acceptance). Its embattled presence in the article, however, serves to remind the reader of the way in which the *constructed* nature of the viral metaphor is denied by more dominant marketing discourses. The key word in Kalyanam et al.'s expository use of the Ebola analogy is "aggression". The phrasing, 'aggressive infection', is a common medical metaphor[1] which speaks of infections as if they had emotional registers which we could, as humans, relate to. When Kalyanam at al. explain that the Ebola virus "kills off its host too quickly" (ibid., p. 81) they are preparing the rhetorical frame for a further extension of the virus marketing metaphor to include this medical metaphor which transfers human emotion to the virus. Thus, they observe that the "viral engine

can be too aggressive and stimulate too many outgoing e-mails" (ibid.),
going on to relate that a principle element of the solution Plaxo instituted
to address this problem was "to make the contact wizard less aggressive"
(ibid., p. 83). Again, the mixing of viral and mechanical metaphors although
potentially confusing the argumentative integrity of the discourse actually
helps to strengthen the presence of the marketing premises of control and
management. The marketing virus is afforded the status of ideal cyborg—
half biological, half mechanical, totally under control. The aggressiveness
of the Plaxo virus is presented as an initial design flaw that is then able to
be selected *out* of its evolutionary growth. The Plaxo marketing department is portrayed in terms of a laboratory, using "a very data-driven, adaptive-experimentation approach to select among various versions of product
features" (ibid., p. 81). Plaxo grows the virus, observes its performance in
the marketing environment and then selects those features which need to
be bred in or bred out of later generations. They "tinker" with "natural
selection" (ibid., p. 78). And like all good (mediated) scientists they have
a formula written on the blackboard. The "viral equation" can be used to
"diagnose and improve the health of the viral engine" (ibid., p. 84) (yet
more demonstration of the authors' cyborgization of the viral metaphor)
and frames the adaptive-experimentation approach of the Plaxo team. The
viral equation may be summarized as: Viral growth equals the number of
update requests sent out by exiting Plaxo users multiplied by the conver-
sion rate of those requests. The viral growth equation gives the authors the
opportunity to portray the evolutionary selection procedures practiced at
the company in highly quantifiable terms, replete with appropriate graphs
and all the other rhetorical accouterments of empirical investigation. The
overall effect of such "data-driven" artifacts is to construct the impression
of managed, scientific work. Indeed, one of the conclusions that Kalyanam
et al. offer is that their study "suggests that viral marketing is hard work"
(ibid., p. 83) and that its success may depend upon "active management"
(ibid.), a finding which they note brings them in accordance with Godin's
viral methodology. The form of "active management" described by the
authors is one clearly portrayed as being a hybridization of methods from
mechanical engineering (required by the "viral engine") and evolutionary
biology. The resulting cyborgization of the marketing virus reflecting the
desire to present such a hybrid as amenable to more detailed human articu-
lation and control.

The final peculiarity of metaphor in the Plaxo case study is the use of the
repeated use of the phrase "natural selection". Darwin's *Origin of Species*
itself contains a large amount of analysis dedicated to the phenomenon of
"variation under domestication" (Darwin, 1985, p. 71) which is clearly and
powerfully contrasted with variation under nature. Indeed, the structure
of Darwin's argument for the existence of the process of evolution is based
upon the initial evidence to be found in humanity's efforts over centuries
to manage the form of its domesticated animals and crops. It is only after

he has marshaled a considerable volume of evidence for the powerful effect of witting and unwitting human selection of variation that Darwin then moves on to the (culturally) more difficult ground of proving that a similar force of selection operates in the natural world. In other words, there is, right at the root of the Darwinian explication of the mechanism of selection, a distinction between human-directed, artificial, selection and natural selection. Given the existence of this distinction, and its importance in the structure of the argumentative case for evolution, what meaning is constructed through the application of the term "natural selection" to the obviously human-directed management of a marketing virus? Given that I have been attempting to demonstrate the significant presence in the Plaxo case study of metaphors and other constructions that convey the implication of human control over nature, it seems curious that the authors would *not* seize the opportunity to underline this pattern through reference to appropriate terminology legitimized by such reputable precedent. Of course, Darwin's choice of terminology is perhaps not very 'sexy' to modern marketing and scholarly ears; the word 'domestication' would probably not set the heart of any copywriter aflutter with excitement. The phrase "artificial selection", rather like 'artificial sweetener', does not convey the richness, the wildness, the power, the *rightness* that "natural selection" does. The rhetorical power of the central medical/biological metaphor of viral marketing lies in its promise of a form of natural, unstoppable inevitability and it is just this sense of a 'force of nature' that the phrase "natural selection" helps to produce. It is indicative, therefore, of a tension in viral marketing discourse between the metaphorical indexing of natural and artificial processes.

With the Plaxo case study, Kalyanam et al. allow us to observe the way in which practitioners and academics can together contribute to the construction of a rich rhetorical discourse for viral marketing that exemplifies the key metaphors generated through the irritation present at the interface between nature and artifice. Irrespective of the level of tension between these two fields of metaphor, however, is the central, continuing presence of the trope of control. The practitioner and academic pitching of viral marketing offers it as a cyborg solution to the issue of community control. The apparently increasing sense that advertisers have that "viral marketing is difficult to execute successfully and measure adequately" (Ferguson, 2008, p. 181) means that effective pitching of the strategy requires both quantitative assurances and a strong rhetorically-derived sense of *rightness* and power. The controlled harnessing of natural forces of growth to the job of managing independent and unpredictable communities is a seductive stream of discourse that carries with it an undeniable trace of revenge. It cannot be forgotten that, in the end, the viral metaphor is an aggressive attack upon the supposedly empowered communities of the Internet. A virus sickens the host, takes advantage of the host, and perhaps even kills the host. Viral marketing initially targets the influential voices of a community in order to more easily make the rest of the group succumb. As we have seen with Godin's language of inducements, though, those initial carriers of the virus stand to benefit at the expense of those further down the line. Procter & Gamble's Vocalpoint and Tremor programs (Ferguson, 2008) reward vanguard armies of mothers and teens respectively with discount coupons, advance product information and promotions in return for their advocacy within their communities. The dynamic is that of turning the community against itself, splitting it up into those who are rewarded advocates and those who are the receivers of the inducement-generated evangelism. Importantly, the basic model of viral marketing countenances no possibility of interaction in the sense of the virus mutating and traveling back to the laboratory. The infection of the marketer is a trope that is entirely absent from the literature (whether practitioner- or academic-focused). It is indeed curious that viral marketing (and its alter-ego, word-of-mouth) has been so enthusiastically embraced in a marketing environment that appears to be predominantly concerned with the need for the creation of interactive relationships between consumers and producers. Viral marketing and word-of-mouth do not pretend to institute dialogs between advertisers and consumers about brands or products; the communication that is envisaged is one-way in the sense that a missile payload is designed to be one-way.

TWO-STEP, ONE-STEP, OR SAME-OLD STEP?

The place of rewarded brand advocates ("sneezers" in Godin's terms) across the many published promotions of viral marketing raises the question of the relationship between the Katz and Lazarsfeld "two-step flow of communication" and the marketing communication paradigms that cluster around the viral model. Katz and Lazarsfeld (1955) held that although mass media messages were aimed at mass audiences they were in fact further mediated by opinion leaders within small social groupings who would explain, frame, and contextualize them. This meant, in their analysis, that communities were protected from outright control and manipulation by the media because all media messages were essentially subject to this re-interpretation. Social interaction in small groups leads to the fragmentation and differentiation of mass media messages as a variety of opinion leaders from different classes, backgrounds, cultural, and political interests filter the original through their own re-telling and commentary. The two-step flow of communication, while optimistically highlighting the limitations of mass media domination of popular knowledge and opinion, also pointed to the pervasive way in which mass media content infiltrated and even set the agenda for much contemporary interpersonal communication. Even when physically away from the radio or newspaper, people were still talking about the messages that they carried. Much of Paul Lazarsfeld's research work was carried out within the context of his Bureau of Applied Research at Columbia University. And much of that research was funded by advertisers searching for more effective market research instruments[2]. Indeed, the obvious immediate lessons from Katz and Lazarsfeld's research lead to the realization in both political and marketing communication arenas that a more nuanced understanding of what people were saying around the water cooler could be vital for the planning of more successful and predictable campaigns. Furthermore, an obvious implication of the two-step flow of communication is that effective political and marketing communication should concern itself with the targeting, education, and use of those opinion leaders who mediate the mass media messages in interpersonal interactions. In order to prevent the amplification of variety in the transmitted message, careful control of opinion leaders is needed. Although Lazarsfeld himself was a socialist and was instrumental in finding the Frankfurt School of critical theory an American home, it has been noted that much of the research he conducted at Columbia "provided techniques for more effective psychological manipulation and exploitation of people" and the advances in survey methods he was responsible for "in the long run have had debatable effects on popular democracy" (Heims, 1991, p. 189). His appearances at the first six Macy cybernetics conferences were motivated predominantly by a desire to "improve his analysis of the statistical data" generated at the Bureau of Applied Research. Heims, a historian of the Macy conferences, notes that the only cybernetic (rather than statistical) approaches that Lazarsfeld seemed to apply in his own work were those derived from the talks given by Alex Bavelas, a psychologist working with statistical modeling of small group interactions, and which emerge in the 1955 text propounding the two-step flow of communication (Heims, 1991, p. 193). My point here is not to argue for some form of uninterrupted historical chain of influence from the Macy cybernetic conferences to the two-step perspective. Rather, it is to contextualize the two-step flow of communication within the contemporary cybernetic and marketing searches for a greater accuracy of measurement and greater control of message fidelity. While Katz and Lazarsfeld's thesis elevated the perception of the community group's power of message interpretation, it paved the way for the systematic attempt to control message fragmentation (and appropriation) through a far more large scale implementation of the principle of feedback-driven control. As Bennett and Manheim (2006) observe, Katz and Lazarsfeld's research "led communicators to incorporate the study of opinion dynamics with that of message effects in developing their art" and therefore was directly responsible for the "heavy reliance we see today on integrated programs of focus group research and public opinion polling in any effort at mass political persuasion" (ibid., p. 214). Despite significant critiques almost from its inception (one thinks of the work of fellow Columbia faculty member, C. Wright Mills [1956], who came to the exact opposite conclusions to Katz and Lazarsfeld, as well as a particularly forthright paper from Todd Gitlin [1978]) the two-step flow of communication became part of the dominant model of communication, helping to reinforce the re-emphasis, from the early 1950s onwards, of the importance of varie-gated social groupings in the understanding of mass media effects, and so ensuring that the "communal and social group character of audiences was restored to conceptual prominence" (McQuail, 2000, p. 362).

Viewed from the perspective of the two-step flow of communication, it becomes difficult to discern exactly what is so new or groundbreaking in the basic communication practices of viral marketing. The use of rewarded brand advocates is at least as old as the Tupperware Home Parties Cor-poration and Avon business models (see Cialdini, 2001) and can easily be extended back to before Katz and Lazarsfeld with the U.S. government's use of the "four minute men" (Ewen, 1996). Godin's "sneezers", Burson-Marstella's "e-fluentials", the "new influencers" of Gillin's blogosphere, the assumption that informs such strategic differentiations between thought-leaders and thought-followers within consumer communities is that opin-ion is formed through the communication dynamics within groups and this is itself a manifestation of the two-step flow of communication paradigm. Viral marketing, therefore, is an instance of the strategic re-fashioning of concepts endemic to the marketing industry since at least the 1950s. There is, however, an important *addition* (or perhaps, spin) to the viral marketing formulation of the two-step model of influence. To appreciate the nature of this spin it will help to briefly consider an alternative proposition: the one-step flow of communication.

Bennett and Manheim have recently argued that, for current networked societies, a one-step flow of communication is a far more appropriate model for audiences who "have assumed more responsibility for managing their own emotional and cognitive realities, often apart from group influence pro-cesses" (Bennett & Manheim, 2006, p. 218). They note that the increasing use of the sort of sophisticated data mining techniques that I have discussed in Chapter 4, has enabled marketers to tailor messages far more effectively to individuals and so ensure that their messages arrive without falling prey to mediated social interpretation. The one-step flow of communication, consequently, describes direct media effect on audiences. Bennett and Man-heim contextualize their argument for the increasing relevance of a direct media effects model by calling attention to the increasing fragmentation of social order in contemporary societies which, they assert, is answered by "increasing individuation in the delivery and reception of information" (ibid., p. 221). The shift away from the consumption of traditional mass media and toward the use of online communication, they reason, mirrors a move toward the construction of small, homogenized audience segmenta-tions who, through the application of data mining, can be targeted by nar-rowcasts of maximum individual relevance. There is therefore no need for consumers to consider their purchasing options through recourse to inter-action within a small social grouping. Bennett and Manheim point to the many formalized social groupings of 1950s and 1960s American society (bowling leagues, veterans associations, pseudo-Masonic lodges, etc.) and concede that the two-step flow of communication is appropriate for such clearly ordered and pluralistic societies. However, in the current online world, they argue, media corporations, marketers, and political campaigners are able to both use technology to reach their micro-segmented-audiences directly and take advantage of the fragmentation and individuation of social order to make sure that their message is not contextualized by out-of-their-control social interactions.

As I will discuss in a later section of this chapter, there are many reasons to question the logical grounds for the one-step flow perspective when so many implementations of Web 2.0 technologies ostensibly revolve around community creation, opinion-leading, and opinion-sharing. However, what I would like to dwell on a little at this point is the idea that the discourses promoting viral marketing represent the fusion of two-step and one-step flow paradigms. The viral metaphor itself implies a one-step flow of communication in the sense that the marketing message is transmitted by the marketer out into the hive where it repeatedly infects consumers. The virus does not mutate—it remains always true to the original design of the marketer and therefore operates in the same way with the same effect. The constant repetition of the same infection pattern cannot result in a multi-step flow of communication precisely because nothing ever changes. The two-step flow of communication posits message mutation as it is represented and contextualized within-group interaction. If the message does not change, but is simply relayed, then the implicit dynamic of Katz and Lazarsfeld's two-step flow is missing: The audience is conceived of as an atomistic, undifferentiated mass with the virus leaping from one atom to the next. On the other hand, the practical application of viral marketing theory revolves around the presence of advocates (sneezers, e-fluentials, etc.) who are chosen for their key, persuasive position within a group. This aspect demonstrates the two-step flow perspective as it does indeed differentiate between members of a group, placing the "influentials" (to use Katz and Lazarsfeld's original term) in an intermediary position between the marketer and the majority of targeted consumers. The message, although designed by the marketer, is mutated by its re-presentation by the influencers; their advocacy adds something to the message that was not there before (credibility, coolness, attractiveness). I must emphasize here that I am not proposing that there are two different types of viral marketing predicated by the two different models of the flow of communication. Rather, I am pointing out that the rhetoric of viral marketing, which is used to explain and promote the use of the strategy to marketing practitioners, marketing academics, as well as clients, combines the two different flow paradigms. The biological/medical metaphor promotes the impression that the medium of transmission is only a carrier, a passive relay, for the virus whereas the reliance on influencer strategies characterizes the medium as the activating key to infection. Furthermore, the two paradigms have implications for the status of the message. In the biological/medical metaphor, the message is active: Exposure to the virus leads to infection because the virus is looking for the opportunity to infect (hence the connotations of the word, 'virulent'). In the influencer section of the viral marketing model, however, the message gains persuasive power, infecting power, depending on who is presenting it (hence the gradation of sneezers in Godin's methodology). Consequently, one either sees the message as primary or one sees the influencer as primary. The biological/medical metaphor promotes the construction of messages which can stand on their own, which have sufficient impact to lead to indiscriminate, exponential broadcasting and which will sit around on YouTube for years to come, waiting for the next casual viewer in search of something interesting to watch. The influencer perspective, however, sees the message as subordinate—there is no need to construct a message which will stand on its own, be useful (or entertaining, or attractive) enough to be passed on, because it is the persuasive status of the re-presenting advocate that is the reason for the growth of infection in a community. Indeed, Godin's insistence on the importance of offering inducements to advocates is an obvious sign that the message is not intrinsically worthy of repetition.

The difference between the two perspectives is indicative of the gap between what we might think of as a memetic approach and a word-of-mouth approach. Memetics, as we have seen above in Dawkins' highly anthropomorphic portrayal of the genetic and memetic replicators, tends to place agency firmly in the (personified) hands of the idea, the meme. Memes get passed on, the dominant memetics discourse goes, due to the comparative fitness of their characteristics; some memes, therefore, do not reproduce successfully enough and fade from memory, passing out of cultural (or sub-cultural) use. Susan Blackmore, perhaps the most influential of the radical memetics theorists, argues that in order to fruitfully understand the way in which memetics can explain human cultural growth and diversity, it is essential to take "the meme's eye view" (Blackmore, 2003, p. 25). Blackmore's theory, very much in line with Dawkins's initial formulation, portrays the meme as a replicating entity that uses humans in order to survive and reproduce. Indeed, she posits that memes are behind the course of evolution of the human brain:

> This is essentially the basis of the memetic drive. Memes compete with each other to be copied and the winners change the environment in which genes are selected. In this way, memes force genes to create a brain that is capable of selecting from the currently successful memes. (ibid., p. 32)

The memetic drive, according to Blackmore, has managed in many areas to direct the shape of human genetic evolution (brain size, for example) and is directly responsible for the richness of human language, because "the function of language is to spread memes" (ibid., p. 33). My point here is not to work through the details of Blackmore's memetic theory, but rather to provide an example of the way in which the memetic approach tends to place agency firmly within the meme. While there are scholars within the study of memetics who reject this position and instead argue for the view that it is the "memetic agent", i.e., the individual human, who is responsible for the replication of the meme (see Conte, 2003), the prevailing view remains that inspired by Dawkins's vision of the idea with a life of its own. This approach is also evident in the way that longtime Web users talk of "Internet memes", neologisms, phrases, and practices that are not spread through a prepped network of advocates but rather seem to appear very quickly as common usage amongst large online subcultures[3]. Many such memes originate as phrases, images, or links on online forums rather than being the subject of forwarded emails and therefore their method of transmission, or infection, represents a significant broadening of the typical viral marketing paradigm. You might, for example, come upon a forum post that uses an apparently nonsensical or inappropriate phrase and put it down to a spelling error, or the fragmented, inarticulate personality of the poster. But then you find another post, by someone else, with the same phrase. So, now you begin to think about its meaning, you Google it and find that it refers to the bad English translation of a line spoken by a character in an *anime* popular last year. Alternatively, of course, maybe you recognized the line right away. Your own use, your imitation, of the phrase will then depend on a number of variables but what is certain is that a few of these memes leap out of the forums and are adopted by far larger communities.

As Paul Marsden (1998) has pointed out, the sudden exponential growth across cultures or sub-cultures of particular behavior or attitudes has been examined through epidemiological analogy since the late 19th century. The spate of imitative suicides that rushed across Europe following the publication of Goethe's *The Sorrows of Young Werther* has often been used as the prime exemplar of such behavior (Cialdini, 2001; Marsden, 1998). Marsden's early work has sought to fuse data from the area of psychological research covering these flash trends, known as social contagion research, with the theory of memetics in order to try and integrate a unified social epidemiological paradigm based upon an evolutionary model. Importantly, Marsden is one of the very few people who bridges the gap between 'strict', social sciences-grounded, empirical memetics research, and marketing practitioner implementations of the viral paradigm. Publishing in both the social contagion/memetics and viral marketing fields, Marsden holds a faculty position at the London School of Economics but also runs a marketing consultancy specializing in the practical applications of his research. His (2006b) account of the current direction in which his own consultancy work is moving constitutes the opening chapter in the collection of essays on connected marketing Marsden edited with Justin Kirby. It provides a number of interesting insights into the connection between the viral metaphor, the word-of-mouth paradigm, and the two-step flow of communication.

Marsden's chapter concerns "seeding trials", which he defines as "targeted sampling with opinion leaders, conducted in the name of research" (ibid., p. 3). The basic principle behind the "seeding trial" is an application of the "Hawthorne Effect" discovered by a group of Harvard Business School researchers under the leadership of Elton Mayo (see Mayo, 1933). The Harvard team discovered that when they involved workers at a Western Electric plant in Hawthorne in trials of new organizational processes and working environments productivity amongst the trial groups invariably increased, no matter what variable the actual trial was testing for. The team's conclusion, known as the Hawthorne Effect, was that involving people in trials gave them a sense of being valued and therefore led to them feeling generally more positive toward their work and working environment during the trial. The act of conducting a research trial, in other words, had a 'positive' effect on the subjects used in the research trial. Marsden describes how the Hawthorne Effect can be used in order to turn "opinion-leading target buyers into product service evangelists" (Marsden, 2006b, p. 6). A "seed trial" offers a product or service to a limited group of people before it is released to the larger target market; the trial group, as a result of the Hawthorne Effect, displays a heightened positive response to, and consequent advocacy of, the product. In leading into a discussion of the clear link this practice has to the Katz and Lazarsfeld two-step flow mode, Marsden downplays the viral connotations of this marketing practice by referring in a rhetorically marginalizing way to Malcolm Gladwell's (2002) *Tipping Point* and its influential use of the epidemic analogy. Marsden writes:

> Although Gladwell uses the language and jargon of epidemiology to unpack the concept of opinion leadership, the idea behind the Law of the Few is an established business truth dating back to the 1940s. (Marsden, 2006b, p. 7)

The use of the word "jargon", with its negative connotations of obfuscation, to refer to something that could just as easily, but more positively, be described as 'language' or 'terminology' is a direct rhetorical attempt to dismiss the viral frame around Gladwell's idea and, indeed, the whole association of viral marketing with the methodology informing "seeding trials". Marsden only uses the word "viral" at one point in the whole chapter, when he uses it to describe the way in which Google enabled trial users of Gmail to further invite their friends into the trial, noting that "this 'snowball' or 'viral' recruitment enhanced the Hawthorne Effect" (ibid., p. 12). In this usage, the descriptive aptness of the viral metaphor is again deflated by using it alongside another common metaphor for exponential dynamism. In his introduction to the *Connected Marketing* collection, Marsden (2006a) comments that the 'viral' term is generally used to describe the *online* use of social networks as opposed to the term 'word-of-mouth' which is applied to their *offline* use by marketers. Having said this, when later in the introduction he describes the quite definitely offline Unilever Dove 'Share a Secret' campaign from 1998, Marsden dubs it "one of the first examples of a *viral sampling* initiative" (ibid., p. xxi, original emphasis), a term which is then erased from the discourse by the time the reader gets to the collection's first chapter where Marsden is now using the phrase "seeding trial". However, buried away in a footnote to the introduction, there is another reference to the link between viral marketing and seeding, as Marsden points out the origins of the term "viral marketing" in the 1989 *PCUser* article we have already seen Kirby citing. The article described the effect of introducing some Macintosh SE computers into a work environment previously full of Compaqs. Marsden notes that the copycat interest in the Macs that ensued demonstrated a product seeding approach to marketing. This makes the absence of any discussion regarding the connections between the viral, memetic, and "seeding trial" discourses all the more obvious when it comes to Marsden's own actual chapter in the collection. This absence of discussion, along with the marginalizing rhetorical strategies noted above, serves as meta-context for Marsden's introduction of the two-step flow as legitimizing historical context for the theory behind "seeding trials". It is, in fact, difficult to ignore the pattern generated by Marsden's devaluation of Gladwell (a populist, non-academic) and his positive re-evaluation of Katz and Lazarsfeld (Columbia scholars with a strong empirical bent). When combined with his use of the Hawthorne Effect (discovered by Harvard scholars with a similarly strong empirical bent) it appears as if there is a significant effort to frame "seeding trials" within a 'scientifically' and 'academically' approved tradition.

Both the established marketing use of the viral metaphor and scholarly engagement with the theory of memetics offer serious challenges to someone wishing to present the impression of established, provable, respectable foundations for a new methodology. The two-step flow of communication and the Hawthorne Effect, however, have the distinct advantage of being *old*, canonical theories generated from top rank American universities. Their aura of authority can be equated to a sort of empirical surety that is very useful (from an evolutionary selection point of view) in a marketing climate growing tired of the lack of measurable return from much viral strategy.

Marsden, then, uses the two-step flow of communication as an "established business truth", even going so far as to implement a stunning piece of visual rhetoric in his "Figure 1.1 Models of media influence" which portrays on the left hand side the 'magic bullet' model, labeled in big capitals with the word "MYTH" and on the right hand side the two-step flow model, labeled with the ominous word "REALITY". Yes, social construction definitely nowhere on the reading list here, I think it would be safe to say. However, I would argue that such language does not demonstrate an unknowing, careless approach to the details and implications of expression. On the contrary, such bold rhetorical flourishes demonstrate a keen appreciation of the persuasive power of language choices. This becomes all the more likely when the exact wording of the footnote in Marsden's introduction is considered in the light of his presentation of "seeding trials". Marsden writes that the *PCUser* article mentioning viral marketing describes an instance of a "product seeding". The advocate-based implementations of the two-step flow model, however, he refers to as "seeding trials". The differentiation, although not made explicit by Marsden, mirrors the division between the use of the viral metaphor and the inducement-based reliance on influencer advocacy that I have been delineating throughout this chapter. The Macintosh SE product trial lends itself to the viral analogy because it illustrates an idea or product that infects a population not by relying on the persuasive power of manipulated advocates but through its own inherent infectiousness. Again, then, I come back to marking implicit, yet elided, distinctions in the viral marketing discourse between a product/service which is in some way capable of infecting a population because of an attractive or fascinating characteristic and a product/service which inherits its infectious nature from the influencers who talk about it. Marsden's texts can be seen as illustrative of the way in which the epidemiological metaphor (as well as the memetic approach that runs parallel to it) is supplanted by the more practical, inducement-led advocacy. This in itself mirrors the move away from the one-step implications of the virus model and toward the two-step flow of communication (explicitly so in Marsden's explication of "seeding trials").

In summary, the viral metaphor implies a repetitive one-step flow model, where the message itself (through the exigencies of its design) displays an active infectiousness akin to communicative agency. This metaphor holds a certain undeniable power in the discourse of contemporary marketing because it offers the same kind of promise that a 'fire-and-forget' weapons system offers a military tactician, namely that a well-designed communication virus can be launched upon a target with no need for further management and with a high expectation of success. However, although this prospect continues to be invoked in the use of the phrase "viral marketing", an engagement with the issue of how such messages can be consistently designed has failed to materialize in the marketing discourse and instead has been supplanted with an emphasis on implementing online and offline inducement-led advocacy programs where agency is firmly in the hands of tightly controlled influencers. Almost from the start of marketing's dalliance with the epidemiological analogy, as evidenced in Gladwell and Godin's early texts, this primarily rhetorical use of the viral figure in the initial pitching of traditional two-step influencer programs has been the norm. From the perspective of the study of interactive marketing this would appear to represent a tension between the seductive pull of the one-step, non-interactive hypodermic model and the equally strong tradition of controlled, two-step, influencer-driven transmission. At this point, it is important to focus on a phrase of Marsden's that we have so far glossed over; the "seeding trial", he notes, is "conducted in the name of research" (ibid., p. 3, p. 13, *inter alia*). In other words, influencers are *told* that the reason a brand is provisioning them with advanced trial products or access to services is that they will be helping them out with a research program. Marketers need the influencers to feel that their opinions are being listened to in order to initiate the Hawthorne Effect. The language and rituals of product and market research are here being used as a means of control, theatrically staged so as to induce target behavior (the influencer's generation of positive recommendations). What appear to be fully functioning interactive systems thus serve as dramatized rhetorics of control. A final issue of language use in Marsden's seeding narrative underlines even further this control emphasis of the two-step flow. Throughout the 20-page chapter, one particular phrasal construction dominates—the influencers chosen for a "seeding trial" will be *transformed* from participants "into advocates for whatever they were trialling" (ibid., p. 6) by the Hawthorne Effect. I would argue that the constant iteration of how the "seeding trial" method will 'transform' or 'turn' the targeted consumers into "loyal" (ibid., p. 12) "evangelists" or "advocates" is an attempt to harness the metaphorical power of the zombie army, intimating that the introduction of such interactive elements into the marketing communication system will actually lead to the magical transformation of these independent, chattering 'opinion leaders' into a vanguard of simple message relays. Marsden's choice of language acts as a persuasive element in his pitching of the "seeding trial" methodology to a marketing audience that requires the maximum control over consumers in an era when consumers appear to be exerting too much influence over the reception of the marketing message.

Marsden's discussion of "seeding trials" leads us on to the area of current marketing practice which appears to most strongly embody the promise of revolutionary interactivity between brands and consumers. The increasing use by marketing practitioners of content produced almost entirely by consumers is held up by many commentators as evidence of a fundamental change in the power relationships that exist between audiences and advertisers, seeming to finally signify the realization that consumers want to be fully involved in a marketing dialog rather than be the passive recipients of a monolog. The next section examines the assumptions concerning community, creativity, and power that such perspectives are built upon.

CO-CREATION AND THE EXPLOITATION OF COMMUNITY

The use of customer communities to lead product development is an area where marketing initiatives appear to demonstrate a highly interactive approach to communication. Some authors (i.e., Ferguson, 2008, p. 182) include such strategies under the rubric of viral marketing, although it is, frankly, hard to locate the viral element in their execution. Manufacturers solicit the opinions of enthusiastic users regarding what particular improvements they would like to see or what new products they could envision and then go on to use such consumer communities to pre-test product prototypes. Lego and Nokia have been early adopters of this innovation in product development which in many ways is inspired by (and sometimes crosses over into) the user communities that have been instrumental in helping to create or develop the major open source software operating systems and applications (the various flavors of Linux, the popular 3-D modeling program, Blender, the Python programming language, etc.). Furthermore, as highlighted by a number of recent studies (Jarrett, 2003; Andrejevic, 2007, 2008; Deuze, 2007; Zwick, Bonsu, & Darmody, 2008), the corporate use of online communities to generate usable content that can then be monetized appears to be a growing feature of Web business.

Following Marsden's logic, all such marketing practices may be perceived to be attempting to implement the Hawthorne Effect. After all, the act of asking a community for its suggestions regarding product design, packaging, or marketing campaign will contribute to that community's positive advocacy of the resulting product or campaign, or so the logic goes. If a community feels involved in a product's development, indeed if it can be made to feel responsible for a large part of the product's final function and form then it would stand to reason that the community would feel all the more connected and engaged with it and so all the more inclined to purchase it. The product would express the community's own desires, perfectly suiting its requirements and so impossible not to purchase. Such a process, in fact, would represent the epitome of the marketing management vision as expressed in a number of canonical, textbook definitions. If we take seriously Kotler's definition that marketing means "identifying and meeting human and social needs" (Kotler & Keller, 2006, p. 5), then the active involvement of user and consumer communities in the creation and development of products, services, and their associated marketing communication is not only desirable but absolutely the foundation of a marketing orientation. The fact that Kotler goes on to approvingly quote Peter Drucker's observation that marketing "should result in a customer who is ready to buy" (ibid., p. 6) emphasizes the core role that the customer should play, from the marketing management perspective, in the design and development of goods. Of course, Kotler identifies this role with marketing research and this might explain why the recent use of consumer content has appeared to be treated as so revolutionary. Marketing research has predominantly treated the consumer as a generator of statistical data that then has to be analyzed rather than as a creator of ideas that should be listened to. For reasons introduced in earlier chapters, marketing research, for the majority of both academics and practitioners, has tended to revolve around quantitative methodologies which assume consumers are entirely 'rational', and generally static, in their expressed reasonings and motivations. Such methodological assumptions reflect the dominant reductionist/

empiricist marketing management paradigm that has held sway over the marketing academy for at least the last 50 years (Arndt, 1985; Chung & Alagaratnam, 2001). Furthermore, as O'Shaughnessy and O'Shaughnessy (2002) have pointed out, even when examined from *within* such an empirical paradigm, many of the assumptions behind apparently empirical or analytical models and dominant theories in marketing (such as multiattribute and hierarchy of effects models and the operational segmentation of markets) can be seen to be the result of the application of inappropriate or inadequate "ways of knowing". On the other hand, recent movements toward the inclusion of critical theory and postmodern perspectives into the apparatus of the marketing academy have resulted in a growing number of voices privileging the creative and interpretive independence of consumers in regard to their reception of marketing communication (O'Donohoe, 1994, 1997, 2001). Accordingly, it can seem as if the growing encouragement of consumer voices in product development, message creation, and brand community management in some sense reflects a moving away from control-orientated, data-driven marketing paradigms and toward more relationship-centered, 'post-modern' models of inclusion. The word that is currently being used to mark this tendency is "co-creation" (Prahalad & Ramaswamy, 2002, 2004a, 2004b), a construction which certainly implies an equal partnership between consumer and brand in the creation process and, in reflecting the common creative industry terminologies of co-producer, co-author and co-director, has a further implication of equal ownership and reward. Both Henry Jenkins (Jenkins, 2006) and Mark Deuze see the co-creation trend as a manifestation of "the convergence of the cultures of production and consumption of media" (Deuze, 2007, p. 244). This "convergence culture" represents an integration of three strands of inclusionary dynamic; an "emerging global participatory media culture", the convergence of production and consumption cultures and movements toward the assimilation of "individual creativity and (mass) production in the creative industries" (ibid., p. 245). The results of this trend have become increasingly visible in the marketing, journalism and software industries where user contributions (in the form of commentary, reviews, articles, video, podcasts, project management, program code, and artwork) are allowing products and brands to flourish within enthusiastic, supportive communities. Zwick, Bonsu, and Darmody (2008) point out that the marketing reaction to this trend has appeared to be surprisingly positive; instead of wistfully longing for the certainties of the tightly-controlled brand management era,

> we see a collective embrace of the idea of a newly empowered, entrepreneurial, and liberated consumer subject, presumably because of the promise such a consumer presents in creating 'competitive advantage' and market opportunities for the discerning 'New Marketer'. (ibid., p. 164)

The enthusiasm displayed by both marketing practitioners and theoreticians for the new era of consumer-led and consumer-generated product and content might perhaps alert us to the possibility that, at least from the vantage point of marketing, not much has really changed. If, as I have been arguing throughout this book, marketing communication is fundamentally premised upon paradigms of control, the emergence of trends that would threaten to disrupt such control would surely be a cause for outright alarm. While Zwick et al. downplay the extent and significance of the hysterical apocalyptic rhetoric that accompanies contemporary marketing's boosting of co-creation and consumer empowerment, they nevertheless go on to describe the continuing, if mutated, concern for power and control that lies behind the enthusiastic adoption of the consumer's creative potential. Using an amalgam of Foucault's definition of government as a form of power which acts through the *construction* of 'free' individuals and the "Marxian labour-theory-of-value" (ibid., p. 179), Zwick et al. argue that

> the notion of co-creation represents a sophisticated technology of government of consumers where the surplus value generated is based on the appropriation of the creative work of often networked and socially cooperative customers. (ibid., p. 182)

They note that consumers involved in 'co-creation' often end up having to pay a premium for the results of that creation; so Nike does indeed give you the ability to design your shoes in just the way you want, but you will pay extra for the time, effort and inspiration *you* have invested in that creative process (and, as Goldsmith's example reminds us, there will always be a limit to how you may express yourself).

For Zwick at al., the convergence of consumption and production actually represents the elimination of one of "the most vexing barriers towards increasing control over markets" (ibid., p. 182). They cite the one-to-one orientation of Peppers and Rogers's version of relationship marketing as the driving marketing theory behind the enthusiastic adoption of co-creation strategies, arguing that such an orientation enables the firm to "more intensely modulate each relationship" (ibid.), and so effect a greater resolution of control over increasingly microscopic segmentations. It is worth adding here that the use of communication technologies to tailor marketing messages according to surfing habits or profile is another example of this search for the one-to-one transmission link and reflects the move toward the sort of one-step flow of communication that Bennett and Manheim (2006) think will characterize the new era of public communication. In other words, it is possible to interpret both the apparently 'empowering' integration of consumer co-creation into corporate production systems and the individualized direct messaging that results from data mining as manifestations of the shift toward a one-step flow of communication where marketing messages are immune to pesky, unreliable and uncontrollable social mediation. The more the consumer can be integrated into the corporation, the less they are embedded within communities that provide contrary contextualization. As we have seen above, however, there are also strong instantiations of the two-step flow of communication in the marketing discourses surrounding viral and word-of-mouth strategies. It would be unwise, therefore, to assert that contemporary marketing communication is founded upon an exclusive implementation of either one-step or two-step models. Instead, below both lie the deeper assumptions of the transmission model and its communication-as-control paradigm.

As I have argued elsewhere (Miles, 2007), the inclusion of consumers within the advertising system (whether it takes the form of focus groups, directed forums, co-created content or copy) necessarily changes those consumers (or has an effect on the construction of those consumers by the stakeholders in the marketing system as well as on the self-construction of these 'tested' consumers); the act of placing them inside the system distinguishes them from the communities that they appear to come from. They become understood and communicated with as "representatives" rather than individual consumers. Both for themselves and for those in communication relationships with them (directly or indirectly) they are re-constructed, re-presented, as representatives with a voice. To bring it back to constructivist principles, the act of observation is a creative act—the focus group is created by a particular person or group of people, according to the particular methodologies of selection and once it is convened the individuals inside its boundaries are now constructed by everyone (including themselves) as representatives whose opinions matter. The act of selection influences the self-construction of each member and the constructions of each individual interacting with the group. Beyond the ramifications that such an argument has for the viability of such qualitative methodologies, there are significant implications for the issues of community construction and content creation in contemporary marketing. Accordingly, I wish to now sketch out a constructivist reading of the co-creation theme in recent marketing discourse with particular emphasis upon the tensions between community and individual that, I will argue, lie at the core of such discourse.

The first aspect of co-creation discourse that lends itself to investigation is the existence of the distinction between producer and consumer. From a constructivist standpoint, as all perceptual distinctions take the form of individual and social constructions, the differentiation between producer and consumer should inevitably be regarded as such a construction (or matrix of constructions). So, if observation leads to the construction of patterns of distinctions, then it seems reasonable to examine the nature of the different observers who might be constructing such distinctions. This is a roundabout way of suggesting that we return to some of the issues raised in Barbara Stern's (1994) revised model of advertising communication. In her model, Stern included within the construction of "consumer" the advertising sponsor themselves, noting that the initial consumer of all advertising messages must be the sponsor because they must sign off on the advertising message before it can go into full production. Agency personnel might therefore be said to spend considerable effort targeting the client with their message rather than targeting the ostensible target audience. So, from the observational standpoint of certain agency personnel, although the word "consumer" might commonly be used to refer to people 'out there', the masses targeted by a campaign, nevertheless the consumer of the agency's services and the initial consumer of all advertising messages would be the client. In a larger marketing communication context, all message streams (press releases, briefings, mailshots, web sites, scripted telesales calls, etc.) will have initial consumers who are not the ostensible target audience. Such initial audiences might very broadly be referred to as "sponsors" in the sense that they sign-off on, and so lend their imprimatur to, the created form that a message has taken. Approvals from a line manager, an executive board, an account director, a consultancy client, or a host of other individuals and groups might constitute the results of such sponsorial consumption. In the traditional marketing communication paradigm, however, there are clear terminological differentiations between such sponsors and the consumers targeted as "consumers". One does communication work "for" such sponsors, whereas one's final presentation of the marketing message is "to" the target audience. The part that sponsors play in creating the message is a well established element of the marketing communication system. The advertising client brief, for example, gives the advertiser the opportunity to significantly dictate the tone and style of the message that they wish to see from an agency. Even within the agency, of course, there is a substantial number of formal opportunities for one layer of personnel to dictate the terms of, and critique, the creative work of another layer of personnel. Such formal systems of goal-setting and commentary make the production of marketing communication a highly diffuse, collaborative affair.

So far, this expansion of the "consumer" designation to include sponsors is something that both evolves straightforwardly out of Stern's work and can even be said to have a certain level of implicit recognition within existing business practices, shared constructions, and linguistic reflections of those constructions. The pitch to the client, for example, although conceived radically differently in many ways from the final presentation of an advertising message to the target audience, betrays certain similar patterns of assumptions and behavior that enable it to be categorized without much argument as an instance of agency production and client consumption. Just like any final presentation of a marketing message, of course, the consumer might choose not to 'buy' the pitch, but they will have sat, comparatively quietly (not passively, because no one listening to someone else communicating can ever be said to be passive) and listened, and watched, while someone tries to sell them a campaign. There are clear differences, too; the client is in the same room and at the end of the pitch will generally let her feelings be known immediately, whereas messages relayed over mass media are subject to far longer and far more uncertain feedback loops. However, once we begin to consider the possibility of broadening the production and consumption categories in this way, we have to re-consider a number of observational stances. For example, all those involved in the 'production' side are at the same time members of a number of target audiences for other marketing efforts (and even for their own). There is no one who is not targeted by some form of marketing communication campaign (I speak as a veteran of cold calling campaigns designed to sell advertising to the directors of advertising agencies). How exactly do we imagine that the shift between producer and consumer works, then? Do we metaphorically change hats, seeing ourselves now as consumers and now as content creators? I think that it is safe to say that few people would be comfortable with such an explanation. Using advertising creativity as an example, it is a long established tenet that a familiarity with a large amount of advertising, films, books, TV content, literature, sports coverage, etc., provides a valuable resource for the working copywriter and art director. As creative director Jim Riswold puts it:

> Everything I have ever done is borrowed, reformulated, regurgitated, turned upside down or inside out, played back at a different speed, and sometimes just plain stolen from either popular culture, music, history, art, literature, the back of cereal boxes, Hegelianism, an athlete's life, a bedtime story my grandmother once read me—whatever. (Quoted in Berger, 2001, p. 157)

The "swipe file" kept by many marcoms creatives is a concrete instance of the amorphous nature of the producer/consumer division; consumption for inspiration is still consumption, after all, but it can often lead to the production of insightful or creative content. Common advertising textbook advice to potential creatives such as pay "visits to the cinema, theatre, art galleries", listen to as many different types of music as possible and read "all types of newspapers, magazines and comics" (Burtenshaw, Mahon, & Barfoot, 2006) tends to reflect the substance of David Ogilvy's observation that the big advertising agencies prefer "to recruit people who have furnished their minds by studying history, languages, economics and so forth" (Ogilvy, 1985, p. 39). In other words, the more your mind has been furnished with the results of a catholic consumption of ideas (and we must remember Ogilvy's rather Classical bias regarding what that would constitute) the more you will be able to use that mind to create interesting ideas for others to consume. James Webb Young's tiny text on idea production, written in the 1940s but famously championed by a revolutionary creative voice of the 1960s, William Bernbach, concisely outlines this approach. Young notes that every great creative mind that he had met in his time in advertising had exhibited the same two characteristics: Firstly, they would be able to get easily interested in "any subject under the sun" and secondly, they were an "extensive browser in all sorts of fields of information". As he summarizes: "it is with the advertising man as with the cow: no browsing, no milk" (Young, 2003, p. 24, I pass over the highly suggestive gender issues in silence). The act of message creation is inextricably bound up with message consumption, then. Professional distinctions between producers/creators and consumers, however, have attempted to maintain a rigid division between those who are paid for their talent and expertise in content production and those who pay for the access to that content. Such distinctions are, of course, reflected in our usage of the terms "professional" and "amateur". Yet these distinctions are based upon economic frames that have little connection with the breadth of activity that can be covered by a consideration of the processes of production and consumption. For instance, leveraging O'Donohoe's work, we can point to the way that "consumers" adapt advertising language and discourse into the construction of their own interpersonal communication; the referencing of an advertising slogan or character in a conversation between two friends is, through its re-contextualization and juxtaposition alongside other disparate referents, an instance of creativity. The 're-purposing' of consumed content into new content for personal use is something that happens not just with "commercial" and "artistic" communication, of course, but is fundamental to the way we build up patterns of language use within any size of social grouping. In-jokes, argot, personal speech peculiarities, distinctive rhetorical styles, and the vast number of other such elements that are adopted, imitated, re-framed, and re-contextualized in everyday interpersonal communication are examples of the way in which people might be said to consume the discourse of others and then use it to create their own. Indeed, from a modern discourse analysis perspective, all the elements of "discursive practice" are used to "actively produce social and psychological realities" (realities which include ourselves) and the choices between the "many and contradictory discursive practices that each person could engage in" (Davies & Harré, 2005, p. 262–263) represent the nexus at which the consumption and production of discourse are continually interfacing. Furthermore, from a more general postmodern perspective, Firat and Dholakia (2006) point out that "all human activity is performative, and needs to be considered as a moment in a perpetual cycle of production" and consequently the distinction between consumption and production must be "largely questioned" (ibid., p. 138). Customers have always been involved in a "process of transforming the product" (ibid.)—the rituals of customization and personalization begin to be enacted often even before we take possession of the product as we imagine what we could do to it, how we might make it our own.

The amalgamation of production and consumption, even the complete collapsing of the distinction between them, might be all very well at the level of discourse analysis and the considerations of identity construction through discursive practice, but what can all this mean for the 'reality' of marketing's apparent embrace of co-creation? In that the distinction

172 Interactive Marketing

between consumption and production is a construction embedded deeply within the discourse of marketing (and the larger discourses of management and manufacturing as well as many others such as engineering and physics) it is difficult to see how the apparent movement toward the extinguishing of such a distinction cannot be anything other than a threat to the fundamental assumptions that buttress its entire intellectual enterprise. And yet, although we are treated to the usual apocalyptic rhetoric surrounding the necessity for adopting strategies of co-creation, there is little indication that marketing as a practice considers itself to be any more under threat from the rise of such perspectives than it usually does. It makes a certain sense, after all, for critical marketing voices such as Fırat and Dholakia to describe the way in which post-modern consumers construct themselves as producers of value and content and so conclude that marketers, in order to build relationships with such consumers, must increasingly involve them in product innovation and content creation. It is quite another for a grand, old voice of business administration such as C. K. Prahalad to be vigorously waving the flag for co-creation. I would suggest that this expression of common cause across the marketing spectrum hides some quite divergent comprehensions of what exactly co-creation is and what it represents in marketing terms. As Adam Arvidsson (2008) notes, for businesses, "customer cooperation is generally seen as a free resource that has no, or virtually no, cost" (ibid., p. 326). There can exist a tendency, therefore, to understand co-creation as an opportunity for the exploitation of a willing volunteer force that may be manipulated into developing and consolidating customer communities into virtual factories. Andrejevic (2008) notes the way, for example, that TV production houses can use fan forum discussion of TV shows to not only gauge audience reaction to particular story arcs and plot points but also to "learn from attentive viewers that an upcoming script includes a continuity flaw or plot inconsistency " (ibid., p. 29). Inevitably, such practices will, as Deuze (2007) asserts, challenge "consensual notions of what it means to work in the cultural industries" (ibid., p. 244). Indeed, such issues do not just concern "cultural" productions; the use, for example, that Nokia has made of the community of programmers, hardware hackers, user interface designers and Linux experts that has coalesced around its Nxxx series of Internet Tablets is a good example of how a brand can support, monitor, listen to, and benefit from the skills of enthusiasts who want nothing more than to have a say in the shape of the next device in the series[4]. The vast majority of this work is done in the spirit of the open source software movement meaning that resulting programs and scripts are available for free download and their source code is available for users to study and adapt. Although Nokia supplies the device with some basic applications, the viability of the Nxxx series has depended on the development and availability of a large repository of programs that have been either specifically written for the devices or ported from other Linux distributions by users. Additionally, its (so far) three major hardware iterations have reflected design and engineering improvements requested by the user community (though some popular requests remain unimplemented, perhaps reflecting some conflict between the company's own sense of where they see the series going and where the users would like it to go). Such an approach has its dangers, naturally, and those users who feel that they are not being listened to or have not received an equal return (for example, in the form of adequate development of the platform) in exchange for their input can turn into quite vocal sources of disappointment and negativity around the brand. A short but telling example of this is provided by Alistair Davidson's (2004) autobiographical case study for *Strategy & Leadership*. The edition of the journal in which his piece appears is largely devoted to enthusiastic articles on Prahalad's theory of co-creation of value and the thrust of Davidson's article is to bring things down to earth a little by illustrating the consequences of relationship problems between customer and firm in a co-production marketing environment. The two-page case study is the story of how Davidson, while initially feeling empowered by being able to continually customize his own monthly contract on the Sprint mobile network via its complex customer web site is then enraged enough to cancel that contract entirely when it becomes clear that the network will not accept any responsibility for the fact that its late processing of some of Davidson's choices led to his missing the deadline for a discount plan sign-up. The details of the case are not as interesting as the spectacle of an influential strategic consultant, author, and customer venting his fury at a company that had ostensibly entered into a co-production relationship with him. Interestingly, Davidson's narrative appears to run counter to the conclusions in Bendapudi and Leone's (2003) study of the role of self-serving bias in consumer participation, in which they suggest that offering customers a choice to participate in co-production may make more sense if the firm believes that there is a significant chance that the outcome of a marketing exchange "will not meet a customer's expectations" (ibid., p. 25). From this perspective, co-creation becomes a strategy for risk management, in which a company uses self-serving bias to manipulate users into sharing the blame for the failure of a product or service that they have been involved in the production of. In an acknowledgement of the postmodern position that consumers are "active co-producers of brand meanings" (ibid., p. 26), Bendapudi and Leone go on to raise the question of just how deeply the effects of the self-serving bias might go in respect not just to solicited chances for co-production managed by the firm but also to the consumer creation of meaning that is an integral part of consumption. Such an invocation of the issue of meaning co-creation is rare amongst marketing academics who are engaged with "empirical" research methodologies. Generally, something of a divide can be discerned between those studies that originate from a critical (or postmodern) perspective, where consumption and production are considered to be in some sense implicit within each other, and those that originate from a more "empirical", strategic management perspective, where consumption and production need to be explicitly re-orientated around the value concept in order to bring about a managed convergence of the two. In addition to these two camps we can also observe a further perspective which sees the trend toward convergence and co-creation as threatening—either to consumers or those working in the traditionally-rewarded creative professions. Banks and Humphreys (2008), for example, speak of the threat to waged labor "of displacement by unpaid amateurs and the loss or redefinition of work" while at the same time questioning whether, for those amateurs, their labor should more properly be constructed as "enabled" or "exploited" (ibid., p. 415). While there is optimism from both the critical marketing and dominant marketing management perspectives regarding the way that co-creation represents, respectively, either a liberating force from the dominating communication modes of traditional control-orientated corporations or a means of engaging with increasingly distant and unreachable demographics, it is striking that mainstream marketing and business theoreticians can regard the same process as the savior of modern capitalism while other, more radical, voices, can portray the same process as the harbinger of a fundamental switchover from capital production to a new social production based upon "ethical capital" (Arvidsson, 2008). In other words, although everyone can agree on what exactly co-creation is (in the sense of what it looks like), there are fundamental differences about what it represents, from the death of capitalism as we know it and the emancipation of the consumer to "the future of competition" (Prahalad & Ramaswamy, 2004a, 2004b) and the phenomenon that will drive the new era of Experience Quality Management (Prahalad & Ramaswamy 2004a, Leavy & Moitra, 2006). In the next chapter I will address the place of interactivity within the discourses of Relationship Marketing and Service-Dominant Logic and I will have occasion to examine the way in which the co-creation of value is presented in the marketing theory texts that constitute the dominant voices in those discourses. For the purposes of this chapter, however, I wish to focus on the way in which C. K. Prahalad uses a construction of interactivity in the explication of his conception of co-creating unique value with customers and how this relates to the form of *community-*focused creation discussed above.

Much of Prahalad's focus is on the way that individual consumers can be engaged in a co-creation process, rather than how *communities* of consumers might work with a company to produce innovation. The examples and case studies that Prahalad favors showcase firms that have found a way of integrating the customer into the process of creating "personalized experiences" (quoted in Leavy & Moitra, 2006, p. 6). Customer communities are explicitly handled in Prahalad and Ramaswamy's (2004a) book length study of the co-creation of unique value with comparatively few examples: Lego Mindstorms, narrated over two pages (ibid., pp. 52–54), the 'co-opting' of Tolkien fans by New Line Cinema (ibid., p. 129), the Hollywood

Stock Exchange, Cisco's Connection Online and Philips Electronics' opening of its Pronto remote control's source code to customer hackers (ibid., pp. 123–125). Reasonably, an approach that emphasizes both experience and personalization is one that will not be naturally inclined to engage with *collections* of consumers. Perhaps, it might even be said that there is a distinct marginalization of communities in Prahalad's theory. For example, when explaining how companies can combine the different elements of their DART model (Dialog, Access, Risk Assessment, and Transparency) to activate new capabilities, Prahalad and Ramaswamy (2004b) illustrate the integration of the Dialog and Risk Assessment components by describing the way in which the risks of smoking have been more deeply understood and considered as public discussion on the matter has been fostered. They conclude by asserting that as a result of this combination of Dialog and Risk Assessment elements, "acting as citizens, individuals are significantly affecting public policy even as they are making informed private decisions as consumers" (ibid., p. 8). For an issue which has been the focus of such concerted public and NGO communication efforts over such a protracted period, and which has perhaps done more than any other case to bring the term "class action" to popular attention, the characterization of the debate on the health effects of smoking as driven entirely by "individual" "citizens" making "informed private decisions" is remarkable for the acute way in which it illustrates the dominance of the trope of individualism in Prahaladian discourse. Similarly, the "Build a Bear" company, used by Prahalad as a model of how a company can allow children to "experience creating their unique toy bear" (quoted in Leavy & Moitra, 2006, p. 5), exemplifies a co-creation of value with individual consumers. One of Prahalad's central tenets is that "experience is unique to an individual" (ibid., p. 6) and this perspective has a strong impact on the examples he chooses to illustrate his conception of co-creation as well as the language that he uses to construct his representations of the theory informing it[5]. Certainly, Prahalad's rhetoric seems to be orientated toward the construction of a discourse in which the individual freedom of the consumer to decide the format of her own experiences becomes the center of all business activity and the examples that he chooses reinforce such a standpoint. The John Deere example used by Prahalad and Ramaswamy (2004a) to illustrate the way in which even a market traditionally thought to be conservative and unwelcoming to change can implement such an approach is couched in highly individualistic terms that seem to purposefully dissolve the need for any sort of farming 'community'. The DeereTrax system, they say, is "built around 'me, the farmer'", "*it champions my farm, my farming productivity, and my unique experiences*" (ibid., p. 94, emphasis in the original). Here, the DeereTrax system is presented as something which doesn't just eliminate the mass templating of farmers and their needs which typifies old-style agribusiness but also eliminates the need for farmers to look anywhere outside the boundaries of their own farm and their own "unique experiences".

Why bother discussing issues with other farmers when, as the DeereTrax representative will tell you, all farmers are different? When they describe the community aspect of the DeereTrax system, whereby "farmers matched on a variety of factors" (ibid.) are 'connected' by the system to "share their knowledge" it seems that John Deere creates the boundaries and sets up the terms on which the diffusion of "unique experience" is achieved. Indeed, when they move on to describing in more general terms how firms such as John Deere act as "nodal companies" in "experience networks" (ibid., p. 95), we encounter a decidedly control-orientated metaphor:

> Nodal companies are like traffic cops, making the rules and allowing for free flow with adequate constraints. (ibid.)

There is a strong tension between Prahalad and Ramaswamy's construction of unique individual consumers and their depiction of the nodal company's engineering of the 'constrained' "free flow" of interaction between such consumers. A nodal company is represented as a communication hub which mediates the individual's expression of individuality to both other individuals and themselves. The authors' suggestion that instead of focusing around acronyms like B2B and B2C, which "miss the point", we should think in terms of I2N2I, individuals to nodal companies "and then back to the individual" (ibid., p. 96), while implying that communication "flow" originates with the individual consumer (a highly contentious position that is not argued for in the text) also undeniably positions the company as a mediator or filter, or more generously, enhancer, of the individual's own experience. The circular nature of the concept behind the I2N2I acronym combined with the metaphor of the "traffic cop" (who both legislates and enforces) suggests a role for the firm that is almost akin to a dialysis machine—the blood is taken, processed, and then re-introduced into the patient's system. A very self-contained loop. And as one reads through Prahalad and Ramaswamy's examples of enterprises like Sephora, REI, and Li and Fung who are all applauded as having designed systems that are able to deal with customers on highly personalized levels, one begins to realize that one of the distinct features of such systems is the way in which they remove the consumer's need to interact with anyone else other than the nodal company and its representatives—the company is able to provide any level of advice, any level of service and any form of customization that the consumer might wish for. The need for a community consequently disappears in such scenarios—if the expertise and personalization is flexible enough then a consumer would never feel the need to go outside the relationship with the nodal company for advice. And, if through some bizarre aberration you do feel the need to speak to a fellow customer about the bewildering choices offered by this wonderful level of customization, well then, the company can put you in touch with someone who has been carefully vetted to fit your unique profile.

Much of what Prahalad and Ramaswamy champion seems on the surface to be liberating and empowering to the consumer, but the basic assumption of consumer control remains. Marketing management might now be called experience management, but it is still a discourse of management wherein the consumer's experience is something to be controlled and kept within tight bounds. Readers of the late Stafford Beer (and Ross Ashby, the cyberneticist who had a tremendous influence on him) will recognize in Prahalad and Ramaswamy's portrayal of the nodal company an attempt to deal with Ashby's Law of Requisite Variety, "one of the really fundamental laws of cybernetics" as Beer put it (Beer, 1994a, p. 279). Put simply, Ashby's Law states that "only variety can destroy variety" (Ashby 1957, p. 207). We can think of variety as meaning "the number of possible states of a system" (Beer 1994b, p. 10) and, translating this into marketing terms, what this means is that there has to be a match between the variety of the firm and the variety of the consumers. If we have a large number of consumers who have a high variety of needs (referred to as the variety of the system) then there has to be an equal variety of "possible states" within the firm (referred to as the regulatory variety) in order to cope with the variety of the consumers. As Beer pointed out, there are two ways that any system can deal with variety—it can either attenuate the system variety so that it matches regulatory variety or it can amplify regulatory variety so that it matches system variety. Beer spent a large part of his life seeking to convince people that the use of computers and telecommunications to amplify regulatory variety was the only sane and humane way for governments and firms to avoid "catastrophic" instability (Beer 1994b, p. 12). In his vision, governments should be "liberty machines" which output freedom rather than organizations that sought to attenuate the variety of their citizens as far as possible. For Beer, cybernetics was a highly positive science, offering the chance for individuals to be freer, more in control of their media content, more able to learn what they wanted to when they needed to. His work stands as an example of the way that cybernetics has often tended to attract optimistic thinkers who see the possibility of using a 'scientific' understanding of the properties of dynamic systems to bring about profound social change. That this book has spent so much time looking at the way in which elements of the cybernetic discourse have been applied to understandings of communication and management that tend to construct the consumer as someone to be aggregated, controlled, and communicated at, is a commentary on the way that the variety of cybernetic approaches has been seriously attenuated in mainstream discourses over the years. Returning to Prahalad and Ramaswamy's thesis, my point is that the customization, the ability to rapidly re-configure the supply chain, the emphasis on reacting to the individual customer all appear to be examples of classic Beer-inspired regulatory variety amplification. So, instead of orientating the marketing system toward attenuating the variety of the customer, they face that variety head on and amplify the regulatory variety. However, I would argue that we should be careful not to characterize this as a 'celebration' of the consumer's variety; Prahalad and Ramaswamy are concerned with the successful management of the challenges that variety, or heterogeneity, provides to the firm. While their adoption of the Ashby/Beer variety amplification approach, and the consequent terminology of heterogeneity and uniqueness, implies the sort of support for and idealization of the freedom of the individual citizen that permeates much of Beer's work, in Prahalad and Ramaswamy it is combined, as I have shown, with two elements that work against such rhetoric of individual liberation. Firstly, the construct of the nodal company is founded upon the assumption that it is responsible for controlling and bounding the communication flow between consumers and between consumers and its own experience enabling elements—this is, in essence, an attempt to attenuate the variety of the consumer and sits uneasily within the discourse of variety amplification that dominates so much of their presentation. Secondly, in emphasizing the heterogeneity of the consumer, Prahalad and Ramaswamy tend to re-define a customer community as a collection of high-variety individuals and nothing more—shying away from addressing what understandings might bind such individuals into something that might be constructed as a community. There is some talk of how the nodal company can create a community of customers in the process of its experience management, but there is a reluctance to discuss how consumers construct themselves as communities and what that might mean for the firm trying to build a relationship with them (the use of the term 'co-opting' to describe New Line Cinema's management of the Tolkien base is indicative of this). Who defines the community and who therefore constructs it are questions which inevitably complicate the shiny, enthusiastic vision offered by Prahalad and Ramaswamy. However, as I began to argue in Chapter 3, a constructivist perspective can help firms explore the ways in which they are constructing understandings of communities that might conflict with the constructions of those who consider themselves to be members of such communities and, furthermore, an appreciation of the recursive nature of communication allows the firm (as well as all the other stakeholders) to reflect upon the ways in which constructing oneself as a member of a community changes the way one understands oneself and the others one observes to be in a relationship with that community.

Prahalad and Ramaswamy's discourse of variety amplification promises a return to some of the more radical and, potentially, liberating ideas emanating from the management cybernetics of Stafford Beer. Yet, the urge to control system variety is strong in cultures that have equated management and communication with the containment, restriction, and direction of message flow. So, while I can applaud, when self-identifying as a constructivist, Prahalad and Ramaswamy's intense focus upon the uniqueness of individual experience and the potentially liberating doctrine of customer co-creation of unique value, I would yet question the extent to which interaction is still bound up with traditional conceptions of management as command and control. Their rhetoric routinely rejects the idea that customers can be 'owned' by the company, citing CRM as an example of a technology which institutes the understanding of customers as "passive 'targets' of the firm" (Prahalad & Ramaswamy, 2004a, p. 133) yet the consistency of their vision is questionable. Perhaps, in their acknowledgement that the real instantiation of dialog in the experience network will need "an altogether different kind of communication infrastructure" (ibid.) we can detect the realization that if marketing systems remain reliant upon existing media and communication formats (and that would include our current Web 2.0 funhouse of social networking and microblogs) then dialog at the level that Prahalad and Ramaswamy desire is going to be forever beyond reach. It is, though, not the technology as such that has to change but the assumptions of control that marketing systems insist on migrating through to their use of every new communication tool.

6 The Autism of Relationship Marketing

The increasing absorption of "interactivity" into the discourse of contemporary marketing theory can be seen as a function of the mainstream struggle to adopt a service rather than product orientation. Relationship Marketing, CRM, the Service-Dominant Logic of Marketing (Vargo & Lusch, 2004), and the gradual prioritizing of value creation within the marketing enterprise (manifesting in such diverse ways as the AMA re-definition and Prahalad's co-creation of unique value) are all networked expressions of a dissatisfaction with, and consequent withdrawal from, a product orientation, or Goods-Dominant Logic. While interactivity appears to be a common central element across all of these variations of the service orientation, there have so far been no studies looking specifically at the part it plays in helping to build the foundations of this increasingly dominant discourse stream in mainstream marketing. Consequently, in this chapter I intend to examine the way in which understandings of interactivity have been developed and used in this service (re-)orientation, specifically in the discourse of Relationship Marketing and the S-D logic that has latterly appeared to bolster it. My contention will be that RM discourse avoids constructing a coherent understanding of interactivity because it attempts to avoid engaging with issues of communication altogether. The constructions that it has put in place of communication (learning, experience, and value) are developed with almost no real concern for the details of the interactivity that is asserted to lie at their center. Relationship Marketing is thus typified by an intense *turning away* from communication that I will metaphorically associate with an autistic response to relationships.

Vargo and Lusch's 2004 paper on S-D logic has served to integrate a number of notable perspectives within the last 20 or so years of marketing theory into a consistent, logical movement away from a goods-dominant logic. Their paper operates, therefore, as a form of foundational history for a revolutionary change in paradigm and, like all such histories, may be read as an attempt to rhetorically construct an expedient narrative that legitimizes the ideological purity, as well as arguing for the inevitability, of the new theory. Consequently, I intend to spend some time examining the place of communication and interaction within Vargo and Lusch's argument in support of the new dominant logic before moving on to close readings of my two exemplar RM texts, Evert Gummesson's *Total Relationship Marketing* and Peppers and Rogers' *Enterprise One to One*, which I have chosen as manifestations of a European and Northern American approach respectively.

I will begin my discussion of Vargo and Lusch's (2004) explication of S-D logic by addressing their choice of metaphors to describe communication and interaction. The authors are noticeably aware of the way that language choices frame and reproduce social and power relationships, as can be seen in their own comments regarding the vocabulary of the goods-dominant logic, in which the description of the market as something which is to be "segmented", "penetrated", or "promoted to" reflects a perspective in which "customers, like resources, become something to be captured or acted on" (ibid., p. 2). This attention to the implications of those metaphors which are chosen to clarify and vivify an intellectual construction would, one presumes, mean that the metaphors used by Vargo and Lusch to present their own theory are calculatedly selected with just such an eye to their rhetorical effect[1]. The treatment of the place of interaction in the new S-D logic can be seen to take place across a number of the "fundamental premises" of Vargo and Lusch's paper. When they discuss their fourth premise, that "knowledge is the fundamental source of competitive advantage", for instance, the authors speak of the way in which information is to be considered the "primary flow" across the "service-provision chain" (ibid., p. 9) in contrast to the traditional goods-dominant perspective that the primary flow is physical. Now, while this premise exhibits the evolutionary nature of S-D logic, its choice of metaphor, or rather its reliance on the metaphor choices of the old G-D logic, means that the communication model that informs the new service paradigm is, at base, identical to that to be found in the goods and production paradigm; information "flows" from one link of the "chain" to the next. The adoption of the chain metaphor is deleterious enough (and is certainly antithetical to the notion of resource network integrator that Vargo & Lusch advance in later premises) but to combine it with the imagery of "flow", a natural metaphor which does not easily lend itself to descriptions of polymorphic, synchronous, multi-level communication interactions, results in a stillborn conception of interaction[2]. Indeed, the understanding of information that is reflected in these metaphors is clearly manifested when the authors define service as "the provision of the information to (or use of the information for) a consumer who desires it" (ibid., p. 9). Information is taken to be something which can be transported from one place to another and so the job of marketing becomes the coordination of the various flows of information within the resource network. Compounding the framing effect of such metaphors is the decision to remain with the exchange paradigm. Vargo and Lusch have the opportunity to argue for the deprecation of the exchange construct as being too bound up with the goods-dominant logic of microeconomics. However, while they note toward the start of the paper that Sheth and Parvatiyar have called for marketing theorists to abandon exchange theory entirely, they frame this as an extreme manifestation of academic dissatisfaction with the state of the dominant marketing paradigm rather than welcoming it as a genuine opportunity. Because Vargo and Lusch stick with the exchange paradigm, merely swapping tangibles for intangibles, their presentation of the interactive relationships that apparently characterize the S-D re-orientation remain grounded in the old metaphors and models of communication that infuse the G-D logic of functionalism and marketing management. Consequently, maintaining the figure of exchange at the core of their discourse allows the authors to describe the provision of services as the "transmission of efforts" (Vargo & Lusch, 2004, p. 7, quoting Frederic Bastiat), and tangible products as "embodied knowledge" (echoing the container metaphor of communication) or "distribution mechanisms for services" (ibid., p. 9). All of these phrases imply a heavy reliance upon the dominant marketing communication and control paradigm.

The final three "fundamental premises" laid out by Vargo and Lusch may all be interpreted as being centrally concerned with communication. FP$_6$, "The Customer is Always a Coproducer", covers the way in which a movement toward customer co-creation is a natural consequence of the "continuous-process perspective" of the new S-D paradigm, "in which separation of production and consumption is not a normative goal " (ibid., p. 11). Referencing the earlier work of Prahalad and Ramaswamy, as well as Oliver, Rust, and Varki's (1998) sketching of a "real-time" approach to responding to the dynamic needs of individuals, Vargo and Lusch's description of co-production is dependent upon an interactive relationship with the consumer that is itself necessarily dependent upon a continuous, personalized discourse which is formed around the invitation to create value together. However, in their summing up of the array of scholarly voices that support the co-production premise, the authors apply their operand/operant distinction in a way that seriously muddies the waters regarding just how far the interaction needs to go. They conclude that the customer "becomes primarily an operant resource (coproducer) rather than an operand resource ('target') and can be involved in the entire value and service chain in acting upon operand resources" (Vargo & Lusch, 2004, p. 11). On the surface this looks like an admirably progressive view; instead of being an operand resource, something to which things are done, consumers appear to be awarded agency by being perceived as *operant* resources and therefore having the status of "active participants in relational exchanges and coproduction" (ibid., p. 7). The distinction between operand and operant however does little to alter the entrenched power relationship between consumer and firm. The act of terming consumers 'resources', whether they are passive or active, implies that there is some element with a higher degree of agency that uses the resource to achieve its goals. This becomes even further apparent when one considers Vargo and Lusch's way of describing the measurement of the firm's success as being constituted by a focus on "marketplace feedback" derived both directly from the customer and through the analysis of "financial performance from exchange" (ibid., p. 5). This is integrated into a larger view of the firm as involved in a "process of continual hypothesis generation and testing" (ibid., p. 6). So, what is being outlined here is a sense in which the firm, as a result of re-orientating itself as a first-order cybernetic processing system, uses the consumer (along with other operant resources like accumulated market knowledge, design skills, relationship networks with other service providers, etc.) to come up with value hypotheses (or propositions) that are then fed back to the consumer, testing for their acceptance. While this process can certainly be characterized as a dynamic and continuous one, it is difficult to say that it adds much to the traditional goods-centered logic conception of the consumer; instead of being the one who is directly *done to,* they become co-opted by the firm into behaving as just another embodiment of knowledge/information (the distinction is not made) who "occasionally" (ibid., p. 7) is returned to being used as an operand resource (presumably when they are sold *to*). The firm gets to have its cake and eat it too, one might say. If there is to be real *co*-production and *co*-creation of value, should it not follow that the use of words like "resource" should really be left on the sidelines? Vargo and Lusch's description of the interaction between consumer and firm under the new service-centered regime is posited on there being someone or something which stands above all the resources, which co-ordinates them. This highly traditional management assumption means that the consumer, while being afforded an equal measure of responsibility for the creative input and production as other workers within the firm, is also, just like those workers, relegated to a subaltern position. The marketer, now lying at "the core of the firm's strategic planning" (ibid., p. 14), designs and builds the "cross-functional business processes" (ibid.) that will enable the knowledge and skills of the "operant resources" to be combined effectively into the presentation and implementation of the firm's "value proposition". This affords the marketer a meta-position, above and separate from the other operant resources and necessarily in a dominating power relationship with them. While Vargo and Lusch acknowledge that the service-centered orientation demands a new "lexicon" that severs its linguistic (and, therefore, conceptual) ties to the goods-dominant logic, the building blocks with which they construct their own S-D structure are unfortunately cast from the molds of that old lexicon.

Traditional marketing communication is addressed in Vargo and Lusch's FP$_7$, "The Enterprise Can Only Make Value Propositions". While approvingly quoting Gronroos' position that "the focus of marketing is value creation rather than value distribution" (Gronroos, 2000, p. 25), the authors continue this reasoning to note that this means that the firm can only provide "value propositions" regarding the services they can provide. The consumer "must understand" (Vargo & Lusch 2004, p. 11) that they are ultimately responsible for the existence of value, in that value only comes into being when the consumer is able to produce value through use. This means that the firm is to be involved in communicating potential values-in-use—namely, propositions. Such propositions need to be "better or more compelling" (ibid.) compared to those of a competitor. Although the word "persuasive" is missing, the implications are clear. In fact, what Vargo and Lusch are describing here is nothing more than the most traditional of advertising strategies, the explanation of the benefit. Advertising agencies have been attempting to sell products and services through the depiction of benefit scenarios since they became more than simple space brokers and began to offer their own creative services. Furthermore, returning once more to Classical rhetoric, the link between utility, happiness, and persuasion is made explicit by Aristotle, when he bases his whole explication of political rhetoric upon the observation that audiences are ultimately persuaded in matters of politics by what is useful for them, which in the end will come down to what makes them happy[3]. As Robert Bly (1990) explains in his classic, *The Copywriter's Handbook*, "a feature is a descriptive fact about a product or service. A benefit is what the user of the product or service gains as a result of the feature" (ibid., p. 57). Now, for Vargo and Lusch, Bly's words must be interpreted as pertaining to the writing of copy which asserts what Gronroos (2000) calls "ready-made value", in that the benefit proposition describes value that resides in the good or service, whereas a "value proposition" within the terms of S-D logic presents a 'good' or 'service' as facilitating the production of possible value by the consumer. Yet, despite their insistence that this is quite a different philosophy, the result will inevitably look exactly the same as traditional advertising forms because, I would maintain, advertising has long revolved around presenting the possible ways in which a product or service can be used by consumers to create value in their life. For example, each of the different advertising formats discussed by Leiss, Kline, and Jhally (1997) can be interpreted as a different way of presenting the basic message of 'this product/service can help you to do, or achieve, or find this thing which we understand is important to you'. So, in what they call the "self-transformation ad", we find the proposition that "people change— make themselves better—through the possession or use of the product" (ibid., p. 254). Regarding what they call the "product-image" format, the authors note that modern photographic techniques have allowed the creators of advertising messages to "place the product within a symbolic rather than utilitarian setting", allowing them to "[explore] the potentialities of products and their meaning in the human world" (ibid., p. 244). When a piece of advertising describes the ways in which a consumer can use a product or service to realize her goals then that advertising seeks to communicate a proposition regarding the potential value that can be realized through her use of the product or service. The consumer is portrayed as an operant resource, using the product to create her own value. But, of course, the problem lies in that phrase "is portrayed". The representation (no matter how indirect or mediated through however many layers) of the consumer as an *operant* resource immediately and inevitably demonstrates that they are an *operand* resource. Such a process creates a token of the consumer which is then *used* by the marketer to present a "compelling" "value proposition" back to them (in much the same way that the marketer asserts the operant nature of the consumer so that they may *use* it to argue for a directing position in the firm's strategic planning). It is difficult to interpret such an orientation as a concerted, serious attempt to understand the consumer as an operator in balanced co-operation with the firm. Vargo and Lusch's use of the word "compelling" is enough on its own to indicate the nature of the power relationship between consumer and marketer that remains in their S-D logic.

The final premise, FP_8, "A Service-Centered View is Customer Orientated and Relational", is naturally heavily focused on the trope of interactivity. Vargo and Lusch speak of the "inseparability" (Vargo & Lusch, 2004, p. 11) of the offerer and the consumer and argue the position that "exchange is relational" (ibid., p. 12). The level of nostalgia that the authors feed into this premise is rather disturbing, exemplified by their comment that an emphasis on individual customer satisfaction rather than on the number of goods sold "harks back to pre-Industrial Revolution days" (going on to quote a glowing description of the highly functional relationship between a Medieval knight and his armorer). Such cloyingly utopian nostalgia, or "romantic fiction" (Achrol & Kotler, 2006, p. 326), does little to clarify the details of the authors' theory of communicative interaction (and see Brown, 2007, for some scathing riffing on the 'retro' spirit haunting this foundational S-D logic text). For, despite all the talk of the "relationship focus" of service-centered marketing, there is precious little offered by Vargo and Lusch in the way of a clearly outlined explanation of how the new interaction differs from an old interaction. It is, in fact, only in the short discussion section after their presentation of the eight fundamental premises that the authors *openly* award the issue of communication with any prolonged attention and even then all we get is a short paragraph based on a large quote from Prahalad and Ramaswamy. For Vargo and Lusch, communication, which they very tellingly refer to by invoking the 4Ps as "promotion", "will need to become a communication process characterized by dialogue, asking and answering questions" (Vargo & Lusch, 2004, p. 13). The development of ongoing dialog, then, is the sum total of the explanation the reader receives regarding how S-D marketing theory views the communication responsibilities of the firm. This is, I would maintain, a glaring ellipsis. If service-centered marketing theory, and the Relationship Marketing and CRM that both feed into and emerge from it, are to be internally consistent they must be able to provide fully worked-through models of marketing communication that are able to demonstrate how dialog and interactivity suffuse the marketing system. As Vargo and Lusch (2004) demonstrate, however, a surface concern with the rhetoric of dialog hides (poorly) the absence of any real attempt to engage with communication issues arising from the fundamental premises of S-D logic.

If relationships are to be the heart of a marketing system it stands to reason that the communication that will allow them to grow and evolve will form the bedrock of such a system. And yet communication is the one aspect of the system that the principle texts contributing to the service-centered discourse refuse to address. As I have shown in previous chapters, the rhetoric of dialog and conversation is rampant across discourses inspired by RM and CRM yet there is a great deal of discomfort evident whenever that rhetoric needs to be deepened, developed and made more nuanced. The assertion of the importance of dialog and interactivity is rhetorically and logically significant but so is the absence, the silence, the turning away from any substantial discussion of its nature, meanings, complications or implications. "Dialog" and "interactivity" are once more seen to be used in a magical way—their incantation is designed to induce a vague sense of optimism and understanding in a reader rather than function as elements of an argument.

I have tried to show above that Vargo and Lusch's foundational text of S-D logic exhibits serious inconsistencies and lacunae in its description of the relational and interactive (and, hence, communicative) premises that are alleged to inform a service-centered marketing orientation. The most concrete lesson that can be drawn from the article with respect to the place of communication in S-D logic is that service-oriented university marketing communication courses should be organized around the teaching of Integrated Marketing Communication—a suggestion that carries no relationship whatsoever to the central questions of how dialog, co-production, and interactivity might be fostered by marketers. This *extreme* unwillingness to engage with communication issues is mirrored in other important texts of the service marketing and RM movements[4] and before I go on to consider my two additional exemplars I need to remark on the one element in Vargo and Lusch's discourse that appears to operate as a form of communication surrogate and which can be observed to function in the same way in the discourses of Gummesson and Peppers and Rogers. This element is the 'learning relationship'. When discussing their final fundamental premise regarding the relational nature of the service-centered view, Vargo and Lusch contend that "service provision is maximized through an iterative learning process" (ibid., p. 12) in which both the enterprise and the consumer take part. This relates back to their opening discussion of the differences between the G-D and S-D orientations, in which the importance of learning in the long-term survival of a firm is hammered home over and over across four paragraphs and two pages. Service orientation marketing is a "continuous learning process" (ibid., p. 5), the firm must use marketplace feedback to "learn how to improve" its offerings (ibid.), core competences are (they quote Prahalad & Hamel, 1990) the "collective learning" within the organization, customers are to be collaborated with and learnt from, as, of course, are outcomes. Vargo and Lusch use 'learning' as a way of obviating the need to engage with issues of communication; there is little attempt to outline the process of corporate learning for the word simply serves as a familiar, push-button, token guaranteed to induce nodding of the head. Of course learning is a good thing, of course it should be front and center in any theory of marketing—who would argue with such a position? And, of course, we're learning *from* the customer, not doing things *to* them. But the learning that is being proposed here is that enshrined in the negative feedback loop. The goal, or reference signal, is customer satisfaction with the service proposition offered by the marketer and in order to achieve this goal the marketer must learn how far away their value proposition is from the value the customer is able (or wishes to) to create with the service. Accordingly, the marketer alters her value proposition until it matches the value-in-use created by the consumer. This cannot be what Vargo and Lusch mean, though, because such a process depends on observing the value created by the consumer, monitoring them in order to determine how they use the service so that the offering can be improved. If we recall that all the firm can offer under S-D logic is a value proposition, this rather seems to translate into the idea that an enterprise must alter its propositions (its marketing communication) according to the knowledge it receives from observing the consumer's value creation—and such alteration can only happen once the proposition has been initially made. But where does that initial proposition come from? And, furthermore, doesn't this mean that an enterprise is always reacting to the consumer's use of its service provision? What place does the accumulation of knowledge (that core competence of the firm) play in a scenario which appears to concentrate on the immediate reaction to consumer's value-in-use?

Ballantyne and Varey (2006) have done an admirable job attempting to provide some expansion on the communication aspects of Vargo and Lusch's logic by way of discussing the dialogical potential within marketing. Their paper is interesting for its implicit constructivist perspective and the manner in which it provides a substantial explanation of the trope of 'learning' relationships, which is itself so vaguely utilized by Vargo and Lusch. Starting with the observation that I have been making throughout this study, that mainstream marketing approaches to communication are all based upon a "monological" control-centered, linear paradigm which is entirely inappropriate to support an S-D logic, Ballantyne and Varey seek to "reconnect communication with interaction" (ibid., p. 225) by broadening the marketing communication paradigm into a "matrix" which encompasses not only one-way communication of persuasive messages *to* the mass market but also two-way dialogical communication *with* and *between* customers which can take the form of either mass-customized interaction integrated with "planned messages" or a fully interactive form producing "co-created outcomes" (ibid., p. 226). Ballantyne and Varey

proceed to describe a truly radical understanding of a dialogical marketing modality which instead of being based upon informational or com-
municational constructions, is built upon the assumption that dialog is
"an interactive process of learning together" (ibid. p. 227) which is "open
ended, discovery oriented, and value creating". Such an understanding of
interactivity is one that is very much in line with my own, although there
are important differences in the way that I am constructing the 'matrix'
of communication. Ballantyne and Varey see dialogical interactive communication as an orientation, a commitment by the participants to relate
to each other in a particular way that can be adopted in order to break
free of the dominant mode of marketing communication which sees the
creation and "regulated transmission" of fixed messages as the be all and
end all of 'interaction'. For them, the dialogical mode is a different way of
going about communication—where each participant seeks to understand
the other's perspective and engages in interaction in order to learn together.
Consequently, Ballantyne and Varey see a difference between the types
of interaction that occur around a traditional print ad campaign, a piece
of CRM-driven direct mailing, and the prospective dialogical interaction
between partners who share trust and the desire to learn. My perspective
would be that all of these forms of marketing communication are dialogical
if we construct them so. Value is constructed by the consumer (and by every
other stakeholder) whether the firm is aware of it or not. The firm can,
through a re-orientation, integrate this co-creation into its understanding
of communication and its relationship with the networks of stakeholders
that it is a part of—but this does not bring co-creation into being. Co-
creation of value (or, in other words, the co-construction of meaning) is
something that happens anyway. A company can pretend as if it does not—
and therefore they will act and create understandings of the market based
upon a solely 'monological', control-orientated, transmission-based communication paradigm. In the final instance, perhaps, it is a choice based
upon the recognition of recursion in communication: As Krippendorff has
pointed out, when one positions "oneself in one's constructions of reality"
(acknowledging the recursive frame) one necessarily "must include one's
constructions of the realities of other human beings" (Krippendorff, 2009,
p. 85). Stakeholders co-create value (and meaning) when they engage with
traditional print ads, CRM-driven direct mailing or when they are involved
in the fully dialogical situations of "key account liaison between two or
more firms" or the "expansion of communities of common interest" on
the Internet (Ballantyne & Varey, 2006, p. 226). Ballantyne and Varey,
it must be said, are clear that all of the modes of interaction are, in the
end, "mental models" (i.e., constructions) but there is a sense in which the
radical nature of their propositions are blunted somewhat by their own
construction of "other" critical voices from the mainstream; they write of
the "charge of naïve altruistic intent" (ibid., p. 228) that might be brought
against their arguments and suggest only that dialog "might find a place"

(ibid.) in a "longer-term view" of marketing. Yet, if we take the ideas of the co-creation of value and the constructed nature of marketing communication models as premises in a re-orientation of marketing (as Ballantyne & Varey do, and as I have done in this book) then dialog must be afforded more than "a place" in it. A consistent working through of the idea of the co-creation of value would naturally spiral out to a consideration of the created nature of all value throughout the marketing network of relationships and the way in which such creation is an integral part of all stakeholders' understanding of both themselves and others.

The focus on learning that Ballantyne and Varey give to their understanding of 'authentic' dialog is one based upon mutuality. They write of "dialogical inquiry" between participants, who will "listen and learn" and therefore "become more reflective of the consequences of past action" (ibid., p. 229), extending this to a "mutual checking of assumptions" that must be "fundamental" to such learning (ibid., p. 230). As such, the authors significantly contribute to creating a real understanding of what learning might mean for an S-D logic, bringing it firmly into a constructivist frame and emphasizing the mutual, constantly dynamic nature of the joint exploration of understandings that dialog entails. Ballantyne and Varey's paper is framed as a "liberating view" in Vargo and Lusch's edited collection of papers on S-D logic and I think it is fair to say that the critiques that the former provide of the latter's original "fundamental premises" speak of the need for quite serious revisions to the service-dominant framework. While I share some of their concern that understanding the co-creation of value as "embedded in any useful communicative interaction" (ibid., p. 232) can, if applied similarly across all relationships in the marketing network, lead to serious questions regarding the delimiting of marketing (and hence impact the perception of the effectiveness of a discipline that appears to have no bounds), I hope to show in my final chapter that such an extension is practical and desirable.

An additional rhetorical aspect to Vargo and Lusch's portrayal of the 'learning' service-orientated enterprise is the heavily ironic light in which it is placed by Ben Wooliscroft's (2008) work delineating the remarkable amnesia that runs throughout their discourse. Wooliscroft compares, premise by fundamental premise, Vargo and Lusch's presentation of S-D Logic with Wroe Alderson's 1965 theory of marketing and finds "considerable overlap in concept" such that he concludes that the 2004 paper "does not herald a new paradigm, merely a return to, or reflection of, a 'lost' paradigm" (ibid, p. 379). For Wooliscroft this is a larger reflection of the way in which marketing theory is taught without reference to its history, making marketing "a discipline with amnesia all too often built into our education" (ibid.). If Vargo and Lusch's own discourse demonstrates such a propensity for forgetting, what are we to make of their contradictory insistence on learning? Is it simply a strategic piece of misdirection designed to distract attention away from their own short-circuiting of the learning loop? Or does the situating of learning at the heart of the service approach serve to forestall engagement with larger issues of communication? Certainly, as Mark Tadajewski (2008) has noted, Vargo and Lusch have latterly been far more open in addressing the historical precedents to their S-D Logic. Furthermore, as I will now show, the importance accorded to 'learning' in canonical Relationship Marketing texts by Gummesson and Peppers and Rogers suggests that it represents more than a passing, expedient rhetorical strategy.

Gummesson's (2008) third edition of *Total Relationship Marketing* represents an attempt to integrate the perspectives and vocabulary emanating from S-D Logic with the precedents set by his own work in service marketing and the Nordic School approach to Relationship Marketing. Gummesson's definition of RM as "interaction in networks of relationships" (ibid., p. 5) clearly foregrounds interactivity as the central process in a service-orientation to marketing. He goes on to explain that by interaction he means that the parties in a network "enter into active contact with each other" (ibid., p. 6). This, unfortunately, tends to raise more questions than it answers; what exactly would 'passive contact' be, how is "active contact" to be characterized and recognized? The binary opposition of active/passive is a common feature in marketing discourse, of course, and is reflected in the notions of 'empowerment' and consumer production that have been examined in earlier chapters. 'Passive contact', if I were to presume what such a construct entails, would refer to situations where representatives of a firm in some way direct consumers to do or think something and those consumers then 'passively' obey the directions without generating any comment, reflexivity, or contextualization. One doesn't need to be a constructivist to react to the absurdity of such an idea. When we use words like 'active', their binary opposites are inescapably invoked; 'active' is used in comparison to 'passive'. Gummesson, in describing interactivity as "active contact" is constructing a rhetorical opposition in which he implies that there are relationships in marketing which are (or have been) passive. This in turn adds argumentative weight to his assertion that Relationship Marketing and the Service-Dominant Logic that buttresses it, are representative of a "paradigm shift in marketing" (ibid., pp. 29, 334). Granted, Gummesson is not saying that the 'reality' of business practice has changed, rather the paradigm shift is occurring in the way that marketing as a discourse constructs what happens in the 'real' world. In this context, 'passive contact' would be the construction of mainstream, G-D marketing theory which understands communication/interaction between the firm and the consumer as a predominantly one-way transmission of information designed to elicit particular pre-planned responses—a view which would approach all customer contacts from the perspective of a control system. In fact, Gummesson is quite clear that Relationship Marketing should be viewed as a construct through which we may choose to see the world and that therefore it is only one of many. This stance is summed up in the "relationship eye-glasses" metaphor, which Gummesson extends into quite a sustained analogy. Theories and models, he explains, are lenses through which we can observe the world and sometimes we might have a set of lenses that are "wrongly curved" and they will lead us to perceive the world as a blur, or perhaps if we wear "tinted" lenses then we will see the sky as "sunny when *in fact* it is cloudy" (ibid., p. 29, emphasis mine). Gummesson continues by arguing that because marketing is a "complex field" we actually need a number of different glasses that can offer us different "perspectives" and then concludes by explaining that his book,

> offers the relationship eye-glasses. If we look through these glasses we can only see relationships, networks and interaction. RM is about what you see through these glasses. (ibid.)

Although the whole passage has constructivist connotations there is an important feature of Gummesson's presentation which should not be over-looked; there is a real world out there that some of our perspectives can get wrong while others can get right. In other words, theory glasses should help us to see particular aspects of the real world, but some theories can be "wrongly curved" or offer us a view of the world that is "in fact" incor-rect. He goes further, indeed, by noting that if readers recognize the view in some way, if his explication of RM leads to a sense of *déjà vu*, then "it means that the text is close to reality and has validity" (ibid.). The unavoid-able implication being that "validity" is bound to "reality". Now, what I can take away from this is that there are some theories, such as RM, which offer different perspectives on the reality of business practice while there are others which are, in some way or another, broken, defective, or biased and these theories offer an incorrect view of the reality of business practice. It might be the case, therefore, that the view of communication and relation-ships which promotes the assumption that consumers can be passive should be considered to be one of those broken theories that does not describe reality correctly. On the other hand, Gummesson does, in passing, make reference to the existence of passive relationships which may be "invisibly embedded" in networks yet still, confusingly, influential (ibid., p. 30). He also, when discussing power as a property of a commercial relationship, states that the Web "as a medium for information and interactivity gives the customer more power", thereby implying that contemporary "relation-scapes" influenced by the Internet would contain more "active contact" than those existing prior to the widespread adoption of such technology (ibid., p. 31). This, in turn, leads one to the conclusion that the evolution of the RM paradigm matches a change in business reality; customers have become more powerful, more active, as they have been able to make use of more interactive technology. This perspective brings us back to the infer-ence that customers used to be more passive, and so less powerful, because the marketing relationships they were involved in left them little room for interactivity and so positioned them as weaker partners in what Gummesson terms an "asymmetrical relationship" of power (ibid., p. 31). Relationship Marketing would, given such circumstances, provide a way for firms to navigate the balancing of power relationships in such uncharted waters.

In previous chapters I have treated the claims of contemporary marketers that the consumer is now in an 'empowered' position as rhetorical strategies designed to maintain a dominant (and dominating) communication as control paradigm. How far, then, might Gummesson's discourse of "active contact" be seen as masking deeper assumptions of control?

Despite (or perhaps because of) both the large number of case studies and stories in Gummesson's text that are designed to exemplify either inspiring RM practice or failure to recognize the importance of relationships in modern marketing, and the soaring super-structure of the 30 relationships, there is surprisingly little space devoted to theoretical discussion of the nature of marketing interaction. The reader is told that "you can only understand customers by regularly meeting them" as this enables the training of "empathy" and leads to the opportunity for "reflecting over your observations" (ibid., p. 105). While this is clearly a description of a *learning* ("training") process there is a strongly one-sided aspect to its presentation: The enterprise meets regularly with the customer in order to learn from them, to use such encounters in order to develop empathy and then go away and, alone, reflect upon what it has learned. In Vargo and Lusch's terms, this is a highly *operand* portrayal of the customer: They are there to be used, to be learned from. When talking of the many interaction "touch points" that exist during service production and delivery processes, Gummesson suggests the a "viable strategy" to use such "points of marketing" is to find those

> which make an impact on the customer's relationship to the company and decide how to best handle them in order to cement the relationship, improve retention and stimulate positive word-of-mouth and referrals. (ibid., p. 87)

The language here is, again, heavy with assumptions of management and control: The company decides, handles, cements, improves and stimulates. The customer is simply someone whose responses can be monitored and learned from. Here, the importance of the role of knowledge in Gummesson's approach to interactivity becomes clear. Following the lead of Vargo and Lusch, Gummesson states that "knowledge and skills are what makes a value proposition" (ibid., p. 188). He goes on to approvingly quote Leif Edvinsson's description of his own role as a Corporate Director of Intellectual Capital, the mission of which Edvinsson sees as being

> "to identify and improve the visibility of intangible and non-material items, to capture and package these items for transfer to users, to

cultivate and develop these items through training and knowledge networking, and to capitalize and economize on these items through rapid recycling of knowledge and increased commercialization" (quote in Gummesson, 2008, p. 194)

The language here mirrors Gummesson's own in treating knowledge as an operand resource that is captured, packaged, transferred, cultivated, developed, etc. If customers, suppliers, and all the other stakeholders of the S-D logic are deemed to be *operant* resources and yet the reason that the firm constructs value in them is that they contain a resource that is regarded and understood as nothing other than an *operand* resource, surely the categorization of stakeholders as operant resources is a rhetorical conceit? In other words, if an RM or S-D approach organizes itself around knowledge as being the primary source of competitive advantage and if it constructs knowledge as an operand resource, then essentially it has not moved marketing even one step forward. The idea of embedded knowledge that Gummesson describes as giving "sustaining competitive advantage" (ibid., p. 190) beautifully demonstrates the way in which the language used to describe the concept betrays and predicates the way in which it is understood. Saying that something is 'embedded' in something else is to use a metaphor from the mining of traditional natural resources to talk about (to others and to oneself) something intangible. Consequently, in comparing knowledge to something physical that needs to be carefully and patiently (and sometimes rather violently) extracted from something else, one treats both it and the surroundings which it has to be separated from as operand resources, and knowledge is no longer something that is a dynamic, fluid, emergent property of relationships. If this is the view of knowledge, then learning becomes a process of extraction and transfer. While Gummesson states that dialogical interaction in stakeholder relationships is the key to successful knowledge transfer and creation, the operand approach to knowledge that is evident in his discourse inevitably reflects upon the understanding of interaction and relationship that is contained in his explication of Relationship Marketing.

Peppers and Rogers' (1999) way of talking about interaction, relationships and knowledge is framed within classically cybernetic language:

> Without individual customer feedback, no collaboration or customization is possible, not is it possible to specify a customer's needs in more detail. Creating dialogue opportunities with customers is a prerequisite for soliciting feedback. But the dialogue itself needs to be integrated into the enterprise's existing knowledge of that customer and its need for additional information. (ibid., p. 25)

Now, while on the surface this passage appears to echo Ballantyne and Varey's understanding of dialog as a learning relationship, there is clearly very little emphasis on the mutuality of the relationship. Firstly, dialog is seen as a "prerequisite" rather than the end in itself. The stark caricature of feedback as something that the firm solicits from the customer (rather than something that is constantly generated by the customer whether the firm hears it or not and which is also constantly generated by the firm itself) demonstrates a decidedly mechanistic approach to interaction. So, while Peppers and Rogers speak of the "Learning Relationship" and "communicating with" rather than *to* (ibid., p. 251), and while they advise that the firm's understanding of the customer should be switched from "passive target to active participant" (ibid., p. 25), when they discuss the practical implementation of such dialogical ideals their understanding of the customer as an operand resource becomes quite apparent. Perhaps one of the most striking instances of this orientation is the way in which Peppers and Rogers explain the significance of knowledge in the "Learning Relationship". Firms should engage in interaction with customers in order to extract knowledge from them. While this knowledge can include the knowledge of what one particular customer has in common with a larger community of customers (to enable the sort of recommendation systems used by Amazon.com and various online music sites), the principle form of knowledge the authors focus on is that of the individual customer's needs and preferences. This knowledge is only worthwhile in so far as it is remembered by the organization, so that any dialog can always be picked up at a later time. For Peppers and Rogers, the purpose of this knowledge-acquiring dialog and "customer-specification memory" is to arrive at a state where you "can create a literally insurmountable barrier to competition" (ibid., p. 177). If customers are put into a position by the firm where they expend significant time and effort in informing the firm of their tastes and preferences, then "the customer is, through his own effort, increasing the *value* of the enterprise, to *him*" (ibid., p. 170). The firm is consequently warned to make sure that customers do indeed "expend effort" (ibid.) in 'teaching' the firm their needs and tastes for it is only through the investment of such effort that they will create a relationship of value to them. More importantly, however, the more effort customers are asked to go through to train the firm, the less likely they are to want to repeat the process with a competitor. As Peppers and Rogers note, the "kind of relationship marketing we are advocating here" is one entirely based upon *convenience* and it is this convenience which provides the competitive advantage by putting up a "barrier of inconvenience" (ibid., p. 179) between the customer and any other competitor. Furthermore, once that barrier goes up it allows the enterprise that shares the relationship of convenience to begin to charge more, justifying the higher price as the relationship has become more valuable to the customer. It is very difficult to not think of this process as a form of carefully laid trap. The marketer lures the customer into divulging more and more information until she has traveled so far down the road that she suddenly finds the "barrier of inconvenience" blocking any prospect of returning back the way she came. The trapped customer now has to live out the rest of her days hostage to the pricing whims of her all-knowing captor. Certainly, it is not as if Peppers and Rogers are trying very hard to dispel such an understanding—not for them the rhetoric of co-creation, co-production, or dialog as mutual learning journey. Interaction is useful only in so far as it leads to the extraction of knowledge regarding customer preferences which can lead to locking a customer into a relationship of convenience. It is noticeable, though, that the whole system works only because the customer is loathe to supply knowledge regarding her preferences to many firms—it is dependent upon the laziness of the customer, or, rather, an understanding of the customer as lazy. Which itself produces a rather paradoxical situation—a faith that a customer will supply her information to only one's own firm. If an enterprise rewards the rendering of preferences and tastes with the convenience of instant customization tailored to those tastes, surely competitors will be doing the same thing. Peppers and Rogers' rhetorically powerful example of a Starbucks and Barista Brava doing business next to each other on the same street works because it places one firm which memorizes customer preferences in juxtaposition to another which does not. Once you have given your personal order at a Barsita Brava it is remembered for the next time you pop in—and that level of convenience can result in greater brand loyalty when compared to the Starbucks experience where you have to re-tell your complicated list of preferences each time you order. But what if Starbucks listens to Peppers and Rogers and begins to institute the same "customer specification memory"? The enterprise has to walk a fine line between making the rendering of personal information costly in effort but at the same time not making it so costly that it will annoy the customer. And in a world of firms all following one-to-one strategies, each enterprise is going to have to look at measuring just how much effort it is asking customers to spend in comparison to its competitors. The "barrier of inconvenience" only works when you have been the first and only firm in your product or service niche to extract the tastes and preferences from the customer. Paradoxically, this situation leads to the obvious attraction of non-interactive, non-dialog-based knowledge-extraction techniques. After all, in a marketspace flooded with one-to-one marketers all playing the relationship game, if you can demonstrate to a customer that they can have the benefit of a long-term, dialog-filled relationship without going through the effort of such a thing (in other words, that they can 'walk in' to a turnkey relationship) then you will offer not only the convenience of instantly appropriate customization but also the extra convenience of *not* having to answer 'just a few more questions'. In following Peppers and Rogers' Convenience-Dominant Logic one has to extrapolate to the uncomfortable possibility that dialog and interaction might not be very convenient for the customer who is, a lot of the time, rushed, distracted, suspicious, and simply bored of questions. Just because customers spend increasingly more time volunteering knowledge about themselves on social networking sites to large networks of friends, followers, and vague acquaintances doesn't mean to say that they wouldn't much rather be twittering about how much a 'griefer' the sales rep is for asking so many questions rather than offering up one more piece of personal information to a brand they are still very much ambivalent about. The extraction of customer knowledge that Peppers and Rogers portray is naturally something that is much more efficiently done through the type of intensive monitoring that I have examined in Chapter 4. As they note, advancing information technologies mean that there are more and more opportunities for firms to increase the "bandwidth" (ibid., p. 256) in any point of contact between customers and the enterprise and this, combined with careful design of the "dialogue interface", will lead to more efficient automation of the knowledge extraction process. They conclude that

> for products that involve significant differences among customers, the bandwidth of a dialogue must accommodate as much automated measurement of these customers' different needs as possible. (ibid., p. 259)

For the sake of convenience, and because the technology allows it, much of this measurement will be tacit.

Peppers and Rogers portrayal of interaction in the Convenience-Dominant Logic of one-to-one marketing presents dialog as a method for knowledge extraction which is easily, and necessarily, superseded by automated measurement and memory technologies. While there are some instances where Peppers and Rogers appear to pay a little more than lip service to the idea of dialog as mutual learning (see Beckett & Nayak, 2008 for a more sympathetic account than I afford them, for example), their construction of the "Learning Relationship" is one predominantly characterized by a mechanistic, one-sided approach to knowledge extraction (rather than knowledge creation) and an understanding of communication predicated upon the transmission metaphor. Furthermore, the logic informing the "Learning Relationship" extrapolates to the gradual substitution of dialog by tacit measurement.

While there are some notable voices contained in the discourse surrounding Relationship Marketing and Service-Dominant Logic which construct understandings of dialog consistently focused around a sense of mutuality between all stakeholders in the marketing system and an appreciation of reflexive communication as the foundation of the marketing enterprise, the general tone is one of *saying* that customers are empowered equals while understanding them as operand resources that need to be mined for every last piece of knowledge that can extracted from them. The way that RM and S-D Logic have highlighted both knowledge as the source of competitive advantage and the concomitant variations upon the "Learning Relationship" that spring from such an understanding is indicative of what I have called at the start of this chapter a 'turning away' from the challenges of communication in a relationship orientation. The fetishization of customer knowledge in the RM and CRM paradigms comes at the expense of any real attempt to examine or change the communication assumptions that underwrite their basic marketing approach. Notable exceptions, such as we find in Ballantyne and Varey, are very much marginalized within the dominant discourse. The rhetoric of dialog and interaction serves to more strongly differentiate RM and S-D Logic from their mainstream antecedents but the failure to seriously and consistently re-examine the basic metaphors and understandings of communication that underlie the new logic has meant that interaction and dialog have tended to simply remain rhetorical strategies of differentiation. The situation that we are now confronted with in contemporary RM, CRM and S-D discourse is one where the basic building blocks of the orientation (interaction and dialog) are almost entirely unexamined. It should not be that much of a surprise, then, if these new approaches end up uncritically reproducing the dominant metaphors and understandings that have characterized the marketing mainstream's engagement with issues of communication since its inception. Yet, within a *relationship* and *service* marketing frame this ironic failure to engage with, re-examine, and re-articulate our basic understandings of communication and marketing communication is a lost opportunity of exceptional proportions.

The comparison of the RM orientation to an autistic model of marketing in my chapter heading is one I make carefully. While acknowledging the controversial nature of autism and autism spectrum disorder diagnosis, the collection of a particular complex of symptoms covering severe difficulties in social interaction and communication under the rubric of autism serves as a particularly fruitful metaphor for the position that, I would claim, RM finds itself in. One of the defining behaviors observed in the autism spectrum disorders is the avoidance of, the turning away from, social interaction. John Richer, using an ethological approach to the examination of autism, notes that in their early development autistic children are particularly likely to avoid interactions which have characteristics of "uncertainty and intrusion" which in turn leads to the child engaging in "little negotiation of shared meanings" (Richer, 2001a, pp. 29–30). Richer connects (though not exclusively) this early developmental feature with research that has observed comparatively poorer 'mindreading' abilities in autistic children. Such abilities require a child to "take the viewpoint of another" (Richer, 2001b, p. 38), understanding that others can believe things that we know not to be true as well as being able to appreciate what, say, person A thinks person B is thinking. As illustrating one of the consequences of this poorer development of what can broadly be termed intersubjectivity, Richer refers to the writing of Donna Williams, who has written of her own autism. Williams finds that "in social relationships she is either in 'receive' or 'send' mode . . . but she has great difficulty in doing both together", facing, in her words, a "complete shutdown in the ability to maintain simultaneous processing of 'self' and 'other'" (Williams quoted in Richer, 2001b, pp. 44–45). Mapping these observations on to the discourse of Relationship Marketing and its accompanying S-D logic, I would argue that they construct an understanding of marketing which, while contextualized within the rhetoric of social interaction, demonstrates a failure to approach that interaction in terms of a communicative integration of self and other. In viewing knowledge as an operand resource that is to be extracted and owned rather than as an embodied construction of mind, RM understands the "learning relationship" as based upon a one-way acquisition of a valuable 'thing'. In doing so, the possibility that a "learning relationship" might be a simultaneous examination of a multitude of one's own and other stakeholders' constructions of self and other is inevitably abandoned. So, while lip service is paid to the idea of co-creation of value, there has been little engagement in marketing theory with how the firm creates value for itself and how it *imagines* it is created by others. The logic underlying the "value proposition" means that it simply becomes the search for "a deeper meaning behind what we are buying and consuming" (Gummesson 2008, p. 325), an evolution of Rosser Reeves's unique selling proposition indexed to an expanded, deeper, more invasive research into the consumer's attitudes, needs, and preferences. It remains, like the USP, something that the firm will transmit to the consumer in order to convince them of its greater viability.

The stereotypical, repetitious behavior of the autistic child, I see metaphorically mirrored in the constant rhetoric of interaction and dialog that is present throughout RM discourse. The words are said over and over again, yet their meaning is not examined—they are frozen tokens for something that the discourse has not been able to connect with, has not wanted to connect with, and so have now become something else—a ritualized reaction to the stress of marketing's current position in the boardroom, perhaps. In the final chapter, I will present an initial attempt to re-connect with the recursive nature of communication, trying to help build a way of understanding marketing that is predicated upon the mutual co-ordination of constructions of self and others across all stakeholders equally.

7 A Recursive, Invitational Model of Marketing Interactivity

In this final chapter I wish to present a model of marketing communication that, while being founded upon continual, mutual interactivity between actors traditionally termed "consumer" and "producer", at the same time rejects the control paradigm that has informed all previous attempts to integrate interactivity into the marcoms system. The model is constructivist in that it assumes that all communication can be seen as building mental models of world, self, and others that are dynamic (in the sense that they are constantly revised) but also tend toward stability (in that our tendency is to seek further consistency between our re-presentations and our observations). The approach taken in this chapter is one which seeks to combine, from a constructivist perspective, a number of discourse streams from disparate fields. The characterization of some of the basic actors or agents in the model originates in earlier work attempting to expand the subtlety of the standard marketing communication schemes (Stern, 1994; Miles, 2007). In addition, the recursive model of communication proposed by Krippendorff (2009) is here adapted and extended to provide a framework for the self-referential aspect of marketing communication hitherto entirely ignored in the literature. In order to engage with a definition of interactivity that challenges assumptions of control, I have attempted to integrate a form of the "rhetoric of invitation" outlined by Foss and Griffin (1995) as well as incorporating some of the implications of Benoit and Smythe's (2003) ELM-inspired study of the rhetoric of message reception. Finally, in order to help bridge the recursive and the persuasive, I have turned to the rhetoric of self-persuasion as formulated by Jean Nienkamp (2001).

In previous chapters I have shown how marketing's relationship with the issue of interactivity is one based upon distinctly contradictory, even paradoxical, forces of discourse. While interaction is held up as a vital component of redemptive approaches such as Relationship Marketing, the Co-Creation of Value, Service-Dominant Logic, and even 'postmodern marketing', their rhetoric of dialog and free conversation is severely undercut by assumptions of management, scripting, direction, and control that inform the deep structure of their discourses. The first-order cybernetic trope of feedback, and its associated elements of reference (or target) signals and the quantitative measurement of communication results, continue to hold sway over marketing's understanding of what interactivity is and how it is to be 'implemented'. While critical marketing theory in general, and constructionist perspectives in particular, are slowly being allowed to take up some form of residency in marketing academia, it is still unclear exactly how much influence they will either wish, or be able, to exert on the day-to-day practice, or understanding-in-practice, of marketing. The following model, therefore, is my attempt to stake a claim for practical relevance by constructing a description of marketing communication in which interactivity is not hobbled by a control or management understanding of dialog as direction but is instead allowed to reflect the way in which all observation is at the same time creation. In doing so, I hope to provide a model which can be used to both investigate previous and current practice as well as bring a new operating perspective to the future convergence of consumption and production.

FOUNDING METAPHORS

Throughout this book I have drawn attention to the metaphors that underlie mainstream marketing discourse on interaction and relationships. I have talked of the ways that communication metaphors of transmission, direction, containment, and linearity have constrained and characterized how marketing, even in its most recent and 'reflexive' forms, has understood the nature of interactivity between firm and customer (indeed, between all stakeholders in the marketing system). It is important, therefore, that any attempt to construct a new model of marketing communication looks first to its metaphors. For, let us not forget, a model is constructed from smaller models, miniature representations, metaphorical shorthand. To try and avoid the assumptions of control, persuasion, and causation that marketing models have generally been founded upon and which their verbal and diagrammatic rhetoric reflect, metaphors that carry connotations of mutuality, creation, co-ordination, observation, and recursion will need to form the building blocks of the new model.

To help me in this search for apposite metaphors I turn to a remarkable paper written by Foss and Griffin (1995) narrating their exploration of "invitational rhetoric", a rhetorical format that seeks to find alternatives to the perception of the audience as an homogeneous conglomerate of an opponent who needs to be persuaded through manipulation and domination. A scholar well-versed in the language of Relationship Marketing, S-D Logic and the co-creation of unique value will be quite taken aback on reading Foss and Griffin's description of invitational rhetoric because so many of the words that they choose to portray the invitational orientation are familiar from the discourse of service-based marketing theories. Foss and Griffin talk of offerings, propositions, joining with the audience in creativity, seeing the audience as composed of unique individuals, and the conveyance of value. Indeed, the following passage, with the substitution of 'enterprise' for 'rhetors', could just as easily have come from an RM encomium on the joys of interactive dialog:

> When value is created in a communicative situation, audience members feel rhetors see them as significant individuals and appreciate and attend to their uniqueness. They feel rhetors care about them, understand their ideas, and allow them to contribute in significant ways to the interaction. (Foss & Griffin, 1995, p. 12)

Yet the context in which these words are framed is rather more alien to marketing discourse. For Foss and Griffin, invitational rhetoric is a chance to eschew the basic pattern of trying to change someone else's opinion. As they point out, "discursive strategies" designed to persuade people to change their mind "constitute a kind of trespassing on the personal integrity of others" (ibid., p. 3). A trespassing which manifests itself in an obsession with control that completely infuses the discourse of traditional persuasive rhetoric (and marketing communication). As an alternative to this combative orientation to communicative interaction, invitational rhetoric "constitutes an invitation to the audience to enter the rhetor's world and see it as the rhetor does" (ibid., p. 5). There is, importantly, no attempt to persuade the audience that they are wrong and the rhetor is right—rather, the rhetor presents her understanding, seeking to most clearly and vividly portray her construction of a situation, a meaning, an event. At the same time, the invitational rhetor is present not only to narrate her own understanding but also to listen to those of the audience. *Kairos*, within the terms of invitational rhetoric, describes the transformative exploration of our own and others' understandings that occurs in the immediate present of invitational interaction; for in narrating our own constructions and in listening to those of others we may come to observe new perspectives which further transform our own. In other words, the practice of invitational rhetoric is just as likely to transform the rhetor as it is members of the audience. Accordingly, the rhetor does not engage in rhetorical strategies of defense designed to belittle the audience's expression of difference. Difference of understanding is not 'wrong'. Ballantyne and Varey (2006) admirably express this in terms of their approach to marketing dialog when they note that "it is quite possible to achieve understanding even if the parties agree to differ" (ibid., p. 230). Foss and Griffin are careful to caution that the end of invitational rhetoric should not be taken to be *change* (whether of the rhetor or of the audience) but rather the offering of the opportunity to mutually explore understandings. Value is framed in invitational terms by the condition that the rhetor values the "intrinsic and immanent worth" (Foss & Griffin, 1995, p. 11) of individual audience members. This worth is embodied in their individual understanding, their unique perspective, and the rhetor honors this value through approaching them as individuals and facing up to their "alterity", their 'otherness' through an intense, committed listening which forgoes any form of interruption in order to let speakers "discover their own perspectives" (ibid., p. 11).

While some of Foss and Griffin's ideas might seem difficult, if not inappropriate, to implement within a marketing paradigm, I would argue that the basic premises are not that far from much of the rhetoric that I have been examining in mainstream RM approaches. If marketing is about creating relationships, if it is about engaging in dialog with stakeholders as co-producers of value, content, and service, if it is about engaging in committed, respectful listening to the value constructs of others, then it is indeed closely related to the concerns of invitational rhetoric. Instead of transmission, containment, direction, struggle, or management, let the metaphor of invitation be the foundation for a theory of interactive marketing.

Foss and Griffin speak of the invitation as an offering of an individual perspective. The rhetor invites the audience to see the world or, more practically, the issue at hand, through her eyes while at the same time offering (through concentrated, committed listening) to explore the issue through the audience's eyes. From the constructivist position that I began to set out in Chapter 3, I would argue that the words 'construction' or 'understanding' offer a clearer sense that each stakeholder *creates* the 'perspective' from which she observes. I also would wish to underline the dynamic nature of such constructed understandings which the word 'perspectives' does not, for me, suggest very strongly. A perspective is a view from a particular position, which tends to imply that whoever looks from that position at whatever time will see the landscape framed in the same way. Yet, as I have been at pains to point out in earlier chapters, and as Foss and Griffin demonstrate in many of their examples of invitational rhetoric, people are constantly changing, their constructed understandings evolving even as they engage in communication. The rhetor changes in the act of rhetoric. In the re-presentation of one's constructed understandings, if the audience listens with committed respect, they give the rhetor the opportunity to, recursively, observe and create those understandings anew. This insight, which is present in Foss and Griffin's invitational rhetoric, the second-order cybernetic communication theories of Krippendorff (1996, 2009), Jean Nienkamp's consideration of "internal rhetorics", and the radical constructivism of von Glasersfeld, must be central to any nuanced model of interactive marketing. To imagine that the various stakeholders of a marketing system are forever constant in their understandings is to do irredeemable violence to the viability of one's model of that system. Recursion and the constant change it invokes have to be situated deep within the interactive marketing model.

The themes of invitation, offering, and recursion and evolution suggest opening, circular, spiraling metaphors rather than linear, simple causations. As interactivity is to be understood as a process which will potentially lead to change in all stakeholders, and as that change is by its very nature almost impossible to predict (as well as never final) the classical marketing depiction of communication as something that transmits messages of influence from A to B, or from A to B to C, will be quite unhelpful.

In order to begin to formalize the model I would like to return to the premises of my constructivist understanding of marketing interactivity as presented in Chapter 3, integrating them with the invitational and recursive elements using metaphors of opening and circularity. Before I can do this, however, I require a way of talking efficiently about tensions that occur when we attempt to co-ordinate with others' understandings that are necessarily dynamic. The most convincing framework for such a discussion that I have found originates in the work of Heinz von Foerster and is generally referred to as his theory of eigenforms. The next section, therefore, will examine how thinking in terms of eigenforms and eigenbehaviours can give us considerable aid when exploring the dynamic nature of constructions of self and others.

EIGENFORMS

The discussion of eigenforms in von Foerster (1981) has been notably explicated and elaborated upon by Louis H. Kauffman (2003) who manages to frame the concepts within broader terms that have more immediate applicability in the social sciences. I have, elsewhere (Miles, 2007), used eigenforms to help construct a second-order cybernetic model of marketing communication and I will here continue my adaption of the eigenform notion into an invitational, constructivist understanding of marketing as interaction.

The idea of the eigenform is based upon the fundamentally constructivist position that "objects are not objects at all, but rather indications of processes" (Kauffman, 2003, p. 73). An "object" (and, naturally, objects include the social world of ourselves and others) takes on 'solidity' for us as a result of its being a symbol "participating in a network of interactions" (ibid.). The pattern of those interactions brings apparent stability, and hence apparent 'solidity', to our understanding of the object. So, as Kauffman, summarizes:

> In the process of observation, we interact with ourselves and with the world to produce stabilities that become the objects of our perception. (ibid., p. 78)

It was von Foerster's contention that this stability was the result of an act of imaginative creation; fixing in the form of a stable "token" the infinite, recursive process of interactions (what von Foerster called the eigenbehaviour). Connecting these ideas to the constructivist perception of marketing scenarios that I introduced in Chapter 3, we may recognize that our constructions of each other, of the customer (as a mass, but also as an individual in a face-to-face context), of the brand, of the market, and of ourselves, are imagined stabilities that we create from our observations of our interactions. Such stabilities, such eigenforms, are the tokens of an "infinite cascade" (Rocha, 1996) of interactions that precede the stabilization, a dynamic stream of observations of ourself and the other. Once we have created an apparent pattern of stability in this stream of observations, this pattern becomes a thing, an object, invested with solidity and inherently resistant to change. Our ideas of our brand, what our service is, who the customers are, how a supplier relates to us, these can all be thought of as eigenforms that are the result of our distinguishing patterns in the observation of our interactions. We can take the apparent stability of such objects as more than apparent, we can think of it as 'real', in the sense that the customer is always the customer. Our tokens become our realities, and our shorthand notes become the entire discourse. Of course, most of the time, as we observe more, as we interact further, we correct our eigenforms, update them if the patterns become too divergent. When we change our opinions of people we have a reference that we can use to measure the new patterns of interaction against: 'You are not the same person you used to be', then, invokes a previous token of 'you' and marks a change in pattern against it. We recognize this in the need for continually updating customer profiles—we might try hard not to behave as if the individual customer is always going to be the same and the constant collection, storage, and analysis of customer interactions *can* allow marketers to dynamically adjust the summary patterns they generate for each customer. However, although current marketing understanding might have room to consider the customer as a dynamic representation of patterns of interaction, there is little sense in which marketers might consider other stakeholders, including themselves, as being dynamically generated tokens. The reflexivity that a constructivist position demands is generally entirely absent from mainstream marketing theory and practice. The notion of eigenforms can be used to call attention to the way in which our constructions of ourselves and the other stakeholders in a marketing system are *all* constructions that are interim tokens, undergoing adaptation, re-creation, or sometimes outright abandonment. If interaction is seen as something that is fundamentally a creative process, in that it is through the observation of interactions that each stakeholder constantly moves toward the stabilization of eigenforms of themselves, others, and all those patterns they discern in the marketing system, then it may be profitably seen as the fundamental process that underlies marketing.

Substituting a constructivist framing of *interactivity* for *exchange* at the heart of marketing allows us to consider the way in which *marketing creates the marketer* as well as creating the other stakeholders in the marketing system. Furthermore, the notion of the eigenform encourages us to consider the dynamic nature of the tokens that we create, helping us to be reflexive about the static nature of the representations we bring to the fore of our discourses, suggesting to us that such stasis is an imaginative convention that can sometimes threaten to mask the unceasing nature of our observation and, consequently, of our patterning. In traditional areas of marketing communication, the fixing of interim eigenforms within the messages presented by stakeholders to other stakeholders can lead to representations of consumers and brand elements that are strongly out of sync with the current understandings such stakeholders have of themselves (Miles, 2007). So, for example, the in-message representation of the target audience is a fixed eigenform—it is a construction created by a number of individuals co-ordinating their separate constructed understanding of the "target audience" for a campaign and then 'freezing' it within an advertising presentation. The fixed nature of the representation within the message means that it cannot undergo the constant re-creation that is a matter-of-course part of the continual interaction process we are all engaged in. The same goes for the in-message (or within-text, as Stern would call it) representation of the 'sponsor' brand—a constantly evolving, co-ordination of eigenforms of the brand becomes 'frozen', static, lifeless. The notoriously fragile relationships between advertising agencies and clients (West & Paliwoda, 1996; LaBahn & Kohli, 1997; Ghosh & Taylor, 1999) as well as the well-documented tensions between managerial and creative elements within marcom agencies (see Hackley, 1999, 2003a, 2003b, and Smith & Yang, 2004) can be seen as consequences of this fixing of eigenforms within commercial messages. There is bound to be a disparity between the frozen tokens of co-ordinated understandings as they exist in the final executions of marketing communication messages and the already-moved-on, re-created, adapted, re-positioned eigenforms that continue to be generated by each stakeholder after the message has been signed-off. This disparity between the stabilized constructions we hold of others and ourselves and those that others hold of us and themselves is, of course, a fundamental source of tension, misunderstanding, and conflict in human society. Interaction is, most of the time, far from the 'perfect' mutual invitation to see each other's understandings through each other's eyes. The difficult search for the viable co-ordination of understandings and their continued parallel evolution is, perhaps, the signature of the human condition. And how terribly presumptuous it is of me to link marketing with such a rich and profound aspect of our existence. But I do not think so. Rather, in seeing marketing as the mutual exploration of constructions of value it becomes both a way to examine our understandings of ourselves, of others, and of our everyday lives. And while some may object that this makes of marketing nothing more than the study of consumer behavior, I would simply say that they would be making the same irreflexive observation that has typified marketing's engagement with the whole subject of interactivity.

EXPLORATIONS OF VALUE

Marketing, in a constructivist frame, is not about divisions between consumer and firm but rather the constant negotiation, amongst all stakeholders, of constructions of value. Each stakeholder can invite the others to explore their understandings of the value that a relationship with them can offer. The firm, for example, might wish a consumer to consider the way a relationship with them will result in a particular perception/construction of value and in doing so they invite the consumer to see this construction of value 'through their eyes'. At the same time, the consumer might wish to invite the firm to explore the sense of value they have constructed around the service (in the broadest sense) that the firm provides them. In exploring these constructions of value, stakeholders can choose to be reflexive about the way in which their constructions contain understandings not just of the value of any offered service but also of themselves and other stakeholders. In other words, the recursive nature of our constructions can be addressed or ignored. But the choice to ignore, or abandon, the implications of the recursive nature of our constructions leads to a 'flattening' of our communicative interactions—we lose track of the way in which we are constantly re-creating ourselves and others and our understandings of value. The consequences of this is a rejection of the essence of dialog—a turning away from *mutual* exploration and a focusing instead upon communicative interaction as a tool for control. The reflexive turn admits that dialog can change both interactants, that in seeking to co-ordinate understandings it is likely that both parties will, recursively, observe their own constructions of self and other, and that in the process of such observation (in the meta-level re-framing it necessarily involves) they construct each other and themselves anew. The 'take-away' insight here, then, is that a constructivist approach to marketing suggests that interaction with stakeholders involves constant re-creation both of our own understanding of who we are, what our 'value' is (as a firm in relationship, or potential relationship, with them) and of who they are. Any attempt a firm makes to define its value for a particular stakeholder should only be a provisional starting point, an invitation to begin dialog. If the firm presents their understanding of the value of their service and, in a traditional control-orientated manner, attempts to 'transmit' that understanding to the consumer with the intention that it will be replicated exactly as a construction of the consumer's, then dialog and conversation are excluded communicative modes. The only form of 'interaction' that such a scenario calls for is the first-order cybernetic feedback loop that the firm will need to implement in order to measure whether *their* understanding can be observed to be replicated in the behavior of the target consumer. As I have described in Chapter 3, however, this 'scenario' is based upon a 'bad faith' model of communication in marketing—the dynamic, highly complex creation, exploration, and re-creation of understandings that marketers themselves are part of every day of their working and non-working lives does not work in this way, so why should their interactions with stakeholders be substantially different? While marketers can choose to construct undifferentiated segments of 'mass' audiences and behave toward them in keeping with their own constructions of themselves as 'persuaders' whose messages are encapsulated in entertaining micro-formats and shot at warp speed along the precisely targeted parabolas of modern communication networks, such constructions will inevitably generate relationships of great tension amongst stakeholders who do not construct themselves as targets and who do not understand the firm as a controlling, persuasive source of direction. Further tension will also be forthcoming when firms with such understandings also appear to behave (through the adoption of particular rhetorics) as if they wish to engage in the co-ordination of long-term relationships with stakeholders built upon dialog (let alone such tropes as "the co-creation of value").

Important to remember is the admission that the co-ordination of under-standings is difficult and unstable. It is not the case, from the constructivist perspective, that disagreement between stakeholders signifies some sort of 'failure'. Lack of co-ordination between understandings is the backdrop against which stakeholders may try to build some form of co-ordination into a relationship. One would consequently predict that unless both stakehold-ers in a marketing relationship observe (and hence re-create) their changing constructions of value, and therefore engage in continual re-co-ordination, the relationship will begin to suffer.

THE MODEL

In offering the following 'model' to the reader I am quite aware that it does not approach the usual form stumbled upon in marketing textbooks. It is not a mathematical model, it is not based upon empirical data, indeed it does not claim to be in any way 'scientific' in the sense that word is usually understood in the discipline. And perhaps far worse: It has no diagrammatic representation. I have given up the arrow, abandoned both the straight and curved line, forsaken the flow chart. If there is one single, simple lesson I have learned during the journey of this study it is that the discussion of communication really should not center around pointing at diagrams, which is not to say that I will be attempting, in a fit of utter insanity, to do without metaphors at all. Quite the contrary. For a model *is* a metaphor. Or more exactly, as Ricoeur reminds us, the "exact analogue" of the model should be the "extended metaphor" or allegory (Ricoeur, 2007, p. 287). Ricoeur notes that a model is a "redescription", a "heuristic instrument that seeks, by means of fiction, to break down an inadequate interpreta-tion" (ibid., p. 283). So, the model I offer below is a redescription of mar-keting which seeks to deconstruct the current "inadequate interpretations" through the construction of an allegory of invitations, explorations, circu-larities, understandings, and values.

THE ALLEGORY

Having introduced some of the characters from this extended metaphor back in Chapter 3, I will now revisit them, fleshing out their details, adding light and shade, and so finish with the more boldly drawn, this time, allegory of their interactions.

PRINCIPLE CHARACTERS (DEFINITIONS AND PORTRAITS)

Stakeholder: someone who engages in the construction of understandings regarding one or more aspects of a relationship.

This definition is obviously not specific to a marketing environment. Anyone 'involved' in any type of relationship becomes a stakeholder in that relationship in so far as they engage in constructing understandings of one or more aspects of that relationship. The recognition that marketing relationships have certain basic similarities of form with other interpersonal relationships is not a new one. Indeed, Gummesson's sometimes rather quaint reliance on the marriage metaphor might well be viewed as the backbone to his whole RM perspective. The definition above, however, uses generality to remind us that marketing relationships are, first and foremost, relationships. Further, stakeholders in a relationship are so by virtue of their creativity: In observation they create their understandings. Reducing the resolution level a little, and connecting back into the discourse of recent studies of social construction in marketing, it is important to remember that such creative observation includes the construction of patterns in group and social discourses, although in the terms of my own radical constructivist orientation such social constructions are played out at the level of individual understandings.

Service: the (re)presentation of a stakeholder's understanding of the value contained in the relationship between them and another stakeholder.

This is, perhaps, a challenging position but one that arises from an attempt to take the logic of service-orientation seriously. It holds that any 'service' a firm offers (and I am aligning myself with the general RM/S-D premise that the production of a good is an example of a service) comes down to a communication process whereby the firm (for example) invites a stakeholder to observe its understanding of the value in their relationship. So, an insurance company or a toy manufacturer or a content management system developer presents their understanding of the value in the relationship between them and a customer. So far, so normal; there is nothing in such a statement that cannot be shoehorned in some way into a standard RM framework. The big change in perspective comes with my assertion that the service the company offers *is* the (re)presentation[1]. In other words, everything else is secondary to the understanding of value and its (re) presentation. A product that is manufactured is, therefore, dependent upon the understanding of value that the firm has constructed into the relationship between its construction of itself and its construction of a stakeholder (or 'group' of stakeholders). The service that the insurer 'presents' to the client *can* be thought of as a financial exchange based upon a calculated risk but it can also be thought of, in this constructivist allegory of marketing interactivity, as being constituted around a firm's (re)presentation of its understanding of the value contained in the relationship between itself and the stakeholder (client). The pricing and terms of the insurance contract (along with everything else) are reflections of that value. Implicit in the firm's understanding of that value are recursive constructions of the firm and the stakeholder.

Interactive Marketing: *the continual process in which stakeholders and potential stakeholders in a network of service relationships invite each other to explore the changing boundaries of the constructed understandings of themselves, of each other and of their own selves within those constructions of each other.*

This understanding of marketing follows logically on from the previous two definitions. At its center is the invitation to exploration. This exploration takes place within a service environment and so the understandings of self and others that are its focus are nested within understandings of value constructed around stakeholder relationships. The definition contains no mention of a target or goal. There is no end point. It is a "continual process" that cannot be said to have ultimately succeeded or failed—only in so far as the process is able to continue might it be called viable. Marketing is, indeed, not something that you can either do or not do: The act of 'setting up for business' begins the invitation to exploration. Certainly, a firm might choose to have a marketing department or not but such a decision might have a bearing only upon the extent to which the firm recognizes what it is doing, the extent to which it is in any way reflexive (and even then, not necessarily). As an activity, as a profession, marketing can be seen as revolving around the invitation to explore the 'service' offered by the employer or client. This *sounds* like a traditional marketing communications role, but (due to the model's re-definition of service) in fact represents a wide-ranging consideration of the value, self, and 'other' constructions of the firm. In other words, in order to (re)present the firm's understandings of value, there must be an awareness paid to the recursive, continuing construction of such understandings. Such an awareness must be structurally coupled with the ability to facilitate a state of continuous invitation that leads to effective exploration (both in the stakeholder and then in the firm). In this model, the marketer is thus the reflexive heart of the firm, concerning herself with the unceasing exploration and mapping of the constructions of value that constitute the relationships between the firm and other stakeholders. Furthermore, as a natural consequence of my redefinition of the stakeholder, it is implicit within the model that *all* stakeholders engage in marketing activities. The marketing relationship does not belong to the firm, it belongs to all its stakeholders. Accordingly, traditional 'customers' can (and often do, whether the firm hears or not) invite other stakeholders (including, but not limited to, the firm) to explore their own understandings of value (and hence their own constructions of self and others). Furthermore, reminding ourselves both of the mutuality integral to an invitational rhetoric and the recursive nature of our constructions, the invitation to explore understandings of value, self, and others will lead to the exploration of how we construct those others seeing us, which in a dialog interaction means that both stakeholders will have the opportunity to try to see each other through each others' eyes. The traditional marketer's concern with how the target audience 'sees' the firm carries within it, from the view of the recursive nature of communication, the issue of how the firm 'sees' the audience, how the firm 'sees' itself and how the target audience 'sees' itself, and then how the audience 'sees' itself 'seeing' itself . . . and so on. The recursive, invitational model of marketing interactivity allows us to travel as far along these roads as we wish—or, as many marketing theoreticians and practitioners do, we might cap the reflexivity, behaving as if our marketing relationships are based upon stable certainties and our customer profiles are empirical realities.

THE PRINCIPLE INTERACTIONS

Invitation

The opening of a business, the founding of an organization, the setting out of a stall—these are all preeminently invitational actions. They invite interaction, which is to say that they invite a consideration of what the business, organization, or stall-holder might mean to the stakeholder. At first, as in any introductory sequence, who actually might be a stakeholder may perhaps be quite unclear. The firm itself will be a group of individuals with a variety of understandings of the firm, the service, and other stakeholders. And each individual within the firm is a stakeholder, of course and 'internal' marketing is focused upon the exploration of and efforts to achieve the viable long-term co-ordination of such constituent understandings. The interaction of invitation is not something, however, that only happens at the start of a stakeholder relationship—it is a fundamental understanding of the model that invitation is a continuous marketing interaction. There can be no final agreement; all co-ordination of understandings is provisional and temporary. The marketer's work is never done. Invitation is an out-reaching that focuses on the present; it is unceasing because the understandings that the firm has of itself, of the value in its relationships and of other stakeholders are themselves dynamic.

Exploration

The marketing invitation is an invitation to explore understandings. Exploration is premised upon the existence of the unknown—the understanding that the firm has of the stakeholder is a shadow-country to the stakeholder. They might not, in fact, recognize themselves there at all. The interaction of exploration, then, is an opportunity to create together a dialog in which both parties can come to new understandings regarding themselves and the other—exploration creates change in the firm and the customer. And this change affects the value of the relationship, which means that it changes the understanding of the 'service' for both parties. So, in this tale, marketing literally creates value—through the exploration of understandings of value, of the value that a relationship between stakeholders might mean, it creates further understandings of the relationship, creating further value.

Recursion

In exploring the understandings of others, stakeholders 'step back' and explore their constructions of who they are and how they 'see' their relationships with other stakeholders. From the perspective of the field of marketing, a recursive approach to interaction means that 'doing marketing' reflexively involves 'thinking about how we are doing marketing'. The disconnection between marketing theory and practice (McDonald, 1992; Robson & Rowe, 1997) is, I would suggest, rooted in the non-recursive approach to communication that infuses both orientations. While there is no shortage of studies (from both academic and practitioner viewpoints) that 'look at' marketing, there are precious few grounded in the perspective of 'looking at how we look at marketing'. If marketing interactivity is understood as recursive, the chasm between theory and practice becomes a non-issue; marketing becomes a process of exploring understandings of value-in-relationships which then recursively looks back upon itself, exploring its own constructions of itself as a constantly re-created part of those understandings.

Co-ordination

The issue of the co-ordination of understandings is the crux of the 'practical' matter. It is also the interaction that appears to threaten the invitational, recursive nature of the whole allegory. I wrote back in Chapter 3 that as a part of exploring understandings "some stakeholders may attempt to co-ordinate their constructed understandings with those of other stakeholders". How does this co-ordination happen? Am I, in the end, simply talking about the "marketing as tricks" (Gummesson, 2008, p. 22) paradigm? Substituting a nice, positive term like 'co-ordination' for the whipping-boy of 'control', when it all comes down to the same thing?

But, of course, that is the whole point behind the process of rhetorical analysis that I have used in this study—using the word 'control' rather than 'co-ordination' implies a very different understanding of what one is observing. Yes, we can use words in a rhetorical way to purposively mask what we really mean, to amplify, or misdirect, or give an advantageous impression—'collateral damage' or 'downsizing' would be good examples. If marketing is understood by marketers as an attempt to control belief, to "trick", then strategies of control and manipulation will dominate their interaction with stakeholders. If marketing is understood as offering the possibility of co-ordinating understandings *in order to generate more viable, longer-lasting relationships*, then there will be little reason to behave as if "marketing is a set of tricks designed to squeeze maximum, short-term profits out of consumers" (ibid., p. 24). Co-ordination can occur if the invitation to explore the understandings of stakeholders moves a stakeholder to integrate another's understanding into her own. Importantly, the model does not mandate that co-ordination is only one-way; the firm might well choose, as an outcome of long-term dialog, to co-ordinate its understanding of the value of the marketing relationship with the customer's. The desire to co-ordinate understandings will have much to do to with how easily they can be integrated into the current patternings of the stakeholder. Integration means, however, that the understanding that a stakeholder co-ordinates with becomes something else once they have 'adopted' it. The act of bringing a (re)presentation into one's own patterning of understandings necessarily alters it, as it connects into and integrates with one's individual matrix of constructions. Additionally, the (re)presentation of an understanding that one co-ordinates with is an eigenform—an approximation of stability that carries with it all the attendant problems of communicating with frozen tokens.

The Tendency Toward Stability

While co-ordination of understandings offers the prospect of longer, more viable marketing relationships, implicit within such integrations is the tension between the homeostatic urge toward stability and the constant change that comes from our recursive, creative observation. The fundamental drama in this allegory of marketing interactivity is that provided by the threat of disappointment, misunderstanding, marginalization, abandonment, or any number of other manifestations of the disparity in understandings between stakeholders who feel they understand each other (and themselves). This model suggests that marketing's job is only just starting when co-ordination between understandings occurs; just as the interaction of invitation is unceasing, so the maintenance of co-ordination requires a constant effort to keep dialog generative, reflexive, and mutual.

CONCLUSION

In this study I have examined the ways in which particular understandings of communication have been reflected in the discourses generated by marketing's engagement with the issue of interactivity and those tropes emanating from it, such as dialog, relationship, and conversation. While contemporary marketing, in both scholarly and practitioner orientations, can perhaps be typified by the positioning of various understandings of interactivity as central to the revitalization of the field in an age of social networking and customer communities, my study has observed a great deal of reliance upon the rhetoric of interactivity coupled with very little willingness to address the tensions between the dominant marketing paradigm of communication as control and the implications of any understanding of what interactivity might mean. Even within the discourses generated by (and constituting) (self-described) revolutionary marketing approaches such as Relationship Marketing, Connected Marketing, and the Service-Dominant Logic, there is a shocking unwillingness to even begin to examine what such interactive elements as ongoing dialog or relationship building might actually mean for marketing.

The radical constructivism that I have employed here is simply one amongst a multitude of possible ways of understanding and exploring interactivity and marketing. It has the virtue of not being a common interpretive paradigm in marketing scholarship and so can perhaps more easily produce fresh perspectives.

On the other hand, its very alterity leaves it open to out-of-hand dismissal and impatient frustration. Yet, I would point out that the marketing academy has to start thinking in unusual ways about these issues. The old ways certainly haven't brought us very far.

So, the model that I have outlined in this chapter is an attempt to begin thinking about the meaning of interactivity in marketing in a way that uses a very different rhetoric from that traditionally associated with the field. It is a construction, not a description of an objective or empirical system. My hope is that it might provide some interesting points of resonance with those who have approached the discourse of interactivity in marketing and found it ripe for deconstruction. Which is precisely what, recursively, I will begin to do with this study once I have typed the final full stop.

Notes

NOTES TO THE INTRODUCTION

1. "Web 2.0" is a phrase created by Tim O'Reilly, founder and CEO of O'Reilly Media Inc. (www.oreilly.com). The term was originally designed to act as a rallying call for web-based businesses and developers after the dot.com bubble burst in 2001, the collection of "Web 2.0" strategies, technologies, and design patterns representing the real potential of online business, as compared to the "pretenders" who had "been given the bum's rush" in the crash (O'Reilly, 2005). The exact components of Web 2.0 are still being argued over. However, O'Reilly describes the common "strategic positioning" as revolving around the idea of "the web as platform", and cites the "user positioning" as "you control your own data" (ibid.). Best of breed Web 2.0 sites are exemplified by Wikipedia, Flickr, YouTube, and Facebook, while some common Web 2.0 technologies would include wikis, torrents, Google's AdSense, and blogs.

NOTES TO CHAPTER 2

1. Aristotle truly deserves to be considered the founder of audience research. His dense strictures in *The Art of Rhetoric* on how a rhetor should approach the common audience segments, what particular emotions can be more easily aroused in what type of audience, and how information regarding the audience's opinions and prejudices should be embedded into the speech are strikingly modern in their outlook (or perhaps, our modern approaches are strikingly archaic). A deep knowledge of the audience is the starting point of successful rhetoric for Aristotle.
2. The choice of the word "stable" here is carefully made. That human beings are, in a multitude of areas, constantly seeking 'stability' is a hypothesis central to General Systems Theory, first- and second-order cybernetics, and theories of autopoiesis. The method by which a system seeks for a condition of stability is termed *homeostasis* and is intimately connected with the process of feedback. Bazerman uses the term "stable" (Bazerman, 1994, p. 185) when referring to the way in which "as a result of long interactional processes, perceptions of many individuals have triangulated in on each other to produce similarities and institutions that hold each other stable as self-fulfilling properties". The construction of stable senses of what other people and institutions represent is an important aspect of previous work I have published on marketing communication models (i.e., Miles, 2007) and also

feature strongly in the theoretical groundwork for the model discussed in Chapters 3 and 7.

3. WordPress is "a state-of-the-art publishing platform with a focus on aesthetics, web standards, and usability", in the words of its own website (http://wordpress.org, retrieved December 17, 2008). The software is designed to make the potentially very complicated task of setting up a webpage in a blog format a smooth and painless experience. It is open source, meaning that users do not have to pay to use it. As well as powering hundreds of thousands of non-commercial blogs, it is also used by a significant number of heavyweight companies (like CNN and Ford) to manage their blogging concerns.

NOTES TO CHAPTER 3

1. There is an inherent problem in writing about radical constructivist ideas. When one talks about a 'brain' or 'research' or 'psychology' one is necessarily using loaded words with long accepted associations and interpretations. Accordingly, the word 'brain' calls into thought the idea of a physical thing with an existence independent of thought, yet a radical constructivist holds that we cannot profitably talk about the existence of any such thing separate from our observations of it because our knowledge of that thing comes from within us, not outside of us. Essentially, constructivism of any sort forces us to be very precise and careful with our language, to continually walk as if on egg shells, as it were. We *construct* our realities through our observations, our patterning, and our language; we do not represent reality with language. Inevitably, constructivists are constantly trying to avoid in their own use of language the implication that their words refer to external, mind-independent realities (often abbreviated to MIRs). Equally inevitably, constructivists delight in pointing out the assumption of MIRs in the language use of their colleagues (see Marco Bettoni's commentary on Butz's 2008 article in the same edition of *Constructivist Foundations*, for example). As Heinz von Foerster has noted, "we are seduced [*by language*] to speak in a way that suggests the existence of a world independent of us" (in Poerksen, 2003, p. 14).

2. I will ignore, in blatant *paraleipsis*, the cunning repetition of Hackley's earlier mirror analogy for constructivism in the later phrase, "this confusion is, I think, strongly reflected in market research".

3. The reference is to J.-F. Lyotard's notion of "svelte discourse" (see Sim, 1988).

4. The following summary sketch is particularly inspired by my reading of Schmidt (2000) and Poerksen (2003).

5. Hans Vaihinger's (1924) *The Philosophy of 'As If'* has had a significant influence upon a host of marginalized, constructivist, reflexive epistemologies in the 20th century.

6. A distinction beautifully illustrated in the pages of *Constructivist Foundations*, wherein "target articles" act as the catalyst for often radically divergent interpretations and understandings which form the bulk of many editions.

7. The nature of this "self" that is re-presented is, naturally, a matter of concern. This book, unfortunately, is not the place for a full exploration of the various constructivist (second-order cybernetic, GST, and autopoietic) models of how the 'self' is constructed. I would advise interested readers to consult the work of Gregory Bateson (2000, 2002), Paul Watzlawick (1984, 1993; Watzlawick et al., 1967), George Kelly (1963), Nelson Goodman (1984), Jerome Bruner (1986), Humberto Maturana & Francisco Varela (1980, 1996), Piaget (1954), and von Glasersfeld (1996).

8. This purposefully echoes the, by-now canonical (in second-order cybernetics, at least), opening sentence of George Spencer-Brown's *Laws of Form*: "We take as given the idea of distinction and the idea of indication, and that we cannot make an indication without drawing a distinction" (Spencer-Brown, 1994, p. 1).

NOTES TO CHAPTER 4

1. Examples current at the time of writing include *Adblock Plus* and *No Script*, both available as free add-ons to the Firefox browser from http://addons.mozilla.org.
2. The origins of this feature speak in a highly granular way to the relationship between commentary and creation on the Web. Randall Monroe, the author of a comic site, www.xkcd.com, beloved of programmers, developers, and the 'slashdotting' intellectuals of the Web, drew a comic strip in which a character creates a virus that will read YouTube comments back to their creators who may then realize what "morons" they sound like. Monroe discovered a couple of weeks later that someone at YouTube had taken matters into its own hands. The thread on Monroe's blog (along with alleged screenshots of resulting YouTube comments on the feature that seem to indicate its effectiveness is only proportional to the level of reflexivity in the commenter) can be accessed here: http://blag.xkcd.com/2008/10/08/youtube-audio-preview.
3. The emergent nature of consciousness is an idea that has coverage in a number of well-known works that have had a large impact in the programming and computer science communities. Chief amongst these would probably be the books of Douglas R. Hofstadter, particularly his original door-stop of a romp through the world of strange loops and self-reference, *Gödel, Escher, Bach: An Eternal Golden Braid* (1984), and his collection with Daniel Dennett, *The Mind's I* (1986).
4. Although when the same techniques are used in the cause of national security, privacy is often cited as a concern by civil liberty organizations. The difference here is that data mining for national security is designed to facilitate the identification of individual suspects or groupings by focusing on profiled patterns. Most marketing data mining is interested in patterns rather than individuals. Although this is changing.

NOTES TO CHAPTER 5

1. There were 830,000 results for a Boolean search on "aggressive AND infection" using the Google search engine on March 27, 2009.
2. Three out of the four areas of influence surveyed in Katz and Lazarsfeld's research on their "midwestern community" can be broadly considered marketing-related (household goods, fashion, and movie-going) with the last category, "public affairs", consequently occupying only a small space in the resulting study.
3. For a large crop of current examples, see http://knowyourmeme.com, while for an attempt at an "interactive" historical presentation of the phenomenon, see http://www.dipity.com/tatercakes/Internet_Memes (a rickroll-free link, I promise). The Wikipedia entry on internet memes is also surprisingly measured, desu.
4. The Nokia Internet Tablets (N710, N800, N810) are wi-fi enabled devices designed to be used primarily to access the Internet. They do not function

as mobile phones (though can be used as such if you install Skype and connect to the net via a wi-fi hotspot) and therefore exist very much outside the company's principle marketing focus. The devices are all powered by a Linux distribution called Maemo and it is in the user provision of software and hacks for this distribution, as well as the highly vocal user evangelism for the series, that Nokia has benefited the most. The user community is centered around the Internet Tablet Talk forum (http://www.internettablettalk.com) and it is a measure of the significance of that community that a number of the forum's regular contributors have been voted on to the council that oversees the development of the whole Maemo distribution (and at the time of writing, the forum itself has been formally integrated into the maemo website at http://talk.maemo.org). Even a casual browse through the forum's archives will give the reader an impression of the large amount of software development and hacking for the device that the user community engages in. It is also worth noting that a number of Nokia employees are regular contributors, some in a very formal capacity, others in a much more informal, though Nokia-badged, manner. Interestingly, at the time of writing (June 2009) Nokia has been suffering a severe backlash amongst many posters on the Internet Tablet Talk community due to rumors that it will not be continuing the tablet device line, refocusing development of the Maemo line toward integrating it with its existing mobile phone business. Inevitably, many members of the Nokia tablet user community have seen this as a betrayal, although Nokia has in no way confirmed these rumors.

5. It is interesting to note that Prahalad's co-author, Venkat Ramaswamy, when writing on co-creation of value as an individual author, tends to be drawn to examples and models that are very much more community-based (Ramaswamy, 2009).

NOTES TO CHAPTER 6

1. Although, even if Vargo & Lusch demonstrated no such awareness, the implications of their rhetoric would be the same: Motivation is invoked purely as a literary conceit.
2. The choice of "flow" here might possibly be an echo of Robert Bartels's (1968) flows and systems approach to a general theory of marketing.
3. For Aristotle, political, or deliberative rhetoric, was persuasion directed at making an audience decide a particular way regarding what *should be done*. In other words, it was rhetoric focused on future action and as such can be related to advertising designed to influence future buying decisions (i.e., what products or services *should be* bought). Modern marketing communication, like most instances of practical persuasion, can be seen as requiring an integration of Aristotle's three different types of rhetoric (judicial, deliberative, and epideictic) just as it clearly calls for an integrated use of the three different 'proofs' of ethos, pathos, and logos.
4. An aversion to communication issues is evident in a number of other contemporary theories of marketing. Shelby Hunt's impressive ability to write a 323-page book (Hunt, 2002) on the foundations of marketing theory without once ever considering the place of communication in such a theory is sadly indicative of the way in which certain streams of marketing discourse are forever trapped in aspects of the microeconomic paradigm no matter how hard they might try to escape. Having said this, it is also the case that Resource-Advantage Theory, and Hunt's presentation of it, is distinctly free of the rhetoric of dialog and interactivity that has been my principle focus

in this book. An investigation into the place of marketing communication within R-A theory is overdue.

NOTES TO CHAPTER 7

1. This constant use of "(re)presentation" might annoy some readers (and it makes some small part of me uncomfortable which is perhaps why I have constructed an annoyed reader). Its purpose is clear, however—to remind the reader that any representation of an understanding to someone else is simple the latest layer of presentation in a long, nested (recursive) series of presentations to oneself.

Bibliography

Abbotts, J. (2001). 'Data, data everywhere—and not a byte of use?'. *Qualitative Market Research: An International Journal, 4*(3), 182–192.

Achrol, R. S., & Kotler, P. (2006). 'The service-dominant logic for marketing: A critique'. In R. Lusch & S. Vargo (Eds.), *The service dominant logic of marketing: Dialog, debate, and directions.* Armonk, NY: M. E. Sharpe, pp. 320–333.

Anderson, J. A. (1996). *Communication theory: Epistemological foundations.* New York: The Guilford Press.

Andrejevic, M. (2007). *iSpy: Surveillance and power in the interactive era.* Lawrence, KS: University of Kansas Press.

Andrejevic, M. (2008). 'Watching Television Without Pity: The productivity of online fans'. *Television & New Media, 9*(1), 24–46.

Aristotle. (1991). *The art of rhetoric* (trans. H. C. Lawson-Tancred). Harmondsworth, England: Penguin Books.

Arndt, J. (1985). 'On making marketing science more scientific: The role of observations, paradigms, metaphors and puzzle solving'. *Journal of Marketing, 49,* 11–23.

Arvidsson, A. (2008). 'The ethical economy of customer coproduction'. *Journal of Macromarketing, 28*(4), 326–338.

Ashby, R. (1957). *Introduction to cybernetics.* London: Chapman & Hall.

Ashby, R. (1960). *Design for a brain: The origin of adaptive behaviour.* London: Wiley.

Baker, S. (2003). *New consumer marketing: Managing a living demand system.* Chichester, UK: Wiley.

Ballantyne, D., & Varey, R. J. (2006). 'Introducing a dialogical orientation to the service-dominant logic of marketing'. In R. Lusch & S. Vargo (Eds.), *The service dominant logic of marketing: Dialog, debate, and directions.* Armonk, NY: M.E. Sharpe, pp. 224–235.

Banks, J., & Humphreys, S. (2008). 'The labour of user co-creators: Emergent social network markets?'. *Convergence: The International Journal of Research into New Media Technologies, 14*(4), 401–418.

Bartels, R. (1968, January). 'The general theory of marketing'. *Journal of Marketing, 32,* 29–33.

Bateson, G. (2000). *Steps to an ecology of mind.* Chicago: University of Chicago Press.

Bateson, G. (2002). *Mind and nature: A necessary unity.* Creskill, NJ: Hampton Press, Inc.

Bazerman, C. (1994). *Constructing experience.* Carbondale & Edwardsville, IL: Southern Illinois University Press.

Beckett, A., & Nayak, A. (2008). 'The reflexive consumer'. *Marketing Theory, 8*(3), 299–317.

Beckett, C., & Mansell, R. (2008). 'Crossing boundaries: New media and networked journalism'. *Communication, Culture & Critique, 1*(1), 92–104.

Beer, S. (1994a). *Decision and control: The meaning of operational research and management cybernetics.* Chichester, UK: John Wiley & Sons. (Original work published 1966)

Beer, S. (1994b). *Designing freedom.* Chichester, UK: John Wiley & Sons. (Original work published 1974)

Bellman, S., & Rossiter, J. R. (2004, Spring). 'The website schema'. *Journal of Interactive Advertising, 4*(2). Retrieved December 12, 2008, from http://jiad. org/article48

Bendapudi, N., & Leone, R. P. (2003, January). 'Psychological implications of customer participation in co-production'. *Journal of Marketing, 67,* 14–28.

Bennett, W. L., & Manheim, J. B. (2006, November). 'The one step flow of communication'. *The Annals of the American Academy, AAPSS, 608,* 213–232.

Benoit, W. L., & Smythe, M. J. (2003). 'Rhetorical theory as message reception: A cognitive response approach to rhetorical theory and criticism'. *Communication Studies, 54*(1), 96–114.

Berger, P., & Luckmann, T. (1991). *The social construction of reality: A treatise in the sociology of knowledge.* London: Penguin Books.

Berger, W. (2001). *Advertising today.* London: Phaidon Press.

Berry, L. L. (1983). 'Relationship marketing'. In L. L. Berry et al. (Eds.), *Emerging perspectives in services marketing.* Chicago: American Marketing Association, pp. 25–28.

Berry, M. J. A., & Linoff, G. S. (2004). *Data mining techniques.* Indianapolis, IN: John Wiley & Sons.

Bettoni. M. (2008). 'Why and how to avoid representation'. *Constructivist Foundations, 4*(1), 15–16.

Blackmore, S. (2003). 'The meme's eye view'. In R. Aunger, (Ed.), *Darwinizing culture: The status of memetics as a science.* Oxford: Oxford University Press, pp. 25–42.

Bly, R. (1990). *The copywriter's handbook.* New York: Owl Books.

Bose, R. (2002). 'Customer relationship management: Key components for IT success.' *Industrial Management & Data Systems, 102*(2), 89–97.

Brown, S. (1993). 'Postmodern marketing?'. *European Journal of Marketing, 27*(4), 19–34.

Brown, S. (1995). *Postmodern marketing.* London: Routledge.

Brown, S. (1998a). *Postmodern marketing two: Telling tales.* London: International Thomson Press.

Brown, S. (1998b). 'The unbearable lightness of marketing: A neo-romantic, counter-revolutionary recapitulation'. In S. Brown, A.-M. Doherty, & B. Clarke (Eds.), *Romancing the Market.* London: Routledge, pp. 255–277.

Brown, S. (1999) 'Marketing and Literature: The Anxiety of Academic Influence'. *Journal of Marketing, 63*(1), 1–15

Brown, S. (2000). 'Theodore Levitt, Morris Holbrook, and the anxiety of influence'. *Journal of Marketing, 63*(1), 1–15.

Brown, S. (2006). 'Buzz marketing: The next chapter'. In J. Kirby & P. Marsden (Eds.), *Connected marketing* (pp. 208–231). Oxford: Butterworth-Heinemann.

Brown, S. (2007). 'Are we nearly there yet? On the retro-dominant logic of marketing'. *Marketing Theory, 7*(3), 291–300.

Brown, S., Bell, J., & Carson, D. (Eds.). (1998). *Marketing apocalypse: Eschatology, escapology and the illusion of the end.* London: Routledge.

Brownlie, D., & Hewer, P. (2007). 'Concerning marketing critterati: Beyond nuance, estrangement and elitism'. In M. Saren et al. (Eds.), *Critical marketing: Defining the field.* Oxford: Butterworth-Heinemann, pp. 44–68.

Bruner, J. (1986). *Actual minds, possible worlds.* Cambridge: Harvard University Press.

Burtenshaw, K., Mahon, N., & Barfoot, C. (2006). *The fundamentals of creative advertising*. Lausanne, Switzerland: AVA Books.

Buttle, F. (1995). 'Marketing communication theory: What do texts teach our students?'. *International Journal of Advertising, 14*, 297–313.

Butz, M. V. (2008). 'How and why the brain lays the foundations for a conscious self'. *Constructivist Foundations, 4*(1), 1–14.

Cammaerts, B. (2008). 'Critiques on the participatory potentials of Web 2.0'. *Communication, Culture & Critique, 1*(4), 358–377.

Chung, E., & Alagaratnam, S. (2001). '"Teach ten thousand stars how not to dance": A survey of alternative ontologies in marketing research'. *Qualitative Market Research: An International Journal, 4*(4), 224–234.

Cialdini, R. B. (2001). *Influence: Science and practice*. Needham Heights, MA: Allyn & Bacon.

Conte, R. (2003). 'Memes through (social) minds'. In R. Aunger (Ed.), *Darwinizing culture: The status of memetics as a science*. Oxford: Oxford University Press, pp. 83–119.

Corcoran, A., Marsden, P., Zorbach, T., & Röthlingshöfer, B. (2006). 'Blog marketing'. In J. Kirby & P. Marsden (Eds.), *Connected marketing* (pp. 148–158). Oxford: Butterworth-Heinemann.

Cruz, D., & Fill, C. (2008). 'Evaluating viral marketing: Isolating the key criteria'. *Marketing Intelligence & Planning, 26*(7), 743–758.

Csikszentmihalyi, M. (1977). *Beyond boredom and anxiety*. San Francisco: Jossey-Bass.

Darwin, C. (1985). *The origin of species by means of natural selection*. Harmondsworth, England: Penguin Books. (Original work published 1859)

Davidson, A. (2004). 'When co-creating value with a customer goes wrong'. *Strategy & Leadership, 32*(3), 14–15.

Davies, B., & Harré, R. (2005). 'Positioning: The discursive production of selves'. In M. Wetherell, S. Taylor, & S. J. Yates (Eds.), *Discourse theory and practice: A reader*. London: Sage.

Dawkins, R. (2006). *The selfish gene*. Oxford: Oxford University Press.

DeFleur, M. (1966). *Theories of mass communication*. New York, David McKay Company.

Deuze, M. (2007). 'Convergence culture in the creative industries'. *International Journal of Cultural Studies, 10*(2), 243–263.

Durham, W. H. (1991). *Coevolution: Genes, culture and human diversity*. Stanford: Stanford University Press.

Egan, J. (2003). 'Back to the future: Divergence in relationship marketing research'. *Marketing Theory, 3*(1), 145–157.

Evans. M. (2003). 'The relational oxymoron and personalisation pragmatism'. *Journal of Consumer Marketing, 20*(7), 665–685.

Ewen, S. (1996). *PR! A social history of spin*. New York: Basic Books.

Ferguson, B. (2006). 'Black buzz and red ink: The financial impact of negative consumer comments on US airlines'. In J. Kirby & P. Marsden (Eds.), *Connected marketing* (pp. 185–196). Oxford: Butterworth-Heinemann.

Ferguson, R. (2008). 'Word of mouth and viral marketing: Taking the temperature of the hottest trends in marketing'. *Journal of Consumer Marketing, 25*(3), 179–182.

Fırat, A. F. (1993). 'The consumer in postmodernity'. *Advances in Consumer Research, 18*, 70–76.

Fırat, A. F., & Dholakia, N. (2006). 'Theoretical and philosophical implications of postmodern debates: Some challenges to modern marketing'. *Marketing Theory, 6*(2), 123–162.

Fırat, A. F. , Dholakia, N., & Venkatesh, A. (1995). 'Marketing in a postmodern world'. *European Journal of Marketing, 29*(1), 40–56.

Fırat, A. F., & Venkatesh, A. (1993). 'Postmodernity: The age of marketing'. *International Journal of Research in Marketing*, *10*, 227–249.

Fırat, A. F., & Venkatesh, A. (1995). 'Liberatory postmodernism and the reenchantment of consumption'. *Journal of Consumer Research*, *22*(3), 239–267.

Fitzgerald, M., & Arnott, D. (Eds.). (2000). *Marketing communication classics: An international collection of classic and contemporary papers*. London: Business Press.

Foss, S. K., Foss, K. A., & Trapp, R. (2002). *A contemporary perspective on rhetoric*. Long Grove, IL: Waveland Press.

Foss, S. K., & Griffin, C. L. (1995, March). 'Beyond persuasion: A proposal for an invitational rhetoric'. *Communication Monographs*, *62*, 2–18.

Gatherer, D. (1998). 'Why the thought contagion metaphor is retarding the progress of memetics'. *Journal of Memetics—Evolutionary Models of Information Transmission*, *2*, Retrieved December 1, 2004, from http://jom-emit.cfpm.org/1998/vol2/gatherer_d.html

Geissler, G. L. (2001). 'Building customer relationships online: The web site designers' perspective'. *Journal of Consumer Marketing*, *18*(6), 488–502.

Ghosh, B. C., & Taylor, D. (1999). 'Switching advertising agency—A cross-country analysis'. *Marketing Intelligence and Planning*, *17*(3), 140–146.

Gibson, W. (1984). *Neuromancer*. New York: Ace Books.

Gillin, P. (2007). *The new influencers: A marketer's guide to the new social media*. Sanger, CL: Quill Driver Books.

Gitlin, T. (1978). 'Media sociology: The dominant paradigm'. *Theory and Society*, *6*, 205–253.

Gladwell, M. (2002). *The tipping point: How little things can make a big difference*. New York: Back Bay Books.

Godin, S. (2000). *Unleashing the idea virus*. Retrieved January 20, 2005 from www.ideavirus.com

Godin, S. (2002). *Permission marketing*. London: Simon & Schuster.

Goldsmith, R. (2002). *Viral marketing: Get your audience to do your marketing for you*. London: Pearson Education Ltd.

Goodman, N. (1984). *Of mind and other matters*. Cambridge: Harvard University Press.

Gronroos, C. (2000). *Service management and marketing: A customer relationship management approach*. Chichester, UK: John Wiley & Sons.

Gummesson, E. (2008). *Total relationship marketing*. Oxford: Butterworth-Heinemann.

Gurak, L. J., & Antonijevic, S. (2008). 'The psychology of blogging: You, me, and everyone in between'. *American Behavioral Scientist*, *52*(1), 60–68.

Hackley, C. (1999). 'An epistemological odyssey: Towards social construction of the advertising process'. *Journal of Marketing Communications*, *5*, 157–168.

Hackley, C. (2001). *Marketing and social construction: Exploring the rhetorics of managed consumption*. London: Routledge.

Hackley, C. (2002). 'The panoptic role of advertising agencies in the production of consumer culture'. *Consumption, Markets and Culture*, *5*(3), 211–229.

Hackley, C. (2003a). 'Divergent representational practices in advertising and consumer research: Some thoughts on integration'. *Qualitative Market Research: An International Journal*, *6*(3), 175–183.

Hackley, C. (2003b). 'From consumer insight to advertising strategy: The account planner's integrative role in creative advertising development'. *Marketing Intelligence and Planning*, *21*(7), 446–452.

Hammond, D. (2003). *The science of synthesis: Exploring the social implications of general systems theory*. Boulder, CO: University Press of Colorado.

Hauser, W. J. (2007). 'Marketing analytics: The evolution of marketing research in the twenty-first century'. *Direct Marketing: An International Journal*, *1*(1), 38–54.

Haydon, T. N. (2009). 'Boing Boing's moderation policy'. Retrieved February 13, 2009, from http://boingboing.net/2008/03/27/boing-boings-mod.html

Hayles, N. K. (1999). *How we became posthuman: Virtual bodies in cybernetics, literature, and informatics.* Chicago: The University of Chicago Press.

Heims, S. J. (1991). *The cybernetics group.* Cambridge: MIT Press.

Hoffman, A. (1971). *Steal this book.* New York: Pirate Editions.

Hoffman, D. L., & Novak, T. P. (1996, July). 'Marketing in hypermedia computer-mediated environments: Conceptual foundations'. *Journal of Marketing, 60,* 50–68.

Hofstadter, D. R. (1984). *Gödel, Escher, Bach: An eternal golden braid.* Harmondsworth, England: Penguin Books.

Hofstadter, D. R., & Dennett, D. C. (1986). *The mind's I: Fantasies and reflections on self and soul.* Harmondsworth, England: Penguin Books.

Hunt, S. D. (2002). *Foundations of marketing theory: Towards a general theory of marketing.* Armonk, NY: M. E. Sharpe.

Iser, W. (1990). *The implied reader: Patterns of communication in prose and fiction from Bunyan to Beckett.* Baltimore: John Hopkins University Press.

Iser, W. (1991). *The act of reading: A theory of aesthetic response.* Baltimore: John Hopkins University Press.

Jardin, X. (2009). 'BB Video: (This is an ad) Soviet Unterzoegersdorf, pt. 1 of 6 / Cheetos Boredom Busters'. Retrieved February 13, 2009, from http://boingboing.net/2009/02/04/bb-video-this-is-an-ad.html

Jarrett, K. (2003). 'Labour of love: An archaeology of affect as power in e-commerce'. *Journal of Sociology, 39,* 335–351.

Jefkins, F. (2000). *Advertising.* Harlow: Pearson Education.

Jenkins, H. (2006). *Convergence culture.* New York: New York University Press.

Jhally, S. (1990). *The codes of advertising: Fetishism and the political economy of meaning in the consumer society.* New York: Routledge.

Kalyanam, K., McIntyre, S., & Masonis, J. T. (2007). 'Adaptive experimentation in interactive marketing: The case of viral marketing at Plaxo'. *Journal of Interactive Marketing, 21*(3), 72–85.

Katz, E., & Lazarsfeld, P. F. (1955). *Personal influence: The part played by people in the flow of mass communications.* New York: Free Press.

Kauffman, L. H. (2003). 'Eigenforms—Objects as tokens for eigenbehaviors'. *Cybernetics and Human Knowing, 10*(3–4), 78–89.

Kelly, G. A. (1963). *A theory of personality: The psychology of personal constructs.* New York: W. W. Norton & Co.

Kennedy, G. A. (1994). *A new history of classical rhetoric.* Princeton, NJ: Princeton University Press.

Key, W. B. (1974). *Subliminal seduction.* New York: Signet.

Kinneavy, J. L. (1984). 'Translating theory into practice in teaching composition: A historical view and a contemporary perspective'. In R. J. Connors, L. S. Ede, & A. A. Lunsford (Eds.), *Essays on classical rhetoric and modern discourse.* Carbondale, IL: Southern Illinois University Press, 69–81.

Kinneavy, J. L., & Eskin, C. R. (2000). 'Kairos in Aristotle's rhetoric'. *Written Communication, 17*(3), 432–444.

Kirby, J. (2006). 'Viral marketing'. In J. Kirby & P. Marsden (Eds.), *Connected Marketing.* Oxford: Butterworth-Heinemann, 87–106.

Kotler. P., & Keller, K. L. (2006). *Marketing management.* Upper Saddle River, NJ: Pearson Education.

Krippendorff, K. (1993). 'Major metaphors of communication and some constructivist reflections on their use'. *Cybernetics &Human Knowing, 2*(1), 3–25.

Krippendorff, K. (1996). 'A second-order cybernetics of otherness'. *Systems Research, 13*(3), 311–328.

Krippendorff, K. (2009). 'A recursive framework for communication theories'. In F. Bermajo (Ed.), *On communicating: Otherness, meaning, and information.* New York: Routledge, pp. 72–85.

Kulikova, S. V., & Perlmutter, D. D. (2007). 'Blogging down the dictator? The Kyrgyz revolution and *Samizdat* websites'. *The International Communication Gazette*, 69(1), 29–50.

LaBahn, D. W., & Kohli, C. (1997). 'Maintaining client commitment in advertising agency–client relationships'. *Industrial Marketing Management*, 26(6), 497–508.

Lakoff, G., & Johnson, M. (2003). *Metaphors we live by.* Chicago: University of Chicago Press.

Lakoff, G., & Núñez, R. (2000). *Where mathematics comes from: How the embodied mind brings mathematics into being.* New York: Basic Books.

Langert, B. (2008). 'What my little league days say to me about the root causes of obesity'. Retrieved February 18, 2009, from http://www.crmcdonalds.com/publish/csr/home

Learmonth, M. (2009). 'Frito-Lay puts Cheetos brand in bloggers' hands'. *Advertising Age.* Retrieved February 11, 2009, from www.adage.com (ID:134558).

Leavy, B., & Moitra, D. (2006). 'The practice of co-creating unique value with customers: An interview with C. K. Prahalad'. *Strategy & Leadership*, 34(2), 4–9.

Lee, N., & Greenley, G. (2008). 'The primacy of *data*?'. *European Journal of Marketing*, 42(11/12), 1141–1144.

Lehmann, N., Qvortrup, L., & Walther, B. K. (Eds.). (2007). *The concept of the network society: Post-ontological reflections.* Frederiksberg, Denmark: Samfundslitteratur Press.

Leiss, W., Kline, S., & Jhally, S. (1997). *Social communication in advertising: Persons, products and images of well-being.* London: Routledge.

Lowrey, W. (2006). 'Mapping the journalism-blogging relationship'. *Journalism*, 7(4), 477–500.

Luhmann, N. (1995). *Social systems* (trans. John Bednarz Jr., with Dirk Baecker) Stanford, CA: Stanford University Press.

Luhmann, N. (2000). *The reality of the mass media* (trans. Kathleen Cross). Stanford, CA: Stanford University Press.

Lury, G. (2001). *Brandwatching: Lifting the lid on branding.* Los Angeles: Blackhall Publishing.

Marsden, P. (1998). 'Memetics and social contagion: Two sides of the same coin?'. *Journal of Memetics—Evolutionary Models of Information Transmission*, 2. Retrieved November 22, 2005, from http://jom-emit.cfpm.org/1998/vol2/marsden_p.html

Marsden, P. (2006a). 'Introduction and summary'. In J. Kirby & P. Marsden (Eds.), *Connected Marketing.* Oxford: Butterworth-Heinemann, pp. xv–xxxv.

Marsden, P. (2006b). 'Seed to spread: How seeding trials ignite epidemics of demand'. In J. Kirby & P. Marsden (Eds.), *Connected Marketing.* Oxford: Butterworth-Heinemann, 3–23.

Maturana, H., & Varela, F. (1980). *Autopoiesis and cognition: The realization of the living.* Boston: D. Reidel Publishing Co.

Maturana, H., & Varela, F. (1996). *The tree of knowledge: The biological roots of human understanding.* Boston: Shambhala Publications.

Mayhew, D. J. (2005). 'A design process for web usability'. In R. W. Proctor & K.-P. L. Vu (Eds.), *Handbook of Human Factors in Web Design.* Mahwah, NJ: Lawrence Erlbaum Associates.

Mayo, E. (1933). *The human problems of an industrial civilization.* New York: Macmillan.

McDonald, M. H. B. (1992). 'Strategic marketing planning: A state-of-the-art review'. *Marketing Intelligence & Planning, 10*(4), 4–22.
McQuail, D. (2000). *McQuail's mass communication theory.* London: Sage.
McQuarrie, E. F., & Mick, D. G. (1992). 'On resonance: A critical pluralistic inquiry into advertising rhetoric'. *Journal of Consumer Research, 19*(2), 180–197.
McQuarrie, E. F., & Mick, D. G. (1996). 'Figures of rhetoric in advertising language'. *Journal of Consumer Research, 22*(4), 424–438.
McQuarrie, E. F., & Mick D. G. (1999). 'Visual rhetoric in advertising: Text-interpretive, experimental, and reader-response analyses'. *Journal of Consumer Research, 26*(1), 37–54.
Miles, C. J. (2007). 'A cybernetic communication model for advertising'. *Marketing Theory, 7*(4), 307–334.
Mills, C. W. (1956). *The power elite.* New York: Oxford University Press.
Mills, C. W. (1959). *The sociological imagination.* Oxford: Oxford University Press.
Moeller, H.-G. (2006). *Luhmann explained: From souls to systems.* Chicago: Open Court.
Nakamura, J., & Csikszentmihalyi, M. (2002). 'The concept of flow'. In C. R. Snyder & S. J. Lopez (Eds.), *The handbook of positive psychology.* Oxford: Oxford University Press, pp. 89–105.
Ngai, E. W. T. (2005). 'Customer relationship management research (1992–2002): An academic literature review and classification'. *Marketing Intelligence & Planning, 23*(6), 582–605.
Nienkamp, J. (2001). *Internal rhetorics: Towards a history and theory of self-persuasion.* Carbondale, IL: Southern Illinois University Press.
O'Donohoe, S. (1994). 'Advertising uses and gratifications'. *European Journal of Marketing, 28*(8/9), 52–75.
O'Donohoe, S. (1997). 'Raiding the postmodern pantry: Advertising intertextuality and the young adult audience'. *European Journal of Marketing, 31*(3/4), 234–253.
O'Donohoe, S. (1998). 'Advertising Research: Sins of omission and inaugurated eschatology'. In S. Brown, J. Bell, & D. Carson (Eds.), *Marketing apocalypse: Eschatology, escapology and the illusion of the end.* London: Routledge, pp. 206–222.
O'Donohoe, S. (2001). 'Living with ambivalence: Attitudes to advertising in postmodern times'. *Marketing Theory, 1*(1), 91–108.
Ogilvy, D. (1985). *Ogilvy on advertising.* New York: Vintage Books.
Ogilvy, D. (2004). *Confessions of an advertising man.* London: Southbank Publishing.
Oliver, R. W., Rust, R. T., & Varki, S. (1998, Fall). 'Real-time marketing'. *Marketing Management, 7*, 28–37.
O'Reilly, T. (2005, September 30). [Blog entry]. 'What is Web 2.0: Design patterns and business models for the next generation of software'. Retrieved June 6, 2009, from http://www.oreillynet.com/pub/a/oreilly/tim/news/2005/09/30/what-is-web-20.html
O'Shaughnessy, J., & O'Shaughnessy, N. (2002). 'Ways of knowing and their applicability'. *Marketing Theory, 2*(2), 147–164.
Ozuem, W. F. (2004). *Conceptualising marketing communication in the new marketing paradigm: A postmodern perspective.* Boca Raton, FL: Dissertation.com.
Ozuem, W., Howell, K. E., & Lancaster, G. (2008). 'Communicating in the new interactive marketspace'. *European Journal Of Marketing, 42*(9/10), 1059–1083.
Peppers, D., & Rogers, M. (1999). *Enterprise one to one: Tools for competing in the interactive age.* New York: Doubleday.

Perelman, C., & Olbrechts-Tyteca, L. (1971). *The new rhetoric: A treatise on argumentation* (trans. J. Wilkinson & P. Weaver). Notre Dame, IN: University of Notre Dame Press.

Phillips, B. J., & McQuarrie, E. F. (2002). 'The development, change, and transformation of rhetorical style in magazine advertisements 1954–1999'. *Journal of Advertising, 31*(4), 1–13.

Phillips, B. J., & McQuarrie, E. F. (2004). 'Beyond visual metaphor: A new typology of visual rhetoric in advertising'. *Marketing Theory, 4*(1/2), 113–136.

Piaget, J. (1954). *The construction of reality in the child*. New York: Basic Books.

Pitta, D. (1998). 'Marketing one-to-one and its dependence on knowledge discovery in databases'. *Journal of Consumer Marketing, 15*(5), 468–480.

Pitta, D. (2008). 'Providing the tools to build brand share of heart: Gydget.com'. *Journal of Product and Brand Management, 17*(4), 280–284.

Poerksen, B. (2003). '"At each and every moment, I can decide who I am': Heinz von Foerster on the observer, dialogic life, and a constructivist philosophy of distinctions'. *Cybernetics & Human Knowing, 10*(3/4), 9–26.

Potter, J. (2005). *Representing reality: Discourse, rhetoric and social construction*. London: Sage.

Powers, W. T. (1989). *Living control systems: Selected papers of William T. Powers*. Gravel Switch, KY: The Control Systems Group.

Powers, W. T. (1992). *Living control systems II: Selected papers of William T. Powers*. Gravel Switch, KY: The Control Systems Group

Prahalad, C. K., & Hamel, G. (1990, May/June). 'The core competence of the corporation'. *Harvard Business Review, 68*, 79–91.

Prahalad, C. K., & Ramaswamy, V. (2002). 'The cocreation connection'. *Strategy and Business, 27*(2), 51–60.

Prahalad, C. K., & Ramaswamy, V. (2004a). *The future of competition: Co-creating unique value with customers*. Boston, MA: Harvard Business School.

Prahalad, C. K., & Ramaswamy, V. (2004b). 'Co-creating unique value with customers'. *Strategy & Leadership, 32*(3), 4–9.

Radford, G. (2005). *On the philosophy of communication*. Belmont, CA: Wadsworth.

Ramaswamy, V. (2009). 'Leading the transformation to co-creation of value'. *Strategy & Leadership, 37*(2), 32–37.

Richer, J. (2001a). 'An ethological approach to autism: From evolutionary perspectives to treatment'. In J. Richer & S. Coates (Eds.), *Autism: The search for coherence*. London: Jessica Kingsley.

Richer, J. (2001b). 'The insufficient integration of self and other in autism: Evolutionary and developmental perspectives'. In J. Richer & S. Coates (Eds.), *Autism: The search for coherence*. London: Jessica Kingsley, 37–53.

Rickman, T. A., & Cosenza, R. M. (2007). 'The feasibility of the weblog: Text mining approach for fast fashion trending'. *Journal of Fashion Marketing and Management, 11*(4), 604–621.

Ricoeur, P. (2007) *The Rule of Metaphor: The creation of meaning in language*. Translated by P. Czerny with K. MacLaughlin and J. Costello, SJ. London: Routledge.

Ries, A., & Trout, J. (2001). *Positioning: The battle for your mind*. New York: McGraw-Hill.

Robson, I., & Rowe, J. (1997). 'Marketing—the whore of Babylon?'. *European Journal of Marketing, 31*(9/10), 654–666.

Rocha, L. M. (1996). 'Eigenbehavior and symbols'. *Systems Research, 13*(3), 371–384.

Rodgers, S., & Thorson, E. (2000). 'The interactive advertising model: How users perceive and process online ads'. *Journal of Interactive Advertising, 1*(1), 26–50. Retrieved November 6, 2005, from http://jiad.org/vol1/no1/rodgers

Rucker, R., Sirius, R. U., & Mu, Q. (Eds.). (1993). *Mondo 2000: A user's guide to the new edge*. London: Thames & Hudson.

Rudall, B. H. (2006). 'Contemporary systems and cybernetics; Innovative applications'. *Kybernetes, 35*(1/2), 209–216.

Rushkoff, D. (1996). *Mind virus*. New York: Ballantine Books.

Scarisbrick-Hauser, A.-M. (2007). 'Data analysis and profiling'. *Direct Marketing: An International Journal, 1*(2), 114–116.

Schmidt, S. J. (2000). 'Ernst von Glasersfeld's philosophy of language: Roots, concepts, perspectives'. In L. P. Steffe & P. W. Thompson (Eds.), *Radical constructivism in action: Building on the pioneering work of Ernst von Glasersfeld*. London: Routledge Falmer, pp. 23–33.

Schwartz, J. (2008a). 'The inside story (Java, Microsoft an MySQL)'. Retrieved February 18, 2009, from http://blogs.sun.com/jonathan/entry/the_value_of_distribution_java#comments

Schwartz, J. (2008b). '(Another win for open storage'. Retrieved February 18, 2009, from http://blogs.sun.com/jonathan/entry/another_win_for_open_storage

Scott, D. M. (2007). *The new rules of marketing and PR*. Hoboken, NJ: John Wiley & Sons.

Scott, L. M. (1992). 'Playing with pictures: Postmodernism, poststructuralism, and advertising visuals'. In J. F. Sherry & B. Sternthal (Eds.), *Advances in Consumer Research*, 19. Provo, UT: Association for Consumer Research, pp. 596–612.

Scott, L. M. (1993). 'Spectacular vernacular: Literacy and commercial culture in the postmodern age'. *International Journal of Research in Marketing, 10*, 251–275.

Scott, L. M. (1994). 'Images in advertising: The need for a theory of visual rhetoric'. *Journal of Consumer Research, 21*(2), 252–273.

Segaran, S. (2007). *Programming collective intelligence*. Sebastopol, CA: O'Reilly.

Shankar, A. (1999). 'Advertising's imbroglio'. *Journal of Marketing Communications, 5*, 1–15.

Shannon, C. E. (1948, July & October). 'A mathematical theory of communication'. *The Bell System Technical Journal, 27*, 379–423, 623–656.

Shannon, C. E., & Weaver, W. (1949). *The mathematical theory of communication*. Urbana, IL: University of Illinois Press.

Shaw, E. H., & Jones, B. D. G. (2005). 'A history of schools of marketing thought'. *Marketing Theory, 5*(3), 239–281.

Shaw, M. J., Subramaniam, C., Tan, G. W., & Welge, M. E. (2001). 'Knowledge management and data mining for marketing'. *Decision Support Systems, 31*, 127–137.

Shih, C.-F. (1998). 'Conceptualizing consumer experiences in cyberspace'. *European Journal of Marketing, 32*(7/8), 655–663.

Sicilia, R., & Ruiz, S. (2007, Fall). 'The Role of Flow in Web Site Effectiveness'. *Journal of Interactive Advertising, 8*(1), 1–15. Retrieved March 18, 2008 from http://jiad.org/article97

Sim, S. (1988). 'Svelte discourse and the philosophy of caution'. *Radical Philosophy, 49*, 31–36.

Smith, C. R. (2003). *Rhetoric and human consciousness: A history*. Prospect Heights, IL: Waveland Press.

Smith, P. R., & Taylor, J. (2004). *Marketing communications: An integrated approach*. London: Kogan Page.

Smith, R. E., & Yang, X. (2004). 'Towards a general theory of creativity in advertising: Examining the role of divergence'. *Marketing Theory, 4*(1–2), 31–58.

Spangler, S., & Kreulen, J. (2008). *Mining the talk: Unlocking the business value in unstructured information*. Upper Saddle River, NJ: IBM Press.

Spencer-Brown, G. (1994). *The laws of form*. Portland: Cognizer Co.

Stern, B. B. (1988). 'Medieval allegory: Roots of advertising strategy for the mass market'. *Journal of Marketing, 52*(3), 84–94.

Stern, B. B. (1990). 'Classical allegory and contemporary advertising'. *Journal of Advertising, 19*(3), 14–26.

Stern, B. B. (1994, June). 'A revised communication model for advertising: Multiple dimensions of the source, the message, and the recipient'. *Journal of Advertising, 23*(2), 5–15.

Stern, B. B. (1996). 'Deconstructive strategy and consumer research: Concepts and illustrative exemplar'. *Journal of Consumer Research, 23*(2), 136–147.

Stern, B. B. (1998). 'The problematics of representation'. In B. Stern (Ed.), *Representing consumers: Voices, views and visions*. New York: Routledge, pp 1–23.

Sun Microsystems (2008). Sun Guidelines on Public Discourse. Retrieved February 18, 2009 from the World Wide Web: http://www.sun.com/communities/guidelines.jsp

Tadajewski, M. (2006). 'The ordering of marketing theory: The influence of McCarthyism and the Cold War'. *Marketing Theory, 6*(2), 163–199.

Tadajewski, M. (2008). 'Final thoughts on amnesia and marketing theory'. *Marketing Theory, 8*(4), 465–484.

Toncar, M., & Munch, J. (2001). 'Consumer responses to tropes in print advertising'. *Journal of Advertising, 30*(1), 55–65.

Vaihinger, H. (1924). *The philosophy of 'as if': A system of the theoretical, practical and religious fictions of mankind*. London: Routledge & Kegan Paul.

Vargo, S. L., & Lusch, R. F. (2004). 'Evolving to a new dominant logic for marketing'. *Journal of Marketing, 68*(1), 1–17.

von Bertanlanffy, L. (2001). *General systems theory: Foundations, development, applications*. New York: George Barziller.

von Foerster, H. (1981). 'Objects: Tokens for (eigen-) behaviors'. In *Observing Systems*. Seaside, CA: Intersystems Publications, pp. 274–285.

von Foerster, H., & Poerksen, B. (2002). *Understanding systems. Conversations on epistemology and ethics*. New York: Carl Auer: Heidelberg and Kluwer Academic Publication/Plenum Publishers.

von Glasersfeld, E. (1990). 'Environment and communication'. In L. P. Steffe & T. Woods (Eds.), *Transforming children's mathematical education* (pp. 30–38). Hillsdale, N.J.: Lawrence Erlbaum.

von Glasersfeld, E. (1996). *Radical constructivism: A way of knowing and learning*. London: Falmer Press.

von Glasersfeld, E. (2000). 'Problems of constructivism'. In L. P. Steffe & P. W. Thompson (Eds.), *Radical constructivism in action: Building on the pioneering work of Ernst von Glasersfeld*. London: Routledge Falmer, pp. 3–9.

von Glasersfeld, E. (2005). 'Thirty years radical constructivism'. *Constructivist Foundations, 1*(1), 9–12.

von Glasersfeld, E. (2008). 'Who conceives of society?'. *Constructivist Foundations, 3*(2), 59–64.

Wang, H., & Wang, S. (2008). 'A knowledge management approach to data mining process for business intelligence'. *Industrial Management & Data Systems, 108*(5), 622–634.

Watzlawick, P. (Ed.). (1984). *The invented Reality: How do we know what we believe we know?*. New York: W. W. Norton.

Watzlawick, P. (1993). *The language of change: Elements of therapeutic communication*. New York: W. W. Norton & Co.

Watzlawick, P., Bavelas, J. B., & Jackson, D. D. (1967). *Pragmatics of human communication: A study of interactional patterns, pathologies, and paradoxes*. New York: W. W. Norton.

West, D. C., & Paliwoda, S. J. (1996). 'Advertising client–agency relationships: The decision-making structure of clients'. *European Journal of Marketing, 30*(8), 22–39.

Wiener, N. (1948). *Cybernetics.* New York: Wiley.

Wooliscroft, B. (2008). 'Re-inventing Wroe?'. *Marketing Theory, 8*(4), 367–385.

Wright-Isak, C., Faber, R. J., & Horner, L. R. (1997). 'Comprehensive measurement of advertising effectiveness: Notes from the marketplace'. In W. D. Wells (Ed.), *Measuring advertising effectiveness.* Mahwah, NJ: Lawrence Erlbaum Associates, pp. 3–12.

Young, J. W. (2003). *A technique for producing ideas.* New York: McGraw-Hill.

Zwick, D., Bonsu, S. K., & Darmody, A. (2008). 'Putting consumers to work: "Co-creation" and new marketing govern-mentality'. *Journal of Consumer Culture, 8*(2), 163–196.

Index

234 *Index*

About the Author

Chris Miles is an Assistant Professor in the Faculty of Communications and Media Studies at Eastern Mediterranean University in the Turkish Republic of Northern Cyprus. His research has appeared in *Marketing Theory*, *Rhetoric Society Quarterly* and *Cybernetics & Human Knowing*.